John N. Mangieri
Cathy Collins Block

~ Power Thinking

How the Way You Think Can
Change the Way You Lead

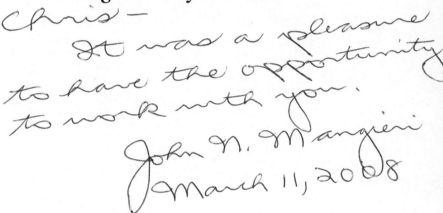

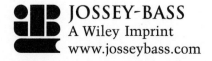 **JOSSEY-BASS**
A Wiley Imprint
www.josseybass.com

Published by Jossey-Bass
A Wiley Imprint
989 Market Street, San Francisco, CA 94103-1741   www.josseybass.com

Jossey-Bass books and products are available through most bookstores. To contact Jossey-Bass directly call our Customer Care Department within the U.S. at 800-956-7739, outside the U.S. at 317-572-3986, or fax 317-572-4002.

Jossey-Bass also publishes its books in a variety of electronic formats. Some content that appears in print may not be available in electronic books.

Library of Congress Cataloging-in-Publication Data

Mangieri, John N.
     Power thinking : how the way you think can change the way you lead / John N. Mangieri, Cathy Collins Block.—1st ed.
        p. cm.
     Includes bibliographical references and index.
     ISBN 0-7879-6882-X (alk. paper)
     1. Leadership—Psychological aspects. 2. Executive ability. 3. Reasoning (Psychology) 4. Insight. 5. Self-perception. 6. Thought and thinking—Study and teaching. I. Block, Cathy Collins. II. Title.
     HD57.7.M355 2004
     658.4'092'019—dc22   2003020018

Printed in the United States of America
FIRST EDITION
HB Printing   10 9 8 7 6 5 4 3 2

—ᴹᴹ— Contents

To the memory of Linda C. Winner,
a great leader and an even finer human being

⟞⟍⟍⟍⟋ Preface

This book began with adversity. Its content, and the subsequent successes that many individuals have enjoyed from it, all came about because first one, and later both, of the book's authors took a step.

Throughout his life, author John Mangieri has been interested in understanding failure. As a child, he was intrigued by broken toys. John was not content merely to recognize that they were broken; rather, he also sought to identify the precise basis for the malfunction. As a student, John had the same curiosity about intellectual tasks. For example, when he and other classmates were given an entire week to learn how to spell fifteen words, John wanted to understand why every student in the class could not spell all fifteen words correctly at week's end. Was it because some had spent little or no time trying to master the task? Was the failure a result of the method they used to learn to spell the words? What *was* the reason?

What began as something of a hobby has evolved over the past two decades into the avid analysis of organizational development and management performance. In 1989, John began a study designed to identify the traits common to organizations that had records of poor performance. His research about poorly performing organizations revealed certain consistent trends. For example, for some organizations, planning did not generate the intended results, leading to duplicated efforts, missed opportunities, and an unceasing drift into chaos. Those organizations lacked focus; their goals were inconsistent, vague, or meaningless, and they seemed to base their decisions on whims rather than strategic reasoning. In addition, such organizations commonly experienced a lack of capital and poor customer satisfaction. One area, however—that of leadership—generated a morass of conflicting data.

Charismatic leaders headed some of the organizations that John analyzed, but other organizations with equally low levels of performance were led by noncharismatic, autocratic, democratic, or even laissez-faire executives. In short, John could find no correlation between one particular approach to leadership and organizational performance.

Frustrated in his attempt to identify leadership styles common to poorly performing organizations, John decided to study this factor from a different perspective: he turned to research on highly successful organizations to ascertain the leadership styles that their managers and executives used.

Once again, the results were contradictory. In some successful organizations, leaders used an extremely authoritarian style of management; their unwritten ethos was clearly "do it my way, or take the highway." But comparable organizations had leaders who used a completely opposite style of management. Although John observed many different leadership approaches and practices, his attempt to identify the holy grail of leadership—*the* significant approach used by executives of successful organizations—was futile. Simply no single best leadership approach existed within these entities.

What John did find was that in virtually every successful enterprise, subordinates commented about the thinking prowess of their leaders. They frequently made comments such as these:

> "Mr. Cannon has the uncanny ability to always make the correct decision."

> "We will be trying to deal with a problem for a long time, and when we are ready to give up, we take it to Mrs. Kettering to discuss. She always seems to suggest a terrific solution instantly."

> "Mr. Lincoln is extremely creative. His ideas are the reason that our competitors copy what we do."

John faced a dilemma. The information that he was uncovering was fascinating, but it did not help him to answer what he was attempting to find out: the style of leadership that managers and executives of highly successful organizations possessed.

John had to decide whether to stop his research or instead alter its direction and attempt to learn more about the thinking process of these leaders. After considering the pros and cons of the situation, he chose to take two steps. First, he decided to abandon his original research and instead sought to find out what special attributes relative to thinking these leaders possessed. His second step entailed inviting Cathy Block to join him in his research efforts.

While understanding the "why" behind failure has always intrigued John, Cathy has had a lifelong interest in how people think. That interest led initially to an undergraduate degree and later to an invitation to serve as a research assistant at the University of Wisconsin Research Center for Cognitive Development. She earned her doctorate from that university and since then has amassed an impressive research record in the field of cognitive psychology. She is the author of several textbooks and articles and is a frequent speaker at national professional meetings. When she joined John in conducting this research, Cathy focused her efforts on collecting and analyzing data on whether leaders of highly successful organizations possess enhanced thinking skills. Her thorough study of these leaders led us to conclude that the answer is a resounding yes.

As the two of us examined outstanding leaders' skills, a clear pattern consistently appeared, regardless of whether they headed a corporation, hospital, school district, government agency, or some other type of organization. These leaders possessed enhanced thinking ability not merely in a single segment of cognition but in all of its components: reasoning, insight, and self-knowledge.

After our initial study was conducted—and totally independent of our work—the Hay Group (Hay/McBer, 1995), a highly respected international consulting firm, initiated an effort designed to identify the qualities of superior chief executive officers. As part of that study, fifty-five people from top-performing corporations in fifteen countries were interviewed in depth. Despite the fact that they led corporations in a broad spectrum of industries and in geographically disparate sites, the study's investigators were able to identify leadership behaviors that these CEOs shared.

The Hay Group's researchers found that "the best executives are able to cut through a barrage of data and pinpoint the issues most important to their company. Their goals were to protect corporate interests from external threats and to pursue business opportunities that positively affected their organization"(Hay/McBer, 1995, p. 19). The researchers also found that these leaders used four competencies when pursuing those broad goals: broad scanning, analytical thinking, conceptual thinking, and decisive insight. Although these labels are different from the ones we use, the areas that they represent are identical to those we explore in this book.

We realize that your life is busy, and so we wrote this book to accommodate your schedule. We recommend that you read the first three chapters in close proximity time-wise. After taking this action, you will have a comprehensive profile of your thinking capacity. You can then read Chapters Four through Ten as your schedule permits.

November 2003   JOHN N. MANGIERI
                                                 Charlotte, North Carolina

                                                 CATHY COLLINS BLOCK
                                                 Fort Worth, Texas

CHAPTER ONE

Why Power Thinking Is a Must and Not a Should for Leaders

When we were growing up, we used to watch episodes of *Perry Mason* on television. Although we knew that Mason's client did not commit the crime, we hung in suspense waiting to discover who the guilty culprit was. Unlike our experience with that program, you will not have to wait until the end of this book to learn our message. It is both a clear and simple one: by enhancing your thinking skill, you will become a better leader, and your organization's performance will concurrently improve.

We can make this assertion about both you as a leader and your organization based on what we have repeatedly witnessed firsthand over the past decade. The strategies that we present in this book have already brought success to numerous professionals by giving them the tools they needed to become power thinkers. We recognize that using these strategies designed to improve your cognitive processes will involve making changes in your life. We also know that change is uncomfortable for many people. It means forsaking long-established modes of behavior as well as some facets of your personality that have brought you a certain degree of past success. Nevertheless, we contend that the strategies set out in this book will enhance you not only as a leader but also personally. We believe you will become happier, more confident, and more satisfied with yourself and your life. This book can help you experience increased success in your work and derive appreciably more enjoyment from it.

WHAT IS A POWER THINKER?

The term *power thinker* describes the skill levels that exemplary leaders possess and regularly use in the performance of their responsibilities. It connotes not only the high level of proficiency they have in the area of thinking but also the manner in which they employ cognitive strategies in their actions as leaders.

In our initial research, we studied 346 individuals who were highly efficient in thinking skill ability and use. In addition, the organizations that they led had high levels of performance. They were characterized by being the top-performing unit in their organization, and competitors emulated their practices. Since our initial study, our efforts have greatly expanded relative to the number of such individuals whom we have both identified and helped to develop. In the past decade, we have worked with over twenty thousand people in business, government, health care, education, and nonprofit organizations.

We found that these individuals, despite working in different professions and having diverse experiences and educational backgrounds, were remarkably similar in that their exceptional level of skill in each dimension of thinking was quite evident to subordinates as they engaged in decision making, problem solving, and creative thought. We noted too that their anticipation of change was an integral part of their leadership strategy.

Our research has also revealed that power thinkers possess exceptional ability in the three major thinking domains of reasoning, insight, and self-knowledge and are highly skilled in the internal and external processes that constitute them. *Internal cognition* refers to the mental strategies used to develop highly effective decisions, problem solutions, and creative thought. *External cognition* refers to the actions these individuals take as a consequence of the thoughts that emanated from their internal cognition.

Reasoning is the mind's way of consciously taking thoughtful actions. The leaders we studied can identify the causes of problems rapidly, correctly delineate the pluses and minuses of possible initiatives and choices, and finish assigned tasks on time regardless of the effort required. They are people to whom both superiors and subordinates frequently come for advice.

We found that exceptional leaders also were quite proficient in *insight,* which is the ability to know and act without prior conscious thought being given to that action. These leaders, when required to make an instantaneous decision, had an exceptional ability to develop instinctively a new and better course of action. In fact, when given choice A or choice B, they would often envision choice C, which was appreciably superior to either of the other two options. We found that they were able to capitalize on the changing conditions that their organizations faced. When their unit or organization had to initiate a new action as a result of external circumstances, they could quickly devise a positive response to the new condition. In addition, they frequently were the catalysts for the change itself. These leaders were skilled at correctly predicting situations that would take place, and as a consequence, their unit or organization often took actions that placed them in front relative to changes rather than in a reactive position.

These exemplary leaders too had excellent *self-knowledge,* by which we mean clearly defined and well-known attitudes and beliefs. Because they were such open books, there was no reticence on their part to talk and share their ideas and experiences with others. They let subordinates and superiors know what they thought and felt about an issue under consideration. They were quickly comfortable in any environment, giving them a real advantage.

We discuss each of these domains in Chapters Four through Nine. Although we present them separately, there are ample instances when they overlap with one another and work in concert.

In the subsequent chapters of this book, we also identify twenty-three thinking subskill components of these three domains. The outstanding leaders we studied regularly and effectively use these subskills. The focus with these subskills is much narrower than that of the domains. When you use them, they will enable you to understand more concretely how enhanced thinking can improve your efforts in areas such as decision making and problem solving.

WHO IS A POWER THINKER?

Jack Covert, the founder and president of 800-CEO-READ, probably knows more about leadership and facets of business than any other person in the United States does. In 1984, he began his career in book sales with an unorthodox approach: he would fill his car trunk with business books and then visit local corporations in the hope that they would buy the books that he was selling.

Today, Covert's company, which is located in Milwaukee, is a far cry from its rather humble origins. It is America's leading direct supplier of business literature and has more than ten thousand corporate and organizational clients nationwide. The company's monthly Top Twenty-Five list of best-selling business books is a frequently cited standard against which a book's popularity is gauged, and the list is distributed to more than six hundred newspapers through the Knight Ridder/Tribune News Service.

Despite the tremendous success that Covert and his company have enjoyed, those early experiences in selling books are very much a part of how he acts and how the company operates. Covert describes his company as a "customer service business that sells books very, very well." Unlike some leaders who merely mouth the words *customer service,* Covert and his team go to great lengths to respond to the needs and wishes of all customers, regardless of whether they are buying a single book for the first time or are large corporations that regularly purchase sizeable quantities of the books he is selling. He also strives to respond to all requests, whether they come from friends, subordinates, or complete strangers. Finally, Covert believes that that his actions should be guided not by whether something might be profitable but whether it is the right thing to do.

Covert, like other outstanding leaders, is strong in all three of the domains that constitute thinking. Let us first consider reasoning, which is the mind's way of consciously taking thoughtful actions.

An important part of Covert's decision-making process as to where his company will or will not head is his daily use of a tracking strategy. He gets a great deal of the data that he uses to make decisions from walking around the company and talking with associates and hearing what books are being ordered. Covert also asks about the types of books that customers say they are looking for, even if they have no specific title in mind. As a result of these strategic conversations, he makes decisions as to what books his company will purchase so that it can more ably respond to customer demands.

What Covert does is much more than a version of managing by walking around: he concurrently keeps his company's financial resources flexible so that they can be used as winning opportunities arise. It was this strategic flexibility that gave him the idea for what has become an important part of his business: his company's superb relationships with authors. Here is what occurred.

Covert attended an event in which the coauthor of a book was signing autographs. The author told Covert that he had orders for books, but they were going unmet because his book's publisher was unable to fill them in a timely manner. Covert told the author that he might be able to help. When he returned to his office, Covert had his staff buy all the copies of the book from every wholesaler they could identify. The effort yielded over seven hundred copies of the book. Some people thought the company would be saddled with unsold copies of the work. Instead, all of the books were sold within three weeks. This experience led to a new part of the business: 800-CEO-READ now contacts authors about its services, and many of them regularly work with the company in the sale of their books.

The second domain in which outstanding leaders are strong is insight—the ability to know and act without prior conscious thought being given to an action.

Covert, insightful in numerous ways, uses two strategies often and especially well in the performance of this skill. Covert often comes up with what he calls "half-baked ideas"—seeds of ideas that are initially planted in his mind after he has read something. He continues to think about the idea while he is walking by himself or playing computer games late at night. After revising the idea in his thought process, he shares it with associates. They discuss the "half-baked idea" at length and as a group decide if the idea should be kept as is, altered, or discarded. Covert laughingly says that about 90 percent of his ideas "never see the light of day" as far as implementation goes. Nevertheless, some of the company's greatest accomplishments have come as a result of this thought process.

Covert, who was once called a "prophet" by former Doubleday/Currency editor Harriet Rubin, regularly engages in insightful actions in a second way: strategy sessions with David Schwartz, owner of Dickens Limited, the parent company of 800-CEO-READ. These sessions are held away from the company's building, and there is no formal agenda for them. The two discuss not profitability but how they want to develop the company and what they want to eliminate, continue, and do better or differently.

Jack Covert additionally has strong skills in self-knowledge, by which we mean well-known values, attitudes, and beliefs. It is the third domain that power thinkers possess.

Rather than worry about what his competitors are doing, Covert states: "Another company can do what we do, but they'd be hard pressed to have the relationships with customers and authors that our company's personnel does." He adds: "You can't win a race backwards. You need to be confident that what you are doing fits customers' needs well. If you do that, then you don't have to worry about sales because they will take care of themselves." Confidence in what he and his colleagues are doing and taking action to see that they continue to serve customers well are far more important to him than keeping up with his competitors.

Jack Covert is a terrific leader who has made a significant imprint in the business world. He has exceptional skill in reasoning, insight, and self-knowledge, and he uses these abilities strategically in his business. In an exemplary fashion, he sells a product that has changed the world: books and the ideas contained in them.

Jack Covert epitomizes the type of leader whose thinking skills are exemplary. He is strong in reasoning, insight, and self-knowledge. He and 800-CEO-READ are the beneficiaries of his skill in these domains and from the decisions that he reaches, the problems that he solves, and the creative ideas that he develops.

AM I A POWER THINKER?

When you begin any venture, it is important to know your starting point so you can plan your route appropriately and assess your progress accurately. In the case of becoming a power thinker, the starting point is your existing skill level in each of the three domains of reasoning, insight, and self-knowledge. Identifying in which of those areas are your strengths and in which are your weaknesses helps you plan and execute a strategy for increasing your abilities and enhancing areas that you have not developed fully.

Unfortunately, most leaders lack objective information regarding their thinking abilities. In research that we present later in this chapter, we show that few leaders have ever had their thinking skill levels assessed or been taught how to think powerfully. Although these findings are both surprising and unfortunate, they are also rectifiable. If you are among the many professionals who lack objective information about their thinking abilities, you can do something to change that situation by taking the standardized assessment, the Yale Assessment of Thinking (YAT) in Chapter Two.

The YAT is a reliable and valid instrument whose previous editions have been administered to thousands of leaders in the United States and other countries. We developed this test in order to provide professionals with accurate and objective data about their performance in the dimensions of thinking that excellent leaders regularly use: reasoning, insight, and self-knowledge. (You can learn more about this test in Chapter Two and the Appendix of this book.)

After you take this assessment and analyze the results, you will know if you already possess the skills of a power thinker. The test results will also provide you with accurate information that affirms your strengths and pinpoints specific weaknesses in thinking. You will be able to compare your existing thinking skills to the levels of outstanding leaders in each of the assessment's twenty-three subcomponents of reasoning, insight, and self-knowledge. Thus, you will know whether you are already a power thinker and will have important data that you can use to plan to become a better leader.

CAN I BECOME A POWER THINKER?

If the YAT determines that you are not now a power thinker, you may be wondering: Can I become a power thinker? Absolutely yes. The YAT is a measure of your *current* skill in thinking, and thinking is a skill that can be readily improved if appropriate corrective strategies are used. Moreover, we have a large and convincing body of data and experience to support what we are saying.

We have noted how few leaders have ever had their thinking skills assessed. A comparable number were never taught how to think in elementary, middle, or high school, or even college. As a consequence, most people do not know how to think as powerfully as they are capable of thinking because they lack knowledge about strategies that will enhance their skill in this area.

According to a 1997 study conducted by the Institute for Effective Management, an estimated 74 percent of university graduates never have been taught formally how to use specific cognitive strategies properly. That is, they do not know how to direct their thoughts effectively to generate the most positive ends.

Since this study was conducted, we have had opportunities to conduct additional research relative to this topic. What we found was both illuminating and distressing.

That almost three out of four professionals who work in business have never been taught how to think is hardly a cause for celebration, yet this abysmal condition is a "best case" when compared to other groups. The following percentages of leaders in the fields shown have never had their thinking skills levels assessed: business, 86 percent; government, 93 percent; education, 90 percent; health care, 96 percent; and other organizations, 92 percent. In these same groups, the following percentages have never been taught how to think: business, 74 percent; government, 87 percent; education, 85 percent; health care, 78 percent; and other organizations, 85 percent. In other words, in the United States, most people do not know how to think as powerfully as they are capable of thinking. They lack knowledge about strategies that will enhance their skills because they were never taught how to think in any of their schooling.

If you are among those who were never taught how to think, it might be illuminating for you to understand when the processes that you use to cognitively reach decisions, solve problems, and think creatively were developed. Research demonstrates that without instruction, the patterns of thinking developed during childhood do not change in adulthood. That means that many leaders are trying to succeed in this rapidly changing, bottom-line-oriented, complex, and highly competitive world using thinking patterns they developed during childhood.

This situation can be changed. We believe that powerful thinking can be taught and that most, if not all, people can learn to do it. Our belief is not mere conjecture. Over the years, we have taught thinking development to many people and have seen some rather remarkable results. You can learn to think better just as you can improve your public speaking, typing, mathematical, golf, or vocabulary skills.

To become more proficient in these or any other skills, you must take action. You must know the requisites for doing the task well, and then you must practice the processes until you master them and they become automatic. As you will discover, power thinking involves accepting new principles and taking simple actions repeatedly until they become an ingrained part of your thinking process.

Our confidence that what we state is accurate comes from the data that we have gathered relative to the significant gains made by thousands of individuals who have participated in the Power Thinking for Leaders programs that we conduct. We could cite several studies that support our assertion, but because the results in each of them are remarkably similar, we will share only one investigation with you. The 3,056 leaders in one of our longitudinal studies who engaged in focused actions designed to improve their thinking ability made the following improvements:

- They have become significantly more effective in decision making.
- They solve problems more quickly and with a higher degree of correctness than they did previously.
- They engage in highly creative thinking more ably and frequently.
- They are more interpersonally skilled and proficient when placed in teaming situations.
- They possess an increased level of job satisfaction.
- They receive higher job performance evaluations from superiors.
- They are absent from work on fewer occasions.
- They are less likely to leave an organization.
- Morale within units that they head has become more positive.
- The units they lead attain higher levels of performance.

A person who significantly benefited from engaging in an effort to improve his thinking ability is Bill Wilder. At the time he initiated this undertaking, he was human resource director for the City of Charlotte in North Carolina. He has over thirty years of experience in human resource management, including having served as the director of the employee compensation program for the state of Florida.

Charlotte, which has fifty-eight hundred municipal employees, has received recognition on numerous occasions for its innovative approach to providing high-quality and cost-effective services to its citizens. The city's Human Resources Department under Wilder's leadership has received national, regional, and local acclaim from the public and private sectors for its exemplary contributions to the efficiency and effectiveness of Charlotte as well as for the department's operations. Wilder has held leadership positions in many human resource organizations and has made numerous presentations. He is a strong advocate of continuous improvement and learning for himself and employees in the units where he has worked. This commitment led him to schedule a program designed to enhance the thinking ability of his department's staff as well as for himself.

Wilder believed that in order to continue to provide maximum support to the city, a more skilled approach to thinking was needed. In making the decision for his staff and himself to participate in such a program, he and his colleagues made a commitment that they would take the actions necessary to become more capable in decision making, problem solving, and creative thinking.

Prescriptive instruction for each participant occurred after they took the YAT. Despite maintaining a very busy schedule, Wilder focused on improving his thinking because this developmental action did not entail great amounts of time. When he was readministered the YAT, he found that in the three months in which he had focused on his thinking, his overall cognitive ability had improved significantly. He had also become appreciably more skilled in decision making, problem solving, and creative thinking, and he became an even better leader for his high-performing organization.

In the organizational world, the bottom line is the only one that seems to customarily be of genuine importance, so we will state our bottom line to you: by reading this book and putting its strategies into practice regularly, you will become not only a power thinker but also an appreciably better leader. This book will introduce you to concepts and strategies that will enable you to become much more effective in decision making, problem solving, and creative thinking if you implement them. You will thereby become a more able leader of an organization that becomes a better and more productive one.

ARE YOU READY FOR THE NEXT LEVEL?

Unlike books that focus on a single dimension of leadership (for example, planning or personnel), the content in this one affects everything meaningful that you do in the performance of your responsibilities. Reaching decisions about issues, solving complex problems, and developing innovative strategies are what leaders do. How well they do them is what differentiates the able from the exceptional leader.

Reading this book and implementing its strategies will represent a major change for you in going to the next level as a leader. Our research, as well as that of Hay/McBer, has shown the relationship between thinking skill and leadership acumen. In programs that we have conducted as well as those initiated by professionals themselves, significant gains have been realized in the internal and external cognitive processes of reasoning, insight, and self-knowledge by leaders who have sought to improve their thinking ability.

In a September 27, 1991, address to the nation, President George H. W. Bush said, "Each day, we write a fresh page in history." By reading this book, you can begin to write a fresh page in your own history as a leader, a decision that will profoundly affect your entire life.

CHAPTER TWO

How Proficient Are My Thinking Skills?

For most readers of this book, learning about your thinking skill levels represents a first. As we stated in the previous chapter, our research shows that few of the professionals in business, government, health care, nonprofits, education, and other organizations have ever had their thinking proficiency evaluated. As a consequence, most of the beliefs that these individuals have about this important facet of performance are based on subjective information.

For example, your boss may have told you that you are insightful, or you may consider yourself to be an excellent decision maker. Either or both of these depictions of your thinking may be true, but if neither is based on objective data, there is an equal chance that what you *believe* to be true about yourself may be erroneous.

You are entitled to have valid information about major factors that affect your performance as a leader. If you became ill, you would consult a physician rather than relying on mere speculation. That physician would undoubtedly order various tests, and the information provided by them would be the basis of your subsequent treatment.

You now have a chance to learn a great deal about why you act as you do. The Yale Assessment of Thinking (YAT) will provide you with in-depth and meaningful data as to the manner in which you think and your effectiveness in performing significant aspects of this cognitive process.

The YAT provides information on four levels. First, your total score will enable you to ascertain the degree to which you already possess the overall thinking skills that are regularly exhibited by the outstanding leaders on whom this test's standards were based. You will be able to determine whether your level of expertise currently stacks up to that of these exemplary leaders.

Second, the YAT is designed to measure your skill in the three domains of thinking (reasoning, insight, and self-knowledge) that research studies have found are crucial to a person's ability to reach a sound decision, solve problems effectively, and think creatively.

Third, within these three domains, there are six cognitive processes that you can develop to increase your leadership abilities. By understanding your proficiency levels in each of them, you can take steps that will significantly enhance your thinking skills and your leadership prowess.

Finally, the YAT will show the actions that you frequently take that are hindrances to your thinking. These behaviors are the antithesis to success. Identifying them and taking actions to reduce their occurrence are important steps for persons in leadership roles or for those who aspire to hold such positions since these actions impede individual and organizational performance.

PREDICTING WHAT THE YAT WILL TELL YOU ABOUT YOUR THINKING

Before you complete the YAT, we ask that you write down in which of the three domains (reasoning, insight, and self-knowledge) you believe the test will find you to be the most skilled, the one in which you are the next most able, and the one in which you are the least proficient.

The following brief descriptions of each domain will aid you in this task:

• Located in an individual's conscious mind, reasoning is where the mind reaches decisions and solves problems after a great deal of thought by using knowledge that it already possesses. It is the mind's way of taking thought-filled action.

- Insight is an individual's ability to know and act without giving prior conscious thought to an issue.
- Self-knowledge encompasses the attitudes, beliefs, and cognitive understandings possessed by an individual.

After you have finished writing down where you think your skills fall in the three domains, we ask that you complete the YAT.

YALE ASSESSMENT OF THINKING

Instructions: This assessment will yield accurate information *if, and only if,* your responses to the items reflect *actual* situational frequencies in your professional life. You should not try to guess what response you should give to an item. Instead, be as precise as possible in using the numerical response that denotes the degree to which each item *actually occurs* in your life. Take as much time as you need to select an accurate response to each item. Remember that this assessment is confidential. No one but you will see your responses unless you choose to share the results. Thus, you should give answers that reflect how you *actually act* rather than to give responses that only attempt to be politically correct. The value of the information you will receive from the YAT is directly dependent on the degree to which your responses accurately reflect your actions.

For each item, give the response that most closely describes the degree to which the situation occurs in your professional life. Be as precise as possible in using the following scale to respond to the items below: 4 = Very Often; 3 = Often; 2 = Sometimes; 1 = Seldom. Place the number that corresponds to your response in the block that precedes each item.

☐ 1. The comments that I make at meetings are better presented than the ones made by others, but my statements do not receive as many positive responses.

☐ 2. When someone challenges my belief, I become even more resolved to retain it.

☐ 3. When I fail to perform a responsibility, I am unclear in my mind what the reason was for my not completing that task.

☐ 4. I talk negatively about myself.

☐   5. My level of self-confidence is lower than it should be.

☐   6. When I am confused or feel overwhelmed, I procrastinate.

☐   7. Past successes have created negative events in my life, and have placed pressures on me that limit my enthusiasm for pursuing new challenges.

☐   8. People compliment me for aspects of my professional life that are less important to me than my other values which they do not recognize.

☐   9. When new ideas are presented to me, I mentally or orally tend to take positions of opposition.

☐ 10. It is difficult for me to identify the reasons why I take certain actions.

☐ 11. When faced with a challenging problem, I wait for events to occur that will make it less difficult to solve.

☐ 12. I become despondent when I fail.

☐ 13. When I face a difficult problem, I like to mull it over for a long period of time in my mind.

☐ 14. When I have to reach a decision by selecting from several options, I choose the one that is closest in substance to past decisions that I have made.

☐ 15. I refrain from conveying to others the hurt that their actions have caused me.

☐ 16. I make decisions about matters in the order in which they are called to my attention by others.

☐ 17. The fear of failure limits me when I am planning future actions.

☐ 18. I have difficulty attaining the goals that I set for myself.

☐ 19. One or more people consistently anger me.

☐ 20. I seek to be involved in initiatives in which my ability exceeds the challenge itself.

☐ 21. While others are speaking at meetings, I write down as much as I can about what they are saying.

☐ 22. I would rather perform routine tasks than think about complex problems.

☐ 23. When faced with an initiative that I do not especially value, I do not establish any goals relative to it.

☐ 24. When asked to perform tasks I'd rather not do, I find it difficult to say "no" to people.

☐ 25. When evidence contrary to my belief is presented, I test this evidence several times before I alter my belief.

☐ 26. When told that I must perform a task for which I have had little or no previous experience, I find it difficult to be successful in such circumstances.

☐ 27. I know it is time to make a decision when people express displeasure with me for not making the decision.

☐ 28. I find that prior knowledge is the best source of information for decision-making.

☐ 29. I am late for appointments with other persons.

☐ 30. When I am criticized, I question my abilities.

☐ 31. When I fail, the confidence that I have in myself decreases.

☐ 32. In meetings, I make impromptu remarks, and share ideas as quickly as I think of them.

☐ 33. I find it difficult to work with individuals who have personalities different from mine.

☐ 34. When I attend a meeting and become confused about what is said, I will remain silent in the hope that I will eventually comprehend what is being said.

☐ 35. I have trouble meeting deadlines.

☐ 36. When I plan, I find it difficult to concurrently analyze multiple courses of action.

☐ 37. Before a major event, my anxiety is higher than that of others.

☐ 38. I believe that statements made at meetings should be intended to persuade others that the perspective of the person speaking is correct.

☐ 39. The plans that I develop are not as successful as I hoped when I originally formulated them.

☐ 40. An individual's beliefs should not be evident in that person's professional actions.

☐ 41. In solving problems, I am impulsive.

☐ 42. When my hard work goes unnoticed, my self-confidence lessens.

☐ 43. I consider myself to be a "worrier."

☐ 44. People have a higher regard for my abilities than I do.

☐ 45. When I become angry about the actions of others, it affects me for a longer period of time than it should.

☐ 46. I have missed opportunities because of self-doubts that I might be unsuccessful in performing these tasks.

☐ 47. My level of self-esteem is lower than it should be.

☐ 48. When I am hearing a presentation in a meeting and I do not comprehend what is being presented, I wait for others to ask questions.

☐ 49. When I am presented with a new idea, I initially try to formulate a mental picture of its shortcomings.

☐ 50. I procrastinate when a problem arises.

☐ 51. I find it difficult to maintain objectivity when I hear ideas presented by people whom I do not like.

☐ 52. I find that prior experience is the best source of information for decision-making.

☐ 53. Because I am aware of my levels of competence in various areas, I avoid activities in which my skills are overly challenged.

☐ 54. I make a decision when I am unwilling to devote any more time or energy to the matter.

☐ 55. When I am unsuccessful at a task, I believe that it is better to give an excuse rather than an apology.

☐ 56. I do not know how to plan so that productive interactions occur among people.

☐ 57. I do not fulfill promises that I make to individuals.

☐ 58. I am forced to reach decisions before I am ready to make them.

☐ 59. It is difficult to finish tasks that do not fall within my areas of strength.

☐ 60. In the past, when I sought to change certain behaviors, I found my efforts were basically a waste of time.

☐ 61. I find it difficult to be motivated to participate in an activity without being the leader of it.

☐ 62. When compared to other people my age, I become more frustrated than they do when things aren't going right.

☐ 63. I find it difficult to understand why the professional goals that I established are not realized.

☐ 64. When I am confronted with problems, other individuals believe that I come up with solutions by discarding alternatives too quickly.

☐ 65. When I failed to complete something that I was supposed to do, it was because I didn't have enough time.

☐ 66. My values are not reflected in the actions I take.

☐ 67. I berate my abilities.

☐ 68. I am better at conceptualizing ideas than in planning the steps necessary to implement them.

☐ 69. I make decisions for other people which they should make for themselves.

Scoring Instructions

Step 1: Enter your responses from pages 13–17 on the Scoring Form (Exhibit 2.1). The numbers in each list correspond to the numbers of the YAT questions. For example, the answer to question 1 belongs in the Reasoning column, the answer to question 2 in the Self-Knowledge column, and the answer to question 4 in the Insight column.

Total your responses for each domain in Exhibit 2.1, and then add them together for your total score.

Step 2: The cognitive processes data entry forms for reasoning (Exhibit 2.2), insight (Exhibit 2.3), and self-knowledge (Exhibit 2.4) that follow list by number the individual items from the YAT that belong to that domain and break them down according to internal and external cognitive processes. For example, question 9 from the YAT refers to reasoning (internal cognitive process), and question 18 refers to reasoning (external cognitive process).

For each of the three forms, enter your score for each item by number.

AM I A POWER THINKER?

At this point, you undoubtedly have many questions about the information that you have recorded on the prior pages. In Chapter Three, we answer those questions. However, we felt it important to address here the most burning question that you probably have: *Am I a power thinker?*

Exhibit 2.1. Scoring Form

Reasoning	Insight	Self-Knowledge
1. _____	4. _____	2. _____
3. _____	6. _____	5. _____
9. _____	15. _____	7. _____
13. _____	16. _____	8. _____
14. _____	17. _____	10. _____
18. _____	19. _____	11. _____
21. _____	20. _____	12. _____
28. _____	22. _____	23. _____
32. _____	24. _____	25. _____
34. _____	27. _____	26. _____
36. _____	35. _____	29. _____
38. _____	37. _____	30. _____
39. _____	43. _____	31. _____
41. _____	45. _____	33. _____
48. _____	46. _____	40. _____
49. _____	50. _____	42. _____
51. _____	53. _____	44. _____
52. _____	54. _____	47. _____
55. _____	58. _____	57. _____
56. _____	60. _____	59. _____
63. _____	62. _____	61. _____
64. _____		66. _____
65. _____		67. _____
68. _____		69. _____

Domain
Totals   _____   +   _____   +   _____   =   ☐

Total
Score

Exhibit 2.2. Reasoning Cognitive Processes Data Entry Form

Item Score for Internal Cognitive Process	Item Score for External Cognitive Process
9. _____	18. _____
49. _____	39. _____
51. _____	63. _____
14. _____	1. _____
28. _____	32. _____
52. _____	38. _____
3. _____	21. _____
55. _____	34. _____
65. _____	48. _____
13. _____	36. _____
41. _____	56. _____
64. _____	68. _____

Total score   Total score

Exhibit 2.3. Insight Cognitive Processes Data Entry Form

Item Score for Internal Cognitive Process	Item Score for External Cognitive Process
27. _____	16. _____
54. _____	24. _____
58. _____	60. _____
17. _____	6. _____
37. _____	35. _____
43. _____	50. _____
4. _____	15. _____
46. _____	19. _____
62. _____	45. _____
	20. _____
	22. _____
	53. _____
☐	☐
Total score	Total score

A Total Score (see Exhibit 2.1) on the YAT of a 94 or below indicates that your thinking skills are comparable to those possessed by exemplary leaders. Thus, the assessment would show that you are indeed a power thinker. And the further below 94 that your score is, the stronger your power thinking skills are.

If your total score was 95 or higher, the assessment shows that you are not a power thinker *at this time.* Your score indicates that there are significant dimensions of thinking that you are using in ways that impede your effectiveness to reach sound decisions, solve problems effectively, and think creatively.

We italicized *at this time* to point out that you can readily improve the thinking skills in which you may not now be as proficient as you

Exhibit 2.4. Self-Knowledge Cognitive Processes Data Entry Form

Item Score for Internal Cognitive Process	Item Score for External Cognitive Process
44. _____	8. _____
47. _____	23. _____
67. _____	66. _____
2. _____	33. _____
25. _____	61. _____
40. _____	69. _____
5. _____	11. _____
30. _____	26. _____
42. _____	59. _____
7. _____	10. _____
12. _____	29. _____
31. _____	57. _____
☐	☐
Total score	Total score

would wish to be. Having said that, we would like to offer some observations to individuals who are currently power thinkers as well as those who are not.

If the YAT showed that your skills are those of a power thinker, congratulations! You were either born with or have subsequently developed exceptional ability in reasoning, insight, and self-knowledge. You are a very able decision maker, problem solver, and creative thinker. These abilities have undoubtedly been invaluable assets to your effectiveness as a leader and to the performance of your organization.

If the YAT showed that you are not *currently* a power thinker, you may be wondering what this means. First, it is important to know what the test does *not* say. A score of 95 or higher does not indicate that you are intellectually deficient or an inept leader. Rather, it shows that your thinking skill levels can be appreciably enhanced by engaging in the strategies presented in the subsequent pages of this book.

THE NEXT STEP

You have just completed an important step in becoming a more skilled thinker. By taking the YAT, you have taken an action that relatively few of your counterparts have: you have had your thinking *objectively* assessed.

In the next chapter, we share with you this test's results relative to other aspects of your thinking ability. The data derived from it are important because they will help you to identify the areas of thinking in which you are already skilled. You will also learn about the segments of thinking in which you will need to become more proficient if you and your organization are going to ascend to the next level of performance. The acquisition of this knowledge and the application of its strategies will be another significant step in your becoming a better leader.

CHAPTER THREE

What Do My Test Scores Tell Me About My Thinking Skill Levels?

I n this chapter, we discuss what the numbers from the Yale Assessment of Thinking (YAT) reveal about other aspects of your current thinking abilities. If you are unhappy with any of them, remember that you can readily change them by following the steps for improvement that we share in this book.

Before you took the test, we asked you to predict what it would reveal about your thinking abilities. For example, are you strongest in reasoning? Do you lack insight? Are you especially clear about your self-knowledge as a person? Why do you act as you do as a leader?

Your test scores may surprise you by identifying strengths you did not know you had or pointing out aspects of your thinking that you can bolster to make yourself a more effective leader. Here we turn to those questions that we asked you to ask of yourself.

IN WHICH DOMAINS AM I PROFICIENT?

The YAT provided you with data about your proficiency in reasoning, insight, and self-knowledge. This objective appraisal is a milestone of sorts for many readers of this book who had never been given objective information relative to their thinking abilities. By consulting your total scores in reasoning, insight, and self-knowledge from Chapter Two and comparing those scores to the guide that follows, you can discern if you are highly skilled or in need of improvement in each of these areas.

In addition to determining your levels of ability in each domain, your scores provide two other important pieces of information. If you would like to learn in which domain you are most proficient, divide your domain total scores as follows. In the areas of reasoning and self-knowledge, divide by 24, and for insight, divide by 21. The domain in which the number obtained is the *lowest* is the area in which you are the most able.

To be sure that you understood our directions correctly, we offer you this example. If your domain scores were 50 (reasoning), 53 (insight), and 54 (self-knowledge), you would divide your reasoning score (50) by 24, and it would yield an average of 2.08. By dividing your insight score (53) by 21, you would have an average of 2.52. Using the same process, your self-knowledge score (54) would be divided by 24, yielding an average of 2.25.

Thus, your average domain scores would be 2.08 in reasoning, 2.52 in insight, and 2.25 in self-knowledge. Since the reasoning score, 2.08, is the lowest, reasoning would be the domain in which you are most able.

By establishing the domain in which you are most proficient, you are able to derive another important piece of information about your thinking abilities: you can determine if your best domain score represents an *overt* or *implicit* area of strength for you.

If, before you took the YAT, you believed that self-knowledge would be the domain in which you were the most skilled and the YAT indicated that it was indeed, then self-knowledge is what is termed your *overt* area of thinking ability. It means you are aware this domain is the one in which you are most able, and you consciously use it as part of your leadership repertoire.

If, however, you identified self-knowledge as your area of greatest strength, but the YAT found insight to be the domain in which you are most proficient, then insight would be an *implicit* area of thinking competence for you; that is, it represents a talent of which you are unaware. For most professionals, the domain got to its level of development with your doing little or nothing to nurture it. Implicit domains customarily do not play a prominent role in our leadership styles because individuals are unaware of them. However, they can become an invaluable tool as leaders use this newly found knowledge in the performance of the myriad responsibilities associated with their organization's performance.

There is one other possibility. Suppose there were two domains (say, reasoning and self-knowledge) in which you had the same or proximate scores (less than a 0.25 difference). If you correctly predicted that one of them would be your area of highest skill, then you would have both overt (self-knowledge) and implicit (reasoning) areas of skill. If you predicted that neither would be your strongest domain, then both self-knowledge and reasoning would represent implicit areas of strength for you.

If your averages were similar (a difference of less than 0.25 from the best to least) in all three domains, then the one that you identified as best before taking the YAT would be an overt area of strength and the other two domains would be implicit ones.

HOW SKILLED AM I IN EACH DOMAIN?

Thus far, we have examined your scores in comparison to one another. Now the question is how your performance in each domain stacks up against that of the outstanding leaders whom we consider to be power thinkers. Before we provide this information, we would like to remind you what we know about power thinkers. Some measures enable us to classify ourselves in only one way, to the exclusion of other elements, as "left brained" rather than "right brained," for example.

Our research, however, has concluded that power thinkers are "and" rather than "or" when it comes to the domains measured by the YAT. They are highly skilled in reasoning *and* insight *and* self-knowledge rather than one of them at the exclusion of the other two.

This does not mean that all three domain scores should be identical. Rather, each of these domains must be in the highly skilled range if you are to be or become a power thinker. Once they *minimally* meet this standard, then differences between and among the domains are acceptable.

Turn back to Chapter Two, and look at your scores on reasoning, insight, and self-knowledge. Use these data to determine if you are in the highly skilled range or need improvement in the domains below. You are highly skilled if:

- Your domain score in reasoning was 36 or below.
- Your domain score in insight was 31 or below.
- Your domain score in self-knowledge was 36 or below.

You are using behaviors that limit your thinking effectiveness if:

• Your domain score in reasoning was 37 or higher.
• Your domain score in insight was 32 or higher.
• Your domain score in self-knowledge was 37 or higher.

WHY ARE THESE THREE DOMAINS SO IMPORTANT?

These domains are important for two major reasons. First, the YAT measures the behaviors that were found to be characteristic of power thinkers. This assessment's normative benchmarks are based on the performance of these individuals. Its items are related to reasoning, insight, and self-knowledge, the domains on which you have just assessed your performance quantitatively and qualitatively.

Second, the three domains are reflected in how we think and act in carrying out our professional responsibilities. Chapters Four, Six, and Eight will discuss the internal cognitive processes of reasoning, insight, and self-knowledge in depth. Chapters Five, Seven, and Nine describe their external cognitive processes. To accomplish these ends, we will explain what constitutes the domain and cognitive process, how they limit persons who lack proficiency relative to them, and how they are reflected in the actions of professionals who are highly skilled in them.

Reasoning

The first cognitive domain assessed by the YAT is reasoning. Located in an individual's conscious mind, reasoning is where the mind reaches decisions and solves problems after a great deal of thought by using knowledge that it presently possesses. It is the mind's way of taking thought-filled actions. People who are highly skilled in reasoning are typically characterized in this way:

• Are the sort that other people come to for advice about problems
• Identify problems rapidly
• Correctly identify pluses and minuses of possible initiatives or choices

- Use people to assist them in making difficult or complex decisions (division of labor or thought)
- Use uninterrupted work time to make lists and draw up schedules
- Are adept at planning
- Can ably coordinate the actions necessary to implement new initiatives
- Finish assigned tasks on time regardless of effort involved to do so
- Do routine and complex tasks well

Individuals who lack proficiency in reasoning are typically characterized in the following ways:

- Don't learn readily from past successes and failures
- Often make disjointed or unprepared comments, so that listeners tend not to heed their comments
- Have trouble seeing the viewpoints of others
- Are often viewed as biased and not objective

Insight

The second cognitive domain is an individual's ability to know and act without prior conscious thought being given to an issue. People who are highly skilled in insight typically exhibit the following behaviors:

- Rely on their "gut" feelings to make decisions
- Are comfortable with abstractions
- Think creatively often and well
- Tend to accurately predict things that happen
- Know they should do something or pursue a course of action
- Think by talking (usually with one or two special people)
- Prefer to deal with problems by reflecting on thoughts and feelings before sharing a decision
- When in a group, will watch or listen before joining in

Conversely, individuals not strong in insight will usually exhibit one or more of the following behaviors:

- Put forth ideas that others often view as narrow in scope and shortsighted
- Often say or think, "If only I had thought of that!"
- Frequently get into ruts in their lives and experience burnout in their jobs
- Are not often the stars of an organization
- Prefer to work on routine or mundane tasks rather than new or creative endeavors

Self-Knowledge

Self-knowledge encompasses an individual's attitudes, beliefs, and cognitive understandings. In our study, power thinkers had clearly defined and well-known attitudes and beliefs. Since they were such an "open book," they had no reticence in sharing ideas and experiences with others. They let subordinates and superiors know what they thought and felt as well. People who are highly skilled in this aspect of thinking typically exhibit the following behaviors:

- Enter any environment and are quickly comfortable
- Are skilled in working in situations requiring teamwork
- Talk and share ideas as well as experiences immediately
- Let others know what they are thinking and feeling
- Are effective in working alone, with close friends, or in large group situations
- Maintain a strong sense of personal space both at work and home

Individuals weak in the self-knowledge domain of thinking typically exhibit one or more of the following behaviors:

- Often feel as if they are not getting a fair shake
- Tend to be a member of a group rather than its leader

- Have more failures than successes on goals they personally design
- Try to live up to and keep up with "the Joneses"

WHAT ELSE CAN I LEARN ABOUT MY THINKING SKILLS?

Thus far in this chapter, we have discussed your thinking skill on a macrolevel, that is, the big dimensions of it. Now we turn to data that focus on a decidedly more micro, but equally important, dimension of your thinking: the test's items themselves.

The YAT has sixty-nine items, each focusing on either reasoning, insight, or self-knowledge. These items were written as they were for another reason: to focus on six crucial cognitive processes that our research found were possessed, and regularly used, by the outstanding leaders whom we classified as power thinkers.

Within each domain, subskill components are classified as either internal or external cognitive processes. (As you will recall, internal cognitive processes refer to the subskill components controlled solely by you as you mentally generate decisions, solutions to problems, and creative thoughts. External cognitive processes embody the manner in which you act as a consequence of the decisions, solutions, and creative thoughts that emanated from others or your internal cognitive processes.) By knowing this information, you can pinpoint the segments of the thinking process in which you are highly skilled, of average ability, or in need of improvement.

The following guide can interpret the scores you obtained for five of the six cognitive processes. The exception is that of insight's internal cognitive process, whose interpretative numbers will be provided later.

If either your internal or external cognitive processes total score from Chapter Two is:

- 18 or under, then the respective cognitive process is one in which you are highly skilled.
- 19 to 24, then the respective cognitive process is one in which you have average ability.
- 25 or higher, then the respective cognitive process is one in which there is a need for improvement.

The following scores should be used to interpret the internal cognitive processes total score for insight:

- 13 or under: this cognitive process is one in which you are highly skilled.
- 14 to 18: this cognitive process is one in which you have average ability.
- 19 or higher: this cognitive process is one in which there is a need for improvement.

Within these six cognitive processes, our research identified twenty-three competencies that power thinkers possess and regularly use as leaders of high-performing organizations. In order to validly assess your own prowess on these competencies, we developed three YAT items relative to each of them. Depending on the competency being assessed, the three items' content varies. In some instances, it is duplicative. In others, each item focuses on a dimension of the competency being measured. These data are the crux of the material presented in Chapters Four through Nine. In Chapters Four and Five, you will learn about reasoning's internal and external cognitive processes as well as strategies that can make you more adept in them. Chapters Six and Seven are similarly organized relative to the internal and external cognitive processes of insight. Chapters Eight and Nine focus on the internal and external processes of self-knowledge. Chapters Six through Nine also provide strategies that can enable you to become a power thinker.

The YAT gave you one additional important piece of information: the individual items that show specific aspects of thinking that you must address if your thinking ability is to be improved. If you responded "very often—4" for any item, you have identified a behavior that is a hindrance to your thinking. You would benefit by learning appropriate strategies to alter and improve your respective thinking actions as described in that item.

THE NEW YOU

In Chapter One, we alluded to the new you that could emerge as a power thinker. You already probably have more knowledge about your thinking skill levels than you have ever had in the past. This information tells you about important dimensions of your thinking that are not only possessed by outstanding leaders but also are the very essence of what you do—reach decisions, solve problems, and think creatively—as a leader.

In Chapters Four through Nine, we present the vehicle for reaching this enhanced standard of performance. We set out ideas and strategies that can be easily developed into your thinking at three levels. First, your objective should be to become highly skilled in reasoning, insight, *and* self-knowledge. It is not enough to be adept in one or even two of them. Second, each domain is discussed comprehensively and separately in subsequent chapters so that you will understand why you are so proficient in the domains in which you are currently highly skilled. In addition, in a domain where your ability is currently lacking, you will find out why your actions hinder your effectiveness in thinking and as a leader. You will also learn strategies that you can employ to turn a domain from being a negative facet of your performance into a positive dimension of it. Third, in Chapters Four to Nine, we describe the internal and external cognitive processes that play crucial roles in our use of the respective thinking domain.

Within each chapter, we discuss the three-item clusters as well as individual items that constitute the respective chapter's either internal or external process. There are twenty-three clusters in which you will discern how proficient you are in them. For the sixty-nine items on the YAT, in instances where you gave a response of 1 (seldom) or 2 (sometimes) to an item, you will read why your existing practice is conducive to powerful thinking. Conversely, you can learn why your responses of 3 (often) and 4 (very often) are negative to effective thinking.

As you read these chapters, we also recommend that you identify, through underlining in the book or note taking, the content you believe is particularly pertinent to your thinking and your role as a leader. In Chapter Ten, we will discuss ways in which you can implement the book's ideas and strategies.

CHAPTER FOUR

Reasoning

Internal Cognitive Process

I n this and the subsequent chapter, we will discuss facets of reasoning, which is located in an individual's conscious mind and is where the mind reaches decisions and solves problems after a great deal of thought, by using knowledge that it possesses. This chapter will focus on the internal cognitive processes that power thinkers use to reach decisions, solve problems, and think creatively. This information is important because our research found that outstanding leaders are highly skilled in these processes of reasoning. Within this subskill of reasoning, power thinkers were especially proficient in their ability to be what we refer to as a fair-minded arbitrator (assessed by items 9, 49, and 51 in the YAT), an unconstricted thinker (assessed by items 14, 28, and 52), an auspicious completer (assessed by items 3, 55, and 65), and a judicious analyst (assessed by items 13, 41, and 64).

In this chapter, we discuss these subcomponents of reasoning. We also provide an explanation of each three-item cluster from the YAT that pertains to these four segments of reasoning's internal cognitive processes. Thus, you will learn "the why" of your responses to these items—either why it is a correct course of thought or why it must be altered to overcome its detrimental effects in the discharge of your leadership responsibilities.

For each group of three items that constitute the four internal cognitive processes of reasoning, you can assess how proficient you are in each of them now by filling out the item cluster graphs in each section of the chapter. Here is how to do that, using as an example the three items that comprise being a fair-minded arbitrator:

1. Next to items 9, 49, and 51 in the Fair-Minded Arbitrator Item Cluster Graph, enter the number that you placed before each when you took the YAT (you will find this information in Exhibit 2.2 in Chapter Two)

2. Add your scores for items 9, 49, and 51, and write their total on the blank next to "Total" in the item cluster graph.

3. On the blank next to "YAT Score Interpretation" in the item cluster graph, use the following guide to write what your total score reveals about your current level of proficiency in this aspect of reasoning's internal cognitive processes:

   If your total score was 5 or under, write "highly skilled."

   If your total score was 6 or 7, write "average ability."

   If your total score was 8 or higher, write "need for improvement."

Item Cluster Graph.   Fair-Minded Arbitrator Item Cluster Graph

YAT Items	Your Response
9	_____
49	_____
51	_____
Total	_____
YAT score interpretation	_____

FAIR-MINDED ARBITRATOR

An arbitrator is a professional who facilitates negotiations and conflict resolution through dialogue. Those who hold this position must be able to cope with conflicting points of view, function under pressure, demonstrate discretion and integrity, and be fair-minded.

The leaders we studied exhibited thinking skills akin to that of an arbitrator when they were presented with new ideas. They were fairminded as they determined the efficacy of possible courses of action, were able to take the best thoughts from conflicting points of view relative to a proposal, and had facility in giving new efforts their approval, altering them for the better, or not implementing them.

We called this facet of their internal cognitive process that of a *fairminded arbitrator* because that is precisely how power thinkers mentally consider new ideas. They have a dialogue in their minds or with others about the initiative before them. Then they analyze the conflicting facets of what they like and do not like about it. While engaging in this cognitive process, they are fair-minded with the goal of doing what is best for the organization rather than rewarding friends and punishing those persons whom they dislike.

Understanding the Fair-Minded Arbitrator

Items 9, 49, and 51 all assess mental objectivity. Both items 9 ("When new ideas are presented to me, I mentally or orally tend to take positions of opposition") and 49 ("When I am presented with a new idea, I initially try to formulate a mental picture of its shortcomings") describe individuals who see the glass as being half-full rather than half-full. By initially establishing a negative mind-set, they are telling themselves mentally, and the person who advances the idea, that it is a poor one. The idea may indeed not be very good. Nevertheless, they are engaging in two other negative behaviors. By taking a position of opposition or formulating a mental picture of its shortcomings at the outset, they have sent their subconscious a powerful message: "The idea is bad, so look for the bad in it." As a consequence, their mind, being the loyal and obedient tool that it is, does exactly that.

In fair-minded arbitrators, a very different cognitive process occurs. These individuals identify segments of an idea that they like first. When warranted, they also pinpoint what features of it are lacking. But by being objective rather than negative, their mind is able to consciously think of alternatives that could shore up the dimensions of the idea that are lacking.

In addition to improving the idea, fair-minded arbitrators have two other positive thoughts. First, by improving rather than merely demeaning a proposal, they are engaging in a strategy that has positive personnel development benefits. Subordinates and peers see how these esteemed leaders think, and they subsequently will use comparable strategies themselves.

Second, the actions of fair-minded arbitrators show employees that their ideas are valued. Even if the ideas are not implemented, subordinates know that they received a fair hearing. Thus, not only does their morale remain positive but they will not be reluctant in the future to present an idea that could turn out to be a real blockbuster for the organization.

Item 51 ("I find it difficult to maintain objectivity when I hear ideas presented by people that I do not like") deals with objectivity too but focuses on a different aspect of it. Individuals who find it difficult to maintain objectivity when hearing ideas presented by people whom they do not like are engaging in stereotypical thinking. In their minds, what occurred in the past will happen again in the future. They label a person who angered them before as an enemy and believe the person cannot do or say anything worthwhile.

Certainly, fair-minded arbitrators have both colleagues and subordinates whom they do not like, but they think in a manner vastly different from the one previously described. These leaders act in a manner similar to the "nothing personal, strictly business" philosophy made famous in the movie *The Godfather*.

They may indeed not like a person, but they realize that they cannot let their personal feelings toward someone whom they do not like interfere with their professional actions. Thus, fair-minded arbitrators give the ideas presented by such persons an objective consideration because they realize that the organization is the loser if they do not.

An Exemplary Fair-Minded Arbitrator: Sue Myrick

We have chosen to write about an elected official, U.S. Representative Sue Myrick of North Carolina, as an example of a fair-minded arbitrator. Representative Myrick, who was elected in 1994 and is now in her fifth term, has compiled an impressive record. She is one of our nation's most highly respected and effective representatives who works well with her constituents, members of her own political party, as well as colleagues from across the aisle. She serves on the powerful Rules Committee, where she is the vice chair of the Subcommittee on Technology and the House. She also chairs the Republican Study Committee and is a deputy whip for the 108th Congress.

Previously Myrick was a two-term mayor of Charlotte, North Carolina. While in this role, she developed a climate where businesses could thrive within the city, as well as went nose-to-nose with drug dealers, telling them to get out of the city's neighborhoods.

When Representative Myrick is presented with a new idea, she listens to it with an open mind. To guide her when she hears an idea, Myrick initially submits it to a litmus test of sorts. She asks: Is this idea good for the United States? If it is, then she will support it and examine ways to improve it if necessary. She has this attitude about objectivity because she believes that it is imperative for leaders to "look for good things to happen." She maintains that such things will not occur if a leader is not receptive to new ideas and points out to colleagues that not all of a proposal's ingredients have to reflect what she herself would have advocated. By not focusing on these potentially negative facets, Myrick is able to decide if the totality of the idea being advanced is one that she can support.

Myrick also believes that a leader should look at an idea rather than at the person who is advocating it. She and those who work in her congressional office objectively consider all ideas brought to them. Myrick does not judge an idea based on her past interactions with someone, but rather will support it as long as the proposed action meets her litmus test. Then she will endorse it and, if necessary, find ways to improve it. The yardstick that she uses—whether it is good for the United States—could be easily adapted for organizational leaders who could use a comparable question: Is this idea good for our company?

Strategies for Becoming a Fair-Minded Arbitrator

If you are not currently highly skilled in this competency, you can take a positive step toward becoming a fair-minded arbitrator when you hear new ideas by emulating the strategies that Representative Myrick uses.

Another way to process information that will prove beneficial to you is what we call the "reason before you speak" strategy. Just as a yellow traffic light cautions us that the light is about to turn red, this strategy reminds us to allow our reasoning process to kick in before we form an opinion or express one about a newly presented idea. Exercising this self-imposed caution will enable you to find inconsistencies in your interpretation of the idea being advanced.

This suspension of judgment will allow the domain of reasoning (rather than emotions) to be employed in your thinking process. You will then be able to determine objectively if your initial assessment of the proposal was based on correct facts rather than hastily formed and incorrect opinions or judgments.

Power thinkers consciously remind themselves to be fair and objective before reaching a decision. In most cases, an immediate judgment is not an optimally effective one unless a person is highly skilled in insight. By exercising caution before reaching a decision, you can make appreciably better ones.

You may enjoy attacking problems right away. For instance, when "complainers" come to talk, you may not want to listen because you have difficulty empathizing with them. Your first thought is, *Stop whining and feeling sorry for yourself. Get busy and correct the situation!* If you remember to actively work to understand the other person's point of view, you can gain helpful insights into an issue and increase your ability to receive information objectively.

During this period when you are exercising caution, seek to use these three internal reasoning strategies:

- Rephrase others' comments using their own words.
- Read body language.
- Traverse new territory from many directions.

REPHRASE OTHERS' COMMENTS USING THEIR OWN WORDS. In order to hold on to other people's words and keep an active mind while listening, pay attention to the exact words people are saying and then use their words in your reply. This action increases your own attentiveness. It also ensures that you are really listening, and those you are listening to will know that you have heard and understood them and will objectively consider their idea.

For example, Andy is the president of a software company. In a discussion with one of his vice presidents about a subordinate who reported to that vice president, Andy asked what the person was like. The vice president said, "a real team player." Andy responded, "I would have thought so," and when the vice president asked why, Andy said, "Because an accurate description of you would include the words 'a real team player,' and I felt anyone who worked closely with you on a daily basis would have a similar attitude." By picking up the same words the vice president had used, Andy communicated that he heard and understood the vice president and also agreed with what was said.

A leader less skilled in this internal cognitive process would have responded quite differently. Such a leader, when told that someone was a team player, might have merely said: "That doesn't surprise me." Without using the additional rephrasing words that Andy said, the other party in the dialogue is left to her own devices to conclude whether the person about whom they were speaking was being criticized or praised. By rephrasing his colleague's exact words, Andy removed vagueness and any possibility for miscommunication.

We encourage you to practice this strategy the next time someone talks to you. Repeat the words the other person uses, and notice the results.

READ BODY LANGUAGE. Power thinkers carefully observe nonverbal communications such as body language and mannerisms because both of these are areas that can be easily and frequently misinterpreted. Fair-minded arbitrators take the additional step of asking questions based on the information that they derive from perceived body language. A conflict between what someone says and the information conveyed by mannerisms can often lead to a misunderstanding. When someone's verbal and nonverbal messages contradict each other or confuse you, act as fair-minded arbitrators do in such instances. These individuals would say: "I'm confused. You said X [what they said] but seem to mean Y [what their body language conveys]. Am I correct?" If you do not ask this question, you are forced to choose between two distinctly different pieces of information: what the individual verbally stated or his or her nonverbal communication. In such situations, you will have only a fifty-fifty chance of responding correctly to the person's intended message.

The next time you believe someone is sending you a mixed message, convey to that professional the conflicting information that you are receiving. The ensuing explanation will enable you to discern the person's true intent. You will also more likely learn about that individual and his idea. You will avoid misunderstandings that could affect the decision that you reach about the idea.

TRAVERSE THE TERRITORY FROM MANY DIRECTIONS. Ideally, you should identify your preconceived viewpoints about an idea early in the power thinking process. (Once you are aware of those predispositions, do not try to convince yourself or others that they are objectively reasoned judgments.) Without this step, you may act on biases rather than facts. With this self-knowledge, you can begin to examine the issue from many different perspectives. We call this approach "traversing the territory from many directions."

Our research indicates that most powerful thinkers have developed methods for taking a wide-frame view. Although it may sound like a simple, commonsense ability, this step cannot be achieved without practicing ways to proactively challenge your own biases about individuals whom you do not like or new ideas. To start to make this internal reasoning cognitive process automatic, we suggest that you complete Exercise 4.1.

As an example, cost cutting has become a crucial issue for many businesses. Donna, a company president, is adept at cost cutting and makes it a high priority in her business decisions. In fact, she tends to make it her highest priority. Donna not only must become aware of her preconceived view of the importance of cost containment but also must examine closely its effect on her actions. A subordinate, Kevin,

---

—✧— Exercise 4.1

FINDING YOUR BIASES

Draw a circle, and label the center with the name of the issue you are working to understand. On the perimeter of the circle, write the names of the people (or departments or factors) affected by the issue. Draw a line from each person or condition to the central issue, and write on it the primary link between them. When all the links are completed, you can discern visually the factors involved in the issue. Your drawing displays the multiple causes and effects that single changes in the issue will precipitate. Knowing these effects in advance of an action identifies one path of information that will become more attractive to you than others. (See Figure 4.1.)

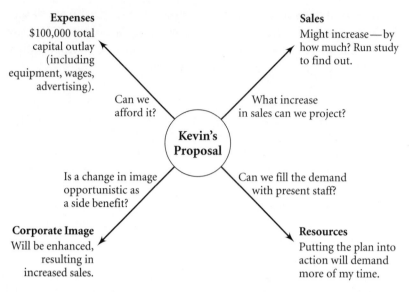

Figure 4.1. Sample Analysis of Biases

approached Donna with a new initiative that would require a capital outlay of $100,000. Donna's usual inclination would be to reject such an "expensive" request immediately. That action would be appropriate if the proposal were frivolous. Kevin's idea, however, had the real potential to yield a million-dollar profit. Donna's predisposition could have seriously restricted the success of her business. Figure 4.1 shows how Donna used Exercise 4.1 to analyze her predispositions. After identifying and setting aside her bias, Donna approved the expenditure, and her company benefited from Kevin's innovation.

Donna did not abandon her views on cost containment for this decision. Rather, she recognized them and made a conscious effort to traverse the territory objectively by examining the ideas that conflicted with her preconceived inclination about this idea.

UNCONSTRICTED THINKER

An *unconstricted thinker* is someone who does not present self-imposed restrictions that hinder his or her ability to think effectively. Power thinkers know that the more frequently that we are influenced by such restrictions, the more detrimental they are to their ability to make sound decisions. Items 14, 28, and 52 of the Yale Assessment of Thinking assess the degree to which you are an unconstricted thinker.

Understanding the Unconstricted Thinker

Items 14, 28, and 52 of the Yale Assessment of Thinking assess the degree to which you are an unconstricted thinker. Fill out the Unconstricted Thinker Item Cluster Graph, entering your scores for these items from Chapter Two. If your total score was 5 or under, write as the YAT score interpretation "highly skilled." If your total score was 6 or 7, write "average ability." If your total score was 8 or higher, write "need for improvement."

When we have several options, our criterion for the one that is selected must be broader than merely whether it is proximate in substance to past decisions that we have made (item 14, "When I have to reach a decision by selecting from several options, I choose the one that is closest in substance to past decisions that I have made"). By having such a viewpoint, our minds will look for the most familiar course of action, rather than the best, when we initiate our thought process. Thus, we might reject an option that is clearly better than an alternative because it departs from the tried-and-true decisions that we have made in the past.

Item 28 ("I find that prior knowledge is the best source of information for decision-making") identifies a similar, but slightly different, impediment to effective decision making: prior knowledge. That which we already know is certainly important. This body of prior

Item Cluster Graph. Unconstricted Thinker Item Cluster Graph

YAT Items	Your Response
14	_____
28	_____
52	_____
Total	_____
YAT score interpretation	_____

knowledge, schemata, is invaluable to our functioning as humans. For example, we know that if we put our hand in an open fire that it will be burned. This prior knowledge keeps us from engaging in this potentially harmful action. When asked to compute $3 + 5$, we do not have to form a cross-functional team or even consult an encyclopedia to find an answer. Our schemata tell us the answer is 8.

Prior knowledge can be beneficial to decision making, but it should not be our sole or even best source of information to decide a course of future action. By adopting this type of viewpoint, as was the case with item 14, you are restricting your thinking to what you already know. Information is now being produced and made available to us at rates unprecedented in history, so relying primarily on that which you already know precludes tapping into this body of knowledge to make the best decision. Since it is unknown to us and we have consciously or subconsciously told our mind that information that we process is what it must use, it will ignore data that could cause us to make a vastly different decision from the one we would make without it.

Like prior knowledge, prior experience (item 52, "I find that prior experience is the best source of information for decision-making") has schemata as its foundation. And for the same reasons previously stated about prior knowledge, prior experience is certainly beneficial to the actions that we customarily take.

The world in which we live, especially since the tragic events of September 11, 2001, is constantly changing. So too is the environment of rightsizing, mergers, CEO firings, and corporate scandals in which contemporary organizations function. As a consequence, there are innumerable events that we have not previously experienced. Prior experience should be one, but not the sole or primary, source on which we rely when reaching decisions.

Thus far, we have discussed the pitfalls of the internal cognitive processes of individuals who engage in the constructed thinking depicted in YAT items 14, 28, and 52. Now we will contrast what they do with the actions of an unconstricted thinker when reaching decisions.

An Exemplary Unconstricted Thinker: Edward G. Boehm

Edward G. Boehm, the president of Keystone College in Pennsylvania, epitomizes an unconstricted thinker. Boehm, one of our nation's most highly respected college presidents, has been recognized for his skill as a leader both outside of higher education as well as within it. In 1995, West Virginia's governor named him a "Distinguished West Virginian" for what he achieved while a citizen of that state. The University of Michigan profiled his leadership style and the positive transformation that has occurred at Keystone College since his being named president in 1995 so that other campus leaders could emulate Boehm's actions.

He has indeed made an impact as the college's leader in using the skills of an unconstricted thinker. During his tenure, Keystone College has grown greatly in both stature and size. The college's enrollment is now 63 percent larger than before his arrival, and the quality of academic programs has been concurrently enriched. Not a single program offered by Keystone College during Boehm's leadership has failed to receive accreditation. Academicians are not the only group who realize what a terrific leader Boehm is. Outside funding from alumni, foundations, and friends of the college has increased by 69 percent since 1995.

Boehm has had to make many difficult and important decisions in getting Keystone College from where it was as an institution when he assumed the position of president to its status today. Since both his schemata from prior knowledge and experiences are ample, Boehm uses them not as the sole source for reaching decisions but rather as one of many resources.

When making difficult decisions, Boehm employs a paradigm that he uses to guard against self-imposed restrictive thinking: he asks three questions for which he seeks answers in a three-step process:

1. For me to make the best decision possible, here are the questions that I must have answered . . .

2. What sources of information (for example, data, people, policy manuals) can I use that will provide me with answers to those questions?

3. What criterion (or criteria) will I use to reach my decision?

He then uses the information that he gathers from these responses to reach a decision about a matter.

Boehm's questions are self-explanatory; nevertheless, a discussion of facets of them may be illuminating. With regard to the first query, Boehm writes the questions down on a sheet of paper as he thinks of them. He employs this strategy because he (correctly) believes that writing the questions his mind has generated frees his mind from the task of having to remember them. Therefore, his thought process can turn its full attention to the identification of other important questions rather than having to remember those he has already thought of. This strategy also precludes his reliance on experience, prior knowledge, and stereotypical thinking in reaching decisions.

To aid him in answering the second question, he has compiled sources of information in areas where his tough decisions are likely to fall. For example, if he faces a budgetary or personnel decision, he has a ready list of resources on which to draw. When a matter falls outside one of his preestablished areas, Boehm believes these sources of information give him ideas as to where he can get comparable assistance and data regarding the unique decision that he faces.

Next, Boehm looks at each question contained in step 1. This action is his step 3: he examines both individual questions as well as all of them as a totality. For individual questions, he will establish a benchmark that the data (in step 2) must support. It may be a response of yes or a numerical percentage, depending on the question being raised. The criteria for the entire group of questions being met will sometimes be 100 percent, meaning that the standard for each question in step 1 must be met. When he is trying to reach a decision about a complex matter, he will sometimes establish a somewhat lower criterion (perhaps four out of six questions must be met) from which he will choose an option.

Strategies for Becoming an Unconstricted Thinker

The strategy that Boehm uses negates the tendency of most individuals to have self-imposed guidelines in the reaching of good decisions. This internal cognitive process and ones similar to it, which will be described next, are indicative of those employed by an outstanding leader who is an unconstricted thinker.

Those who need improvement in this area would do well to remember the words of James Comer (2003), a professor of psychology at Harvard University: "Thinking development doesn't require investments in expensive new programs or infrastructure; rather, it is a mindset change. Such a focus reduces behavioral problems and acts as an organizing theme that enables staff members to carry out the daily collaboration, problem solving, and creative exploitation of opportunities" (p. 421).

Our research regarding power thinkers concurs with Comer's viewpoint. Generally, examining and making modifications in two areas can significantly improve this aspect of internal cognition: how we consider decisions before us and when we reach them.

HOW WE CONSIDER DECISIONS BEFORE US. If you are not now an unconstricted thinker, it is quite likely that one or two tendencies impinge on the way in which you make decisions: judging things as either black or white and stereotypical thinking:

• Black-and-white thinking. When individuals are faced with a choice of two or more options, they want their decision to be clearly the best of them. As we know, though, decisions are rarely that black-and-white. How individuals deal with this ambiguity separates the unconstricted thinker from a less able counterpart. Those who are less able in this area attempt to minimize the complexities of issues facing them. When they make a decision, they will downplay its ambiguities and categorize them by saying they are either a result of this or that. By failing to recognize the complexities of the decision, they are ignoring the variables that can have ripple effects on its efficacy. Thus, unforeseen problems will arise that will derail success during the implementation process.

If you tend to be a black-and-white thinker, you must begin to look at each option differently than you are at present. Instead of constricting your thinking by categorizing an option as merely this or that, examine its positive and negative features in a quantitative fashion. To accomplish this objective, we suggest you use the weighted characteristics test presented later in the chapter as Exercise 4.4 to provide you with this data before you reach a decision.

• Stereotypical thinking. A second malady that adversely affects good decision making is stereotypical thinking. You can tell if you practice it by asking yourself a few questions: Have others told you that you group people, places, or ideas only by their most generalizable characteristic? Do you find yourself automatically saying no when asked to take an action that will cause you or your organization to repeat an experience that will likely fail, as it did before? Do you not reattempt an initiative if you are displeased with some segment of it?

If you answered yes to one or more of these questions, then stereotypical thinking is limiting the success of your decisions. To overcome it, you must first understand why you have the tendency to think about things in such a generalizable fashion. You cognitively use this process because human nature tries to put complexities into familiar patterns or gestalts (that is, simple concepts) as rapidly as possible.

Our human nature can be easily and effectively reined in by consciously addressing our tendency to think stereotypically. We can do so by asking ourselves, when faced with a decision, "How is this different from comparable decisions that I have reached in the past?" Building this important question into your habitual process of reasoning is easy to do, and it will be a positive step toward becoming a more proficient decision maker.

WHEN WE REACH DECISIONS. If you are not yet an unconstricted thinker, you could make significant improvement by making changes in two areas. We just addressed the first of them: how we consider the decisions before us. We now address the second of them: when we reach decisions.

Most leaders for whom this area is not one of strength use an identifiable pattern as to when they reach a decision. To see where you stand, respond yes or no to these two questions:

- Do I make decisions regarding things that I like to do before those things that I do not?
- Do I make decisions about matters about which others are making noise before decisions that are more important?

An unconstricted thinker will answer no to the questions. Their less able counterparts in this area of cognition would likely respond yes to one or both of these queries.

If your answer was yes to the first of these questions, we recommend that you use the process described below, which will enable you to make decisions more readily in the future about matters that you do not like:

1. List the issues that you do not like as well as facets of your position about which you are not particularly knowledgeable.
2. Identify the very best resources (for example, people, software programs) that you can tap when you are confronted with a difficult or unpleasant decision in one of the areas you identified in step 1.

3. Employ a decision-making strategy such as the paradigm used by Boehm, the weighted characteristics test, or another one presented in this book.

4. If a major decision has to be made in a few weeks, field-test segments of the decision reached in step 3 to assess its efficacy.

5. Where warranted, make revisions based on this field-test before implementing a tentatively identified decision.

The second question that we raised earlier was, "Do I reach decisions about matters about which others are making noises before decisions that are more important?" Our research found a very clear differentiation between unconstricted thinkers and non–power thinkers relative to this question. Non–power thinkers answered this question affirmatively. This group cited that they wanted to "get someone off their back" or to promote organizational harmony as the factors responsible for having such a viewpoint. An unconstricted thinker sometimes will accede to external pressure such as the preceding situation and reach an inconsequential decision ahead of a more important one. These instances are rare, however. To keep expedience from precluding importance as to the order in which decisions are reached, unconstricted thinkers use planning as a vehicle for prioritizing matters requiring action.

Unconstricted thinkers realize that when seemingly every second of their time is scheduled, it is virtually impossible to find free time in the confines of a workday, and that which is unscheduled is frequently not acted on. To ensure that the preponderance of their time is not spent in deciding trivial matters, unconstricted thinkers make appointments with themselves for the purpose of reaching important decisions, such as ones that will strengthen the organization's performance. By setting aside time for making an important decision, you can overcome indecision and ensure that your decisions are not ad hoc or made under pressure. In this way, you will maximize your internal cognitive processes by consciously using the decision-making paradigm regularly employed by Edward Boehm or another strategy presented in this section.

AUSPICIOUS COMPLETER

In functioning as an *auspicious completer,* power thinkers identify the reasons that they do not complete a task or attain a goal. When they are unsuccessful, they do not offer excuses but strive to have an understanding as to how they can be successful. And when they fail to perform a responsibility, they seek to honestly discern why they did not complete the assigned task. Items 3, 55, and 65 of the Yale Assessment of Thinking assess the degree to which you are an unconstricted thinker.

Understanding the Auspicious Completer

Items 3, 55, and 65 of the Yale Assessment of Thinking assess the degree to which you are an auspicious completer. Fill out the Auspicious Completer Item Cluster Graph, entering your scores for these items from Chapter Two. If your total score was 5 or under, write as the YAT score interpretation "highly skilled." If your total score was 6 or 7, write "average ability." If your total score was 8 or higher, write "need for improvement."

Tasks that we do not often complete include things for which we have little aptitude or that we dislike. When non–power thinkers fail to perform such tasks, they concoct excuses as to why they did not complete them instead of analyzing what they could do to not be asked to do them in the future. If you are often trapped into performing tasks for which you have little aptitude and even less interest in doing, we recommend that you learn to replace excuses with explanations.

To help you to better understand the auspicious completer aspect of power thinking, consider George Santayana (1863–1952), a philosopher, poet, critic of culture and literature, and best-selling novelist. He was considered an eminent philosopher during his lifetime, but his

Item Cluster Graph.   **Auspicious Completer Item Cluster Graph**

YAT Items	Your Response
3	_____
55	_____
65	_____
Total	_____
YAT score interpretation	_____

work did not receive the acclaim then that it since has because his ideas were ahead of the times in which he lived.

Santayana's list of publications is impressive, and a significant group of scholars today study his work. He is probably best known for a line from his 1905 book, *The Life of Reason: Reason in Common Sense:* "Those who cannot remember the past are condemned to repeat it" (p. 284).

Over the years, these words have been quoted often. Some individuals have written or said variations of this quotation, and there have certainly been many interpretations as to the meaning of it. The explanation that is probably the most widely accepted version of what Santayana wrote is that people, like countries, will err by repeating mistakes that they or others have made because they failed to learn from them. Our research showed that power thinkers do indeed learn from these lessons of history, while their less skilled counterparts typically do not.

YAT items 3, 55, and 65 all deal with individuals who do not "remember the past" as to why they really were unable to perform a responsibility. By not understanding this reason, they "are condemned to repeat it" often—and to the detriment of their stature as leaders.

Our research on power thinkers revealed that they are decidedly different in their approach to the completion of tasks from individuals who are not auspicious completers. For one thing, they complete tasks. Second, they learn from the past when they were unsuccessful and modify their thinking accordingly to produce success the next time they are in a similar situation. It is this blending of success and the completing of tasks that led us to characterize a power thinker as an auspicious completer.

The YAT contains three items (3, 55, and 65) that deal with the areas discussed in this section.

Item 3 states, "When I fail to perform a responsibility, I am unclear in my mind what the reason was for my not completing that task." While not doing what was assigned adversely affects the well-being of an organization, that individual's inability to determine the reason for his or her failure to perform this task has even more dire long-term consequences. Since the person did not identify the negative behaviors that precluded him or her from doing what was assigned, there is a high degree of probability that this individual will use these very same cognitive processes in the future—and, in all likelihood, with the same level of nonsuccess as in the prior task.

In item 55 ("When I am unsuccessful at a task, I believe that it is better to give an excuse rather than an apology"), the offering of an excuse rather than an apology is an erroneous use of the reasoning internal cognitive process. By developing an excuse, the conscious mind is absolving the person of wrongdoing in connection with his or her lack of success in completing a task. Instead of remembering the past and learning from it, such individuals are attributing their failure to factors external to themselves, such as other individuals or the circumstances. Thus, rather than learning the shortcomings within their own cognitive processes that let them down and taking action to ameliorate them in the future, these persons have categorized their failure as being caused by a unique external circumstance.

If item 65 ("When I failed to complete something that I was supposed to do, it was because I didn't have enough time") is an area in which you very often find yourself, you are not alone. "I didn't have enough time" is the most common excuse offered by professionals who fail to complete tasks. Although it is accurate to say that many people have a heavy workload, it is equally true to state that many leaders use reasoning's internal cognitive processes in an ineffective manner as they perform these responsibilities. People who employ such procedures have never been taught effective ways to think. The reason they did not have enough time to complete the task was the inefficient internal cognitive processes that they continue to employ.

An Exemplary Auspicious Completer: W. Austin Ligon

W. Austin Ligon, the president and CEO of Car Max Inc., regularly demonstrates the internal cognitive processes used by auspicious completers. Car Max began in 1993 as an innovative car-selling concept. After losing money in its first six years of operation and receiving criticism for some of its practices, the company earned a profit for two consecutive quarters for the first time in 1999.

Today, Car Max generates over $2 billion in sales and has more than five thousand employees at its sites in eighteen markets. An example of the company's impact is that in 2002, it was responsible for 89 percent of the used cars sold in that year in the United States.

The catalyst for this success story is W. Austin Ligon. It was he who developed the vision for Car Max and he who sought to learn why the company was failing rather than offering excuses for its lack of profitability.

Ligon learned that the company's formula for the placement of stores where Car Max vehicles were sold was erroneous. It was treating midsize and metropolitan markets similarly. Car Max learned that customers in midsize markets would drive up to twenty-five miles to buy a car, while customers in metropolitan markets will not drive that far to purchase an automobile because of traffic congestion.

Ligon could have continued with his original strategy, and Car Max would probably have failed. Instead, he analyzed the lessons of history that were keeping the company from attaining its desired objective, and he altered his thinking to not repeat these lessons. Car Max sites in metropolitan areas are now located within no more than fifteen miles of one another, rather than the former twenty-five miles between sites.

Did it take courage to admit that his original thinking was wrong? You bet. Did Car Max benefit from Ligon's analysis of the company's failure to accomplish its profitability vision? Once again, the answer is yes.

Strategies for Becoming an Auspicious Completer

If this segment of reasoning is one in which you are not highly skilled, you can improve your ability by learning to replace excuses with explanations. Excuses that we state to others and to ourselves are equally detrimental to becoming a powerful thinker. Excuses are offered to others to avoid taking responsibility for our own failure to do something. Since what we do not do is typically that which we dislike doing, our failure to provide the real reason for our inaction means that we will likely be asked repeatedly to do the same undesirable tasks in the future. Thus, giving an excuse reduces your success.

Excuses come in two forms: those we give others and those we give ourselves. Both can have adverse outcomes relative to the completion of tasks for which we are responsible. This section describes how to replace excuses with explanations.

REPLACE EXCUSES WITH EXPLANATIONS. An *excuse* can be defined as a pretended reason for conduct. The goal of any excuse is to avert responsibility for one's behavior by instead placing blame on another person or event. In contrast, *explanations* are statements of reasons that support one's conduct. The difference between the two concepts is significant. When you feel a need to offer an excuse for your decision, we encourage you to offer an apology instead. Some people may give excuses rather than apologies because excuses appear easier, at least on the surface. Being honest about the reasons for our behavior requires courage to accept the fact that we are not perfect and to risk revealing our true, deeply held reasons for our inaction. It takes courage to state, "Because of X, I decided Y," rather than, "I really wanted to do it, but [someone won't let me, or something happened, or . . .]."

You may think that an excuse helps to avoid hurting another person, but it does not. Giving excuses, in fact, has a negative outcome: it increases the frequency with which others ask you to do things you do not want to do. When you give an excuse, people believe that your excuse is the real reason you are declining their request. In the future, they will make the same request again because they believe that you really wanted to do it, but that the reason you gave for your inaction was why you were unable to do it. Consequently, they will think that if they just plead more urgently or that if whatever obstacle you gave as an excuse is removed, you will do what they want. All they have to do is to ask continually until they discover when this opportune time occurs.

Excuses can also create a mismatch between your nonverbal language and your words. For instance, even if you say how sorry you are for not meeting someone's request, your nonverbal language may demonstrate that you could have met the request if desired. When you make excuses, power thinkers often notice the discrepancy and judge you to be inconsistent or even dishonest. By providing an honest explanation for your decision, you show that you are trustworthy. In the future, others will value your decisions and assistance more highly because they know you will do only what you really want to do or what is in the best interest of the organization.

Also, by stating the true reasons for your decisions, you will not waste mental and physical energy trying to create—and remember—believable excuses. Excuse giving can become a strategy for avoiding reality, which will distract your subconscious and decrease your power of insight. Because subconscious mental processes cannot discern excuses from truth, the former is treated by your subconscious as facts. Thus, excuses can become reality.

Equally destructive are the excuses you give yourself. As you see from the list in Exercise 4.2, excuses that you give yourself usually involve negative self-talk (for example, "I can't because I don't do well in that area," "I don't have time," "I forgot"). When you use them, you

~~~~ Exercise 4.2

WRITING STATEMENTS THAT REPLACE EXCUSES

Read the list below to identify the most common excuses you have used in the past. Then write a statement you can use in the future as an effective substitute for each excuse. Put that explanation in a prominent but private place, so that it will be readily available when you need to utter these words instead of offering excuses. Your goal should be to make these statements enough times that they become an automatic part of your approach to decision making.

For excuses you give yourself, begin the replacement statement with the words: "I can [a positive action you will take to counteract negative self-talk] whenever I [describe the situations in which you may be tempted to use that specific negative self-affirmation]."

I Can't/Don't Because . . .   *I Can and Will Because . . .*

1. I've done it before and it didn't work, or it [or I] wasn't good.

   _____

2. No one told me that it was okay to begin.

   _____

3. That isn't my job.

   _____

4. I'm too busy [or tired].

   _____

5. I don't have time.

   _____

6. I forgot.

   _____

7. I didn't know it was so important.

   _____

8. It was already good enough for them, so it should be good enough for me.

   _____

9. I just can't seem to get started.

   _____

(Continued)

Exercise 4.2 (Continued)

I Can't/Don't Because . . .   *I Can and Will Because . . .*

10. I would if I just didn't have
    so much to do right now.   _____

11. _____ isn't worth the
    time, energy, or effort.   _____

12. It bores me.   _____

13. I'll do it later.   _____

14. I'm too inept [inexperienced,
    lazy, or something else].   _____

15. I have too many
    responsibilities at . . .   _____

16. If I were in complete control
    of my time, I'd . . .   _____

17. It makes me feel
    uncomfortable.   _____

18. I don't want to.   _____

19. It wasn't important.   _____

20. I'm scared [or ashamed,
    or mad, or something else].   _____

21. I can't find . . .   _____

22. _____   _____

23. _____   _____

demean yourself. Therefore, if you use excuses too frequently, you convince yourself that you really cannot accomplish a goal because they have become a reality in your mind.

This statement bears repeating: excuses block your ability to assume larger responsibilities and face challenges honestly. As we will discuss in Chapters Six and Seven, honesty is an important ingredient in strengthening insight. You can eliminate excuses by completing Exercise 4.2, analyzing what you have written, and making a conscious effort to use what you have learned from this exercise.

JUDICIOUS ANALYST

A *judicious analyst* is a power thinker who uses time as an ally, not an enemy, when solving problems. These individuals do not get stampeded into coming up with precipitous solutions before they have had adequate time to develop appreciably better ones. And while attempting to solve a problem, they do not engage in practices that will squander time and make their busy schedules become even more harried.

Understanding the Judicious Analyst

Items 13, 41, and 64 of the Yale Assessment of Thinking assess the degree to which you are a judicious analyst. Fill out the Judicious Analyst Item Cluster Graph, entering your scores for these items from Chapter Two. If your total score was 5 or under, write as the YAT score interpretation "highly skilled." If your total score was 6 or 7, write "average ability." If your total score was 8 or higher, write "need for improvement."

The late Red Skelton was once asked what trait was most important to being a great comedian. He responded "timing." Skelton said that most comedians, whether they are just beginning their careers or are famous, have comparable senses of humor. What separates great from adequate comedians is timing: great comedians know how long to wait before saying the punch line, when to use a grimace or some other bodily gesture to enhance a joke, and depending on the audience's reaction, the order in which to deliver a monologue.

The exemplary leaders whom we studied, like the comedians about whom Skelton spoke, know just when a problem has been solved.

Item Cluster Graph. **Judicious Analyst Item Cluster Graph**

YAT Items	Your Response
13	_____
41	_____
64	_____
Total	_____
YAT score interpretation	_____

These judicious analysts take the requisite amount of time so that they can properly use reasoning's internal cognitive processes that they regularly employ in solving a complex problem. By using a strategy that is conducive to problem solution, they then engage in subsequent action in a confident manner. Their confidence is based on their knowledge that what they are about to do is the proper solution to the problem that is confronting them.

In the assessment presented in Chapter Two of this book, items 13, 41, and 64 all focus on the issue of time in the problem solution process. The length of time is the major variable that separates the aspect of reasoning that each of these items addresses.

To many leaders, item 13 ("When I face a difficult problem, I like to mull it over for a long period of time in my mind") appears to be a prudent course of action. In fact, they are making two mistakes when using this internal cognitive process.

First, while engaged in trying to find a solution to a difficult problem, nonjudicious analysts mentally mull over both the problem and possible recourses of action. Doing this processing in their mind is akin to a clothes dryer that spins endlessly. While the mind is engaged in remembering the same information and the continuous rethinking of it, reasoning's internal cognitive process is hindered in its ability to generate new thoughts. The mind is also impeded in its capacity to look analytically at the solutions that are in its "clothes dryer."

Second, there is a fallacy that spending a great deal of time in thinking about a problem will lead to a correct solution. Time alone causes neither good nor bad courses of action to be generated in the mind. What leads to sound decisions is the use of effective problem-solving strategies, such as the ones presented in this book.

Judicious analysts do two things when confronted with a difficult problem: they decide what strategy they will use to solve it and then write down ideas as they think of them. By writing ideas down as they are generated, they free the mind from the task of remembering them. Thus, it is able to come up with additional possible solutions and to analytically assess the soundness of the ideas that have been developed during the problem-solving process. When judicious analysts have completed the preceding process and are satisfied that they have the requisite information pertinent to the problem, they decide the course of action that they will take to solve it.

YAT items 41 and 64 focus on another malady of poor problem solution: formulating a plan to address it too quickly. Leaders who reach solutions impulsively (item 41—"In solving problems, I am impulsive") or discard alternatives too quickly (item 64—"When I am confronted with problems, other individuals believe that I come up with solutions by discarding alternatives too quickly") would do well to remember the time-honored fable of the tortoise and the hare. Just as the faster of the two animals, the hare, did not win the race, quickly conceived plans of action usually do not effectively solve complex problems.

Whereas item 13 addressed spending an appreciable amount of time to solve a problem, items 41 and 64 focus on precipitous action. Many people grew up watching John Wayne westerns. In these movies, when confronted with a problem, Wayne never formed a cross-functional team to study its issues. Rather, he provided an immediate response as to what he would do to solve the problem.

Many leaders erroneously think that by emulating John Wayne and reaching solutions immediately, they are showing their strength to subordinates. But unless these individuals have exceptional skill in insight or have faced this particular problem before, their precipitous action usually results in the implementation of ineffective solutions. Thus, instead of being respected by subordinates, such leaders are viewed as loose cannons and not worthy of trust.

As was the case with item 13, we once again are suggesting that leaders have a proven strategy that they can employ whenever they are confronted with a difficult challenge. The strategy must be one that will enable them to consider all segments of the problem objectively. By using such a process, they can develop comprehensive alternatives, revise them, and choose and implement a positive solution.

Quickness is not what makes an effective problem solver. When discussing item 13, we stated that taking a great deal of time does not automatically lead to good problem solutions. The same is true about quickly deciding on courses of action to problems. You would do well to remember that it is not the speed with which a solution is developed but how you use the time being spent to consider alternatives that will determine whether the solutions devised will produce subsequent positive outcomes.

Items 13, 41, and 64 of the YAT focus on the issue of time when individuals are solving problems. Our research found that judicious analysts use an established strategy to derive a solution. After analyzing an idea and the information that this process yields, these power thinkers decided on not just a course of action to address the problem but rather the best one for its solution. While they were engaged in this reasoning cognitive process, they did not establish artificial time boundaries by making instant decisions about what they were going to do or taking an inordinate amount of time to choose a solution. Rather, they used time judiciously as they implemented their designated problem solution strategy. Hence, we identified this aspect of reasoning's internal cognitive process to be that of a judicious analyzer.

An Exemplary Judicious Analyzer: Sharon Allred Decker

Sharon Allred Decker has been an enormously successful leader in both the nonprofit and for-profit sectors. Her accomplishments led to her being named, along with such luminaries as Sandra Day O'Connor and Oprah Winfrey, as one of "America's Fifty Most Successful Women" by the *Feminine Fortunes Magazine.* Anyone who knows or who has worked with her would agree that she is truly a power thinker.

Decker was named president of Doncaster, a division of the Tanner Company, in 1999. Doncaster is a direct seller of high-end women's apparel. The company, whose origins trace back to 1935, designs, sources, distributes, and sells its products to over twenty-five hundred independent contractors located in every state.

At the time that Decker was hired, Doncaster needed to reposition its products and its image as one that sold matronly and outdated apparel. Being an outsider at the time of her hiring presented both an opportunity and a challenge for Decker. She could address this problem objectively and without any emotional ties to the company's past efforts. Conversely, her prior leadership positions were not in this industry, so in the minds of some, she lacked the credibility to solve Doncaster's problems.

She decided to use the ladder strategy to address the challenge facing her company. Just as a ladder has rungs that enable a person to ascend to a desired elevation, this strategy's steps facilitate moving a situation from problem status to solution. This strategy entails asking three questions:

1. Why do I consider this matter to be a problem?

2. What would I consider the condition to be for me to consider it to be solved?

3. How can I get the situation from its existing condition to its desired condition?

In using this approach, Decker established that she considered the company's situation to be a problem because sales were down. She was also concerned about the company's future. If Doncaster was to continue to be typecast as a seller of matronly clothes that featured outdated styles, then the likelihood was that not only would the company experience downward sales, but also the market appeal of their clothing line would lessen even more in the future (the *why* of the ladder strategy).

After engaging in this process, Decker decided that for this condition to be solved, the following would need to occur (the *what* of the ladder strategy): (1) more appealing fashions needed to be in the company's clothing line, (2) the perception of Doncaster in the market needed to be changed to reflect its image of selling "forever chic" rather than matronly clothes, and (3) sales needed to be increased.

Decker tackled the *how* of the ladder strategy—getting the situation from its present status to the *what* established in the prior step—with both purpose and enthusiasm. She began a series of visits across the country in which she met with sellers, managers, and others who could help her to move the company to its desired position. Decker assured them that Doncaster's values as a company and its positive relationship with them would not change. She also asked for ideas they had, regardless of how slight the step forward, that would move the company toward the objectives she had established for the problem to be solved. She chose from the best of their ideas and implemented them.

Since Decker's selection as president, Doncaster has grown significantly in profitability, net sales have increased, and morale is high. The company has also shed its image as a supplier of matronly apparel.

Three other aspects of Sharon Allred Decker's approach to problems are worth mentioning. First, she sees problems not as something to be avoided but rather as "opportunities to build on my strength." Decker believes that each time she goes through an experience such as the preceding one that she learns new knowledge and skills that she can use in the future.

Second, when asked if she ever regretted not selecting alternatives that she discarded, she replied: "You decide on a solution based on the information that's available to you. Sometimes it's 30 percent off, and maybe if I implemented an alternative action, it would have been better. But I've always believed as a leader that it's much worse to do nothing about a problem than to follow a strategy that made our company 70 percent better."

Third, Decker correctly believes that most difficult problems have multiple solutions. Therefore, rather than trying to develop one cure-all for them, she devises multifaceted solutions as she did to address the situation that she encountered after she was named president of Doncaster. For each of these multiple solutions, she establishes "lines in the sand," which are the accountability standards that each facet must reach.

Strategies for Becoming a Judicious Analyst

If you are not yet highly skilled in using time judiciously to deal with problems or strategically analyze possible solutions to them, you would do well to emulate Decker. In addition, we present two strategies that can aid you in your efforts to become a judicious analyst who solves problems effectively: double think and the weighted characteristics test.

DOUBLE THINK. In situations where it would be beneficial to reflect while attempting to solve a problem, you should use the strategy of double think, which enables you to comprehensively analyze the situation before you and helps you to do the following more effectively: (1) imagine positive outcomes, (2) select preferred alternatives, (3) adopt a long-term perspective, and (4) experiment with options before taking action.

Without double thinking, choosing options can become extremely difficult. You may miss the optimal resolution of a problem because no matter how hard you try to dispel such a feeling, the worry that other choices might be better than the one that you favor looms over you. These nagging fears can distract your reasoning from properly occurring as you think. The use of the double think strategy also limits your use of unproductive shortcuts as well as an overreliance on old experiences during problem solving. Although your past experiences should be one piece of information on which you can rely, previous knowledge may be based on outdated assumptions. Those experiences will not reflect your growth as a professional since these past experiences occurred or enable you to take into account the factors unique to the situation at hand.

Some solutions to a problem emerge within a few seconds, but others take appreciably longer to develop. We encourage you to use the Double-Think Checklist in Exhibit 4.1 when you have an important

Exhibit 4.1. Double-Think Checklist

1. Do I have enough information to solve this problem?   ☐ Yes ☐ No
   If not, how can I get the information required to come up
   with a solution?

   _____

   _____

2. Do I know what I need or want from this problem's solution?   ☐ Yes ☐ No
   If not, I must wait until I do. If so, how can I use my
   motivation and talents to receive what I want without
   causing damage to other positive purposes?

   _____

   _____

3. Before I decide, can I test alternative choices on a small scale
   or seek advice from an expert in the field?   ☐ Yes ☐ No
4. What could I do to make this problem's solution easier and
   more effective? For example, what resources have I used in
   the past to solve similar problems? Writing a letter to the
   people involved to "write away my negative thoughts"
   and then not mail it?   ☐ Yes ☐ No
   Talking to significant others to gain new perspectives?   ☐ Yes ☐ No
   Taking longer to decide?   ☐ Yes ☐ No
   Establishing a time in the future when I will reassess
   conditions around the problem until I have good
   indicators that the optimal time for deciding upon
   a solution has arrived.   ☐ Yes ☐ No
5. Have I imagined what will occur if each possible
   alternative is implemented?   ☐ Yes ☐ No
6. Have I considered all the people who will be affected and
   the viewpoints of both women and men?   ☐ Yes ☐ No
7. Have I developed a backup plan in case the result I expect
   does not come about?   ☐ Yes ☐ No
8. Is there a risk involved?   ☐ Yes ☐ No
   If so, what support do I have?

   _____

   _____

9. Am I basing my solution solely on past experiences?   ☐ Yes ☐ No
10. Is this the right time to make the decision about this
    problem?   ☐ Yes ☐ No
    Can I take more time to think?   ☐ Yes ☐ No
11. Have I fully assessed alternatives that I might have
    discarded too quickly?   ☐ Yes ☐ No
12. Have I considered how Murphy's Law ("Anything that can
    go wrong will go wrong") could affect the outcome of each
    of the choices I am considering?   ☐ Yes ☐ No

(Continued)

Exhibit 4.1. (Continued)

13. If I take the first option (and it turns out to be the best solution), what is the greatest good that could be accomplished?

_____

_____

If I take the second option, what is the greatest good that could be accomplished?

_____

_____

14. Do I feel that it is less threatening to be undecided about a matter than it is to force a solution relative to it?   ☐ Yes   ☐ No

15. Is this my problem and my responsibility, or am I trying to make it someone else's problem?   ☐ Yes   ☐ No

16. Have my feelings on this matter affected my choice of options?   ☐ Yes   ☐ No
    If yes, have they had a positive or negative influence?

_____

_____

Alternatively, have my emotions of anger, doubt, or fear minimized the opportunities represented by solving the problem?

_____

_____

17. Can I think of only one course of action?   ☐ Yes   ☐ No
    If so, I will proceed through these questions again until other possible alternatives emerge to make sure I am not overlooking options.

_____

problem to solve. To understand the power of the checklist, complete Exercise 4.3. Using the checklist as early as possible in the problem-solving process will help you to identify the critical elements of it, and narrow the options from which you ultimately will attempt to solve the problem.

Our research relative to this checklist has found several important ramifications when it is used. One is that the checklist enables you to isolate feasible alternatives. In addition, it forces you to consider different courses of action before you decide on one of them. One of the strongest features is that people who are adept in using this strategy delay action when the double-think checklist reveals that more information is needed. For example, a corporate leader stops by subordi-

---

Exercise 4.3

USING THE DOUBLE-THINK CHECKLIST

1. Write on a notepad a problem that you currently face. Read the checklist in Exhibit 4.1, and answer each question as it relates to it. For each *no* answer, consider using the strategies for power thinking discussed in this chapter.
2. On the same sheet of paper, write down the two or three preferred options that emerged from this process. How did double-think improve the solution that you developed?

---

nates' offices during implementation of group decisions, asking double-think questions to find out what other information is needed before the deadline for reaching a solution. This action enables him to take necessary steps if a problem has occurred or if procrastination is occurring so that the initiative will be on time and successful.

When using the checklist, you are likely to identify some questions that are especially useful in the problem-solving process. Learn to ask these questions automatically of yourself and of others before you attempt to reach solutions to significant problems quickly.

We encourage you to refer to the double-think checklist in the future as you consider all the elements of a problem that you must resolve. The answers you develop will help you to better understand the nature of the issues involved and identify some options or alternatives. Once you have identified these potential solutions, you can assess the merit of each on the basis of both its totality as well as its individual components. This step in the problem-solving process generates information and options as well as analyzes how your emotions may be influencing reasoning's internal cognitive process. Your goal is to find as much information as you can, set aside sufficient time to read and reflect on the options you have identified, listen attentively to the various viewpoints about those options, and analyze the data before you.

WEIGHTED CHARACTERISTICS TEST. If you wish to consider the efficacy of a possible course of action, we recommend using the weighted characteristics test, which is a way of thinking about the interaction of the many variables within a challenging situation. It allows you to see the total picture of the outcomes that could occur with each option you are considering. Exercise 4.4 describes how to do a weighted characteristics test.

One of the benefits of this approach is that it enables you to see what the most important issues are when you are faced with a problem. To demonstrate, do a weighted characteristics test with the following example:

> You have been offered a new job. You and your family have deep roots in the town in which you now live, and the job will require a move across the country. This potential job will double your current salary, and you will receive a substantial annuity. The company is internationally known. This is the job you've wanted all your life. Your wife is reluctant to move because she has a job where you are living now, and your son is a sophomore in high school. The climate is not as good in the new location, and commuting time to work would be considerably longer than it is now.

After you have identified your possible options (move away or do not move), follow the instructions in Exercise 4.4, and then look at our solution in Exhibit 4.2 to see how your rankings compare with ours. To practice this strategy a second time, use the weighted characteristics test to analyze your options concerning a problem that you are facing now.

Exhibit 4.2. Sample Weighted Characteristics Test

This is how we completed the test and weighted the advantages and disadvantages. How did our responses compare with yours?

Do Move		Do Not Move	
1. Double my salary	10	1. Value of deep roots	4
2. Substantial annuity	5	2. Wife will be happier	9
3. Internationally known firm	6	3. Son could finish school	8
4. Always wanted this job	7	4. Climate is better here	1
5. Commute could give me time to work on subway	3	5. Commute could take time from family	2
Totals	31		24

—〜〜— Exercise 4.4

WEIGHTED CHARACTERISTICS TEST

1. Draw a line down the middle of a sheet of paper to make two columns. At the top of the left column, write down a phrase that describes one of your preferred options; write a phrase for an alternative preferred option at the top of the right column—for example, "Do Move" and "Don't Move."

2. Under each option, list the positive outcomes that could occur if you chose that option based on all the information and knowledge that you have at this point. Once you have identified outcomes for each variable, list the negative consequences that could occur if either of the courses of action were selected. For example, you might consider that moving to a new city would require investing time in relocating, and you would view that loss of time as a negative consequence of moving. Because "staying here in town" would eliminate that negative, you would write "not having to invest time in relocating" as one of the positive consequences of "staying here in town," and you would list it in that column. In summary, if you view an outcome as having a negative effect, write that outcome as a positive reason for selecting the opposite option.

3. After writing down all the possible outcomes or consequences, count the number of statements you wrote. Select the outcome or consequence of most importance to you, and write the number of the total to the right of that consequence. For example, if you wrote down ten possible outcomes, the number to the right of your most important outcome would be 10.

   Next, find the consequence that is second in importance to you, and assign it the next lower number, which will give that consequence the second highest weight in importance (if you have ten items, the next most important one would be assigned a value of 9). Continue in this manner until all consequences on both sides of the scale are assigned a number.

4. Total the number of points of the statements on each side of the balance. The option with the higher score is the preferred solution for you to pursue using the information that was available to you at the time the decision had to be made.

Once you understand how to use the weighted characteristics test, you may wish to modify it. Some judicious analysts prefer a variation of the weighting we used. They list more than two options in columns and allocate 100 points among the possible outcomes. The ones of greatest importance are assigned the highest weights, and factors of lesser importance are given smaller weights. They use this process because they believe that this system allows them to differentiate better among the weights given to items. This method pits alternatives against one another so that the best choice can be made.

The weighted characteristics test allows you to identify specific reasons for choosing a course of action to a problem. These assessments can be also used when more than two choices are being considered. For example, you could compare option A to B, and then compare the one found to be the better of the two to option C.

SUMMARY

In this chapter, we have explored how thoughts are generated during the internal cognitive process of reasoning. You have been presented with twenty-one highly effective strategies that power thinkers frequently use:

1. Identifying segments of an idea that you like

2. Improving rather than demeaning proposals

3. Showing employees that their ideas are valued and have received a fair hearing

4. Employing the "reason before you speak" strategy

5. Rephrasing others' comments using their own words

6. Reading body language

7. Traversing the territory from many directions to analyze your predispositions as well as those of others

8. Implementing paradigms to reach decisions such as the one employed by President Boehm

9. Avoiding the judgment of things as either black or white

10. Eliminating stereotypical thinking

11. Field-testing and revising segments of decisions before they are implemented

12. Making appointments with yourself to consider and reaching important decisions

13. Identifying the reasons that you do not complete tasks or attain goals

14. Taking actions to avoid repeating mistakes that you have made because you failed to learn from them

15. Replacing excuses with explanations

16. Using time strategically when solving problems

17. Writing down possible courses of action as you think of them

18. Overcoming the tendency to reach quick decisions

19. Employing the ladder strategy

20. Engaging in double thinking

21. Taking the weighted characteristics test

Using these strategies will help you to become a more effective leader, and your organization will become more successful as a result.

Finally, we also described the four subcomponent skills that constitute the internal cognitive process of reasoning: fair-minded arbitrator, unconstricted thinker, auspicious completer, and judicious analyst. On the next two pages, we have provided space to write your reflections as to steps you plan to take in order to become more proficient in each of these segments of internal cognition.

REASONING INTERNAL COGNITIVE PROCESS THINKING ENHANCEMENT

Fair-Minded Arbitrator

Unconstricted Thinker

Auspicious Completer

Judicious Analyst

CHAPTER FIVE

Reasoning

External Cognitive Process

⟨ω⟩ I n Chapter Four, we presented information about reasoning's internal cognitive process, which the mind uses in order to develop thoughts. In this chapter, we discuss its other segment: the actions the mind takes as a consequence of the decisions, solutions, and creative thoughts it generates. This facet of reasoning is called the external cognitive process.

Our study of power thinkers found that these individuals were highly skilled in four dimensions of this aspect of cognition. As a consequence, we classified their proficiency in these areas to be that of a bold pioneer (assessed by items 18, 39, and 63 of the YAT), provocative communicator (assessed by items 1, 32, and 38), resolute questioner (assessed by items 21, 34, and 48), and planning implementer (assessed by items 36, 56, and 68).

Each of these segments will be described in this chapter. As you did in Chapter Four, you can assess how proficient you are in each of them now by completing the item cluster graph at the start of each section.

BOLD PIONEER

U.S. history is replete with stories of the men and women who lived when our country was in its early years of existence. These early settlers established an ethos for which our country came to be known: a pioneering spirit that focuses on lofty aspirations that are pursued creatively and relentlessly until they are realized.

America's pioneers encountered obstacles as they strove to attain their aspirations, but they did not abandon their goals when confronted with adversity. They fearlessly and confidently worked at the tasks before them.

We relate this information about our country's past because it remains relevant today. Although many leaders do not exhibit the can-do attitude that made our country great, that attitude exists abundantly in power thinkers. Like the pioneers who lived in the United States many years ago, these leaders set significant objectives for themselves and their organizations to attain. Then they work toward their realization boldly and in an undaunted manner. That is why we classify these leaders as *bold pioneers.*

Ernst and Young state in their company's advertisements that the "most dangerous day in the life of a business is when it reaches all of its goals." The same could be said about leaders.

Understanding the Bold Pioneer

Items 18, 39, and 63 of the Yale Assessment of Thinking assess the degree to which you are a bold pioneer. Fill out the Bold Pioneer Item Cluster Graph, entering your scores for these items from Chapter Two. If your total score was 5 or under, write as the YAT score interpretation "highly skilled." If your total score was 6 or 7, write "average ability." If your total score was 8 or higher, write "need for improvement."

In research conducted by the Institute for the Power of Positive Students (1998), it was reported that only 3 percent of the professionals who are not power thinkers formulated and wrote goals. We have found this statistic to be consistent in our own work with non–power thinkers. Certainly, they established goals (and frequently) because their boss said they had to, but they did not have a strong commitment to them. As a consequence, the lack of attainment of these objectives (conveyed in item 18—"I have difficulty

Item Cluster Graph.   Bold Pioneer Item Cluster Graph

YAT Items	Your Response
18	_____
39	_____
63	_____
Total	_____
YAT score interpretation	_____

attaining the goals that I set for myself") is a frequent occurrence for these individuals.

Goals are the keystone of how power thinkers act. They expend time and give careful consideration to their formulation. When difficulties occur, they nevertheless boldly continue to seek its attainment; in contrast, their less skilled counterparts will abandon the goal with the excuse that it was "unrealistic" or they will state it is impossible to attain because some external condition has changed. Power thinkers may alter their plan as to how they will achieve it, but they never abandon the goal itself. Power thinkers firmly endorse what was developed, and they believe its realization is important to their and the organization's success.

Item 39 ("The plans that I develop are not as successful as I hoped when I originally formulated them") focuses on a related, but slightly different, aspect of goals: what occurs when they are met. If you responded either "very often" or "often" to this item, your planning is likely flawed. It lacks vision and importance. There is a myth in some organizational circles that "more is better." Such a philosophy is wrong when it pertains to planning. If a plan contains numerous trite elements, then its successful implementation will mean that much was done, but to what purpose?

Unlike the "much ado about nothing" plans of less skilled leaders, the ones developed by bold pioneers create the level of success that was envisioned when they were developed because the plans that power thinkers create contain an important and exciting goal. Bradford and

Cohen (1997) term such a priority "an overreaching goal that is a meaningful description of the purpose that captures the unique thrust of the specific unit" (p. 85). It is this unrelenting effort toward the realization of meaningful ends, rather than attaining a collage of insignificant objectives, that differentiates the plans of bold pioneers from ones developed by their less skilled counterparts. Like the pioneers, what they seek to accomplish is important. When it is, a high level of success occurs.

If item 63 ("I find it difficult to understand why the professional goals that I established are not realized") is frequently true for you, there can be many reasons for it. Aside from the ones previously stated, our research found that two factors were dominant. First, when goals are not met, power thinkers take actions to discern why. They want to learn the causes of their nonattainment, so that they will not engage in similar counterproductive strategies in the future. Less skilled leaders place blame on other people and conditions.

The second difference is the tenacity with which goals are undertaken. Since the goals they establish are important, bold pioneers work unceasingly until they are met. Power thinkers embody what Prime Minister Winston Churchill told the Harrow School students on October 29, 1941: "Never, ever, ever, ever, ever, ever, ever, give up. Never give up. Never give up. Never give up." Power thinkers rarely give up when seeking to attain a goal. In contrast, goal abandonment is a significantly more frequent occurrence for leaders who are less skilled in this dimension of thinking.

An Exemplary Bold Pioneer: Billy Payne

A power thinker who characterizes how leaders should act relative to goals is Billy Payne, who attained fame first as a lawyer and later as the person responsible for the selection of Atlanta as the site for the Summer Olympic Games held there in 1996. Payne is a bold pioneer who establishes significant things to be accomplished (overarching goals) and pursues them boldly. When they are realized, few would argue that what was done was not important.

Payne knew precisely what goal he wanted to accomplish when he sought to have the Olympic Games held in Atlanta. He quit his lucrative law practice and went into debt as he worked without a salary for three years in order to pursue his goal.

Although he faced plenty of obstacles, he never listened to naysayers and abandoned his goal. The fact that Atlanta hosted the Games, in spite of the fact that it had been given little or no chance of doing so, is a direct testament to Payne's belief in what he was seeking to accomplish, as well as his skill as a goal developer and attainer.

Strategies for Becoming a Bold Pioneer

If you are not adept in the bold pioneer aspect of reasoning, you would do well to rethink your viewpoint relative to goals. Certainly they serve little or no purpose if the organizational ethos is such that they are mere window dressing. However, their stature can be easily reversed if bold goals are instead established. Goals that are substantive and have organizational importance can play a crucial part in an organization's vitality.

John W. Gardner, perhaps our nation's foremost authority on leadership, had this to say about the setting of important goals to an organization: "Unless the leader has a sense of where the whole enterprise is going and must go, it is not possible to delegate (or carry out personally) the other functions. To have 'a sense of where the whole enterprise is going and must go' is . . . the very core and essence of the best leadership" (Gardner, 1990, p. 20).

Gardner is correct. Subordinates are not going to rally around a meaningless set of goals. Nor are they going to be motivated to expend extra time and energy toward the realization of an organizational blueprint for the future that is laden with insignificant objectives.

Power thinkers set goals that are important and serve as a source of motivation for those whom they lead. They realize that it will take planning and effort to attain these goals. They also know that when these objectives are achieved, their organization will be a decidedly better one.

If you set high goals and have difficulty in reaching them, it is likely that your shortfall is in the details. Careful consideration is usually given to the launching of new initiatives. Where goals go unmet in a different segment of their implementation: after the action to meet the goal is initiated.

If your efforts customarily go awry during this segment of an undertaking, then the strategy we set out next, using backward reasoning, can aid you immeasurably. Many leaders do not give adequate attention to the conceptualization of the actions that need to occur after a plan has been initiated. When adversity occurs, they will choose lesser goals. Instead, we urge you to focus your thoughts on each step necessary to achieve the important goals that you have established and these steps will stretch your organization to make it better. To improve your track record in the implementation of the goals that you establish, use the backward reasoning strategy after you have established a goal.

USE BACKWARD REASONING. Backward reasoning is valuable when the desired outcome is clear, but the actions to achieving the goal are not. This strategy can also help you analyze the efficacy of a proposed initiative. In backward reasoning, you work backward from your desired end to figure out what your first and subsequent steps should be. By forcing your mind to think in a manner in which it is unaccustomed—backward—it becomes appreciably more analytical. It will focus on each step needed to reach the intended target rather than skipping over them. This attention to steps later in the implementation process will cause you and your colleagues to identify potential obstacles with a specificity that will enable you to erase these roadblocks before they keep your goals from being achieved.

Exercise 5.1 gives you the opportunity to try this strategy. After you do this exercise, we encourage you to use it relative to planning actions necessary to attain an important goal that you wish to realize.

PROVOCATIVE COMMUNICATOR

Power thinkers not only develop important goals to be met, but they also raise the bar of the quality of ideas advanced by others. That is why we call them provocative communicators.

Understanding the Provocative Communicator

Items 1, 32, and 38 of the Yale Assessment of Thinking assess the degree to which you are a provocative communicator. Fill out the Provocative Communicator Item Cluster Graph, entering your scores for these items from Chapter Two. If your total score was 5 or under, write as the YAT score interpretation "highly skilled." If your total score was 6 or 7, write "average ability." If your total score was 8 or higher, write "need for improvement."

Item 1 ("The comments that I make at meetings are better presented than the ones made by others, but my statements do not receive as many positive responses") measures how well others perceive your statements. If they are not positively received, typically there are two reasons for this occurrence.

~~~ Exercise 5.1

BACKWARD REASONING STEPS

Think of a problem you currently face, and write the desired outcome to the situation:

Vision: _____

List the step that would have to occur immediately before it, and then the step that would have to occur right before that. Continue to reason backward until you can write a step that you can take tomorrow to set this new goal in action.

Step that will have to take place directly before that desired outcome, or vision, can be attained:

_____

Step before that: _____

Step before that: _____

Step before that: _____

Step before that: _____

Step before that: _____

Step before that: _____

Step I can take TODAY to start working to reach my vision:

First, the idea being advanced by that individual may have several holes in it. These shortcomings usually occur when a leader has not adequately thought through an idea. Such individuals believe they are showing strength as a leader by providing a rapid response to the matter under consideration, but in fact, they are engendering a perception of themselves that is the precise opposite.

A second reason for a negative response to one's comments is the manner in which they are delivered. The statements made by leaders who are not provocative communicators frequently convey

Item Cluster Graph.   Provocative Communicator Item Cluster Graph

YAT Items	Your Response
1	_____
32	_____
38	_____
Total	_____
YAT score interpretation	_____

that they are prattlers who talk seemingly endlessly and of things lacking substance.

What power thinkers at meetings say is almost always well received by others. Provocative communicators are rarely among the first persons to speak at meetings. They listen to others, and they carefully weigh the merits of what has been said as well as the ideas being advanced. Power thinkers give the external cognitive reasoning process time to kick in so that it can perform its function effectively.

When provocative communicators do speak, it is not because they are enamored with the sound of their own voices. Rather, their remarks are concise, accurate, and substantive. Is it any wonder that the comments they make at meetings elicit positive responses?

If you frequently make impromptu remarks at meetings (item 32, "In meetings, I make impromptu remarks, and share ideas as quickly as I think of them"), it would serve you well to understand why you do so and why such actions are detrimental to your stature as a leader. Our research has found that those who make impromptu comments rely heavily on past knowledge and experience for the content of their remarks.

In Chapter Four, we discussed at length why such a reliance could hinder your effectiveness as a decision maker, problem solver, and creative thinker. To review, when your mind forms judgments based exclusively on the past, it is preventing you from considering new information, limiting your ability to be visionary and to devise new approaches to issues. You would do well to remember that impromptu remarks reflect your mind's endorsement of the tried and true rather than that which you have not experienced in the past.

Moreover, unless you are strong in insight, impromptu remarks tend to be negative and reactive rather than visionary. This mind-set is deleterious not only to the ideas that you endorse but to those advanced by others. If you do not give new ideas fair and objective consideration, then the remarks you make at meetings will not reflect those of a provocative communicator nor will they raise the bar of the quality of ideas advanced by others at meetings. Instead, what will be discussed will be the familiar and the unimportant.

If item 38 ("I believe that statements made at meetings should be intended to persuade others that the perspective of the person speaking is correct") elicited a response of "very often" or "often," you would do well to follow the advice Thomas Jefferson gave to his grandson: "When I hear another express an opinion which is not mine, I say to myself, he has a right to his opinion, as I to mine. Why should I question it? His error does me no injury, and shall I become a Don Quixote, to bring all men by force of argument to one opinion? . . . Be a listener, keep within yourself, and endeavor to establish within yourself the habit of silence . . ." (McCullough, 2001, p. 113).

Power thinkers are exemplary listeners. When they ask a question, it is not to exhibit their brilliance or to claim ownership of the idea being discussed. Rather, they listen attentively and in silence. When they do speak, it will not be to sink an idea but to push the bar of the discussion up by asking a provocative question (for example, "What would happen if . . . ?"). Their goal is not one of self-advocacy, but to create an organizational ethos where all ideas are discussed at a high level.

An Exemplary Provocative Communicator: Richard K. Hoerner

Richard K. Hoerner is a power thinker who embodies what it means to be a provocative communicator. Hoerner is the managing director and senior portfolio manager of Black Rock Incorporated, a global investment management and risk management products firm. Black Rock's clientele includes companies located in every state, as well as in Canada, the United Kingdom, Ireland, Japan, and Australia.

Hoerner was appointed to his current position in 2000. He oversees the portfolios management of all liquidity products, including money market funds, short-term customized portfolios, and offshore liquidity funds. Since his appointment to this position, assets have increased by $17.5 billion. The liquidity assets under his management now total approximately $78.6 billion.

As a provocative communicator, Hoerner not only makes sound comments at meetings, but he also masterfully provokes others to do similarly. Hoerner believes that meetings can serve an organization in two ways: they can be a vehicle to advance ideas and a forum where employees grow. To those ends, he recognizes the power of his position and knows that he could dissuade colleagues from expressing their ideas if he was confrontational at meetings. In keeping with this philosophy, he does his utmost to encourage people to make statements and present ideas by not putting them on the spot.

When others advance ideas, Hoerner employs a "leading the witness" strategy in which he makes comments intended to get a colleague to amplify the ideas being advanced. His comments focus on areas where the person's viewpoint has not been adequately explained. His remarks and the response they provoke give those listening to the idea a clearer understanding of it so that they can add their thoughts for making it better.

A second strategy Hoerner uses is to ask, "Do I understand you correctly?" In this way, he is able to elicit significant information. Hoerner correctly believes that initial comments made at meetings focus on the what—that is, the planned action, cost, time line, and other facets—of an action. He believes that great ideas occur when groups also address the why (such as the rationale) and the what-if (such as possible outcomes) of it. By asking, "Do I understand you correctly?" he seeks to help his colleagues explain their views relative to these realms of an idea. Hoerner believes that when the what, the why, and the what-if of an idea have been fully addressed, then a group is ready to reach a decision relative to the implementation of a meaningful course of action.

In performing both his "leading the witness" and "do I understand you correctly?" roles, Hoerner is careful not to convey a viewpoint as to whether he favors an idea. At meetings, he strives to stimulate discussion, but he also does not make a judgment about the soundness of a matter until he has gained sufficient information. Hoerner maintains this philosophy because he believes that he can best judge an idea after he has examined it in depth.

Hoerner's other strength is his prowess in speaking at meetings. His comments are rarely impromptu. They are formulated in what he calls his strategic speaking thought process. Before he speaks, he seeks to be quite clear in his mind as to what he will say, why he will state it, how he will deliver his remarks, and what he expects to occur as a result of his remarks. By giving others the opportunity to express their views prior to his speaking, he can enhance his comments from what he has heard. This strategic speaking process enables him to fully use his reasoning ability in the words that he utters.

Strategies for Becoming a Provocative Communicator

Hoerner's leading the witness, "do I understand you correctly?" and strategic speaking strategies have served him well as a leader, and they can aid you in becoming a provocative communicator. So too can the use of another strategy, which we refer to as the CAP strategy: speaking concisely, accurately, and precisely.

Our research found that power thinkers state the reasons for their judgments and move ideas forward by presenting them effectively. Before speaking, they stop to think through their position, and they then present it concisely, accurately, and precisely (CAP). The effectiveness of their remarks at meetings is based on their adherence to the three premises that constitute the CAP strategy:

- Concise speakers eliminate irrelevant details.
- Accurate speakers avoid misleading statements, verify facts, and remain silent unless they are absolutely sure that their information is valid or their opinion is honest.
- Precise speakers eliminate overgeneralizations, exaggerations, and unwarranted superlatives.

Power thinkers use CAP language because they know that when they gain the reputation of providing specific, valid, and truthful information, other people will trust their words. Here are the steps you can take to implement the CAP strategy when you speak:

- Make your statements productive, not self-defensive.
- Have your point clear in your mind before you speak.
- Learn to assert, illustrate, and stop.

- Use specific, concrete nouns and precise verbs.
- Avoid generalizations.
- Do not preface your comments with disclaimers.

The CAP speaking strategy will improve your ability to communicate positively and effectively, even with those who hold opposing positions. As Napoleon said, "The people to fear are not those who disagree with you, but those who disagree with you and are too cowardly to let you know."

MAKE YOUR STATEMENTS PRODUCTIVE, NOT SELF-DEFENSIVE. To use CAP speech, avoid entering meetings with the objective of merely championing your own opinions throughout the meeting. By speaking concisely, accurately, and precisely, you will be less likely to speak only to convince others to join your predetermined position. Enter the meeting intending to identify how participants' comments change your preconceived position about an issue; and use reasoning strategies each time before you speak as described subsequently.

If arbitrariness or apathy exists within a group or if someone pleads for acceptance of his or her perspective above the greater good, use CAP speech to appeal to people's sense of fairness and impartiality. For example, imagine a meeting involving a hiring decision in which one member of the group wants to hire a specific person and pleads that person's case from a biased position. You can appeal to the group's impartiality by saying, "If we want to add another member to our team who has the same strengths as several of us do, we will choose candidate X. If we want our unit to increase the effectiveness with which we respond to challenges we are likely to encounter in the future, we will choose another candidate."

CLARIFY YOUR POINT IN YOUR MIND BEFORE YOU SPEAK. With CAP speech, your mind acts before your mouth opens. Before you speak, answer (perhaps in your notes to yourself) the following questions:

- What is the point I want to make?
- How can I best phrase this point to move us forward?

If you cannot discern the answers clearly before you speak, this is a signal that your mind has not completed its work. Answering the two questions prioritizes your thoughts and points them in the direction you choose. It is crucial to determine in advance the effect you want your words to achieve because the moment you begin to speak, listeners mentally classify your message as one for attention or dismissal. This ability is a prerequisite for the successful usage of the next strategy in CAP speaking.

LEARN TO ASSERT, ILLUSTRATE, AND STOP. Based on your choice of words, listeners instantly form an opinion about how important your message is. Effective CAP language makes your statements stand out. To discover what is the essential core of your message is an exceedingly challenging task, but one you can accomplish. (Many lawyers, for instance, are trained to give powerful opening and closing statements in a few succinct sentences.) To convey your intent skillfully, tell people your thoughts and what you suggest in only two sentences:

> *Sentence 1:* Formulate a statement that portrays your message and intent concisely, accurately, and precisely. For example, say: "I've charted our steady 10 percent annual increase in sales," rather than "Wow! Our sales sure are growing, thanks to all your hard work." Do not overstate your case or say more than you know.
>
> *Sentence 2:* Provide an illustrative fact, summary statement, or example of that image in action rather than trying to restate your intention through additional general and descriptive sentences. For example, follow the first statement with "For the last seven years the largest percent of increase has arisen from our marketing campaign to our eighteen-to-twenty-five-year-old market segment, a fact we will build on in today's meeting."

In other words, express your main message in one sentence, use a second to support it, and then stop talking. If people want to know more, they will ask. (Waiting for their response before you continue is the second and harder step.) For example, if you feel that an action is imperative and have determined that two points summarize your main message, say: "Taking an action on X is essential. Without it, Y will recur." Without CAP speech, you will convey a less powerful message through indecisive statements such as, "I think we all might want to think about X. It's really kind of important, and maybe we should think about what we most want to do about it. What do you think, or do you want me to tell you what I believe we should do?"

USE SPECIFIC, CONCRETE NOUNS AND PRECISE VERBS. Taking the time to say exactly what you mean eliminates miscommunication. Choose easily visualized nouns and vivid verbs. For example, instead of simply telling an employee to write a report, ask for a report similar in writing style to another report (which you then give the employee as a sample). Add that the report should end with a persuasive concluding paragraph and that the final sentences of it should specify the precise actions the people reading it are being asked to take.

AVOID GENERALIZATIONS. If you constantly use superlatives like *best, most, all, never,* and *always,* people will judge you to be either irrationally extreme or weak and imprecise. To avoid this impression, continue to use double thinking until a vivid example or specific point can be expressed concisely, accurately, and precisely. Taking this step means that you will leave many meetings having said less than other people. Speaking less often than others is not a loss, however. When you cannot describe an idea specifically, it is often too weak or vague to share except with trusted mentors and friends. Through discussions with friends and mentors, you can shape your idea into a succinct and powerful example. When this occurs, you will be able to present sound ideas at a meeting that others can readily understand and use to pursue a positive purpose.

DO NOT PREFACE YOUR COMMENTS WITH DISCLAIMERS. A disclaimer is a phrase that gives a reason to reject an idea. Here are some examples:

> "This may be a stupid idea, but . . ."
>
> "I know it probably won't work, but . . ."
>
> "I've been wrong before, but . . ."
>
> "I know I don't have much experience, but . . ."
>
> "You may disagree, but . . ."

Phrases like those weaken your message. They supply reasons that others should not buy into your ideas. They also direct listeners to disavow your comments before they have even heard them. Disclaimers immediately encourage listeners to search for reasons to disagree with you. After all, you begin by asserting that arguments already exist that oppose your position, so your listeners will help you find them. Similarly, if you say that your idea could be wrong, many individuals will invent reasons why it *is* wrong.

To keep disclaimers from creating this nearly instantaneous mental response on the part of listeners, state your idea directly, without an opening phrase. If you nevertheless feel the need to preface your remarks, make comments that are positive. For example, instead of saying, "I haven't had much experience, so I may be wrong . . ." say, "From my perspective, I see the following benefits. . . ."

Disclaimers often are used when people lack the courage to support the ideas they are about to express. You can eliminate disclaimers by stopping to clarify to yourself the intent of your message and allowing time to have confidence in what you are about to say. Although some people use disclaimers to communicate their sensitivity to positions that others hold, even this use of them is counterproductive. It conveys that you are an indecisive or impulsive thinker, not a powerful one.

Besides monitoring your own speech for disclaimers and other unhelpful patterns, you can analyze people's responses to your comments to detect if you are projecting weakness. For example, if others remove their eye contact in meetings or rarely act on your suggestions, then you are not speaking concisely, accurately, and precisely.

RESOLUTE QUESTIONER

At first glance, the items associated with being a resolute questioner all seem like positive actions to take at a meeting. Individuals probably believe that they are being "good citizens of the organization" when they write down as much as they can about what others are saying (item 21), remain silent when they become confused about what is being said (item 34), and wait for others to ask questions when they do not comprehend what is being presented (item 45).

What they are doing is harmful to reasoning's external cognitive process and to the contribution that they can make to the organization. They are neither asking questions to clarify their cognitive uncertainties nor are they pursuing their desire to understand these ambiguities with firm determination. As the next section explains, a resolute questioner acts differently by not only asking questions but doing so boldly, regularly, and strategically.

Understanding the Resolute Questioner

Items 21, 34, and 48 of the Yale Assessment of Thinking assess the degree to which you are a resolute questioner. Fill out the Resolute Questioner Item Cluster Graph, entering your scores for these items from Chapter Two. If your total score was 5 or under, write as the YAT score interpretation "highly skilled." If your total score was 6 or 7, write "average ability." If your total score was 8 or higher, write "need for improvement."

Item 21 ("While others are speaking at meetings, I write down as much as I can about what they are saying") describes a practice that is negative for two reasons. First, by writing as much as you can about what is being said at a meeting, your mind is acting as if it is a word processor. As such, it does not critically judge the merit of what it is hearing; rather, its purpose is to record on paper the words being uttered. By using your mind in this fashion, you are not thinking of questions that you have about the content that you are hearing, you are not raising the level of the discussion, and you are not making a contribution to the meeting.

If you typically write as much as you can at meetings and then review your notes later, you are falling into a second trap: wasting time, a commodity in short supply. In today's fast-paced world, those who use such a practice are devoting twice as much time to this process as they should. What they are doing is making the recording of a meeting (by taking copious notes) be their priority activity. They are then reading these notes and giving thought to them.

Item Cluster Graph.   Resolute Questioner Item Cluster Graph

YAT Items	Your Response
21	_____
34	_____
48	_____
Total	_____
YAT score interpretation	_____

Power thinkers act quite differently. At meetings, they do not merely record what they are hearing; they engage their thought processes to judge its efficacy. They write only key words or phrases about what is being discussed. They write them so that they will be able to recall the key facets of what was said. Thus, their primary activity is generating questions that are intended to look between and beyond the parameters of what they are hearing.

For example, power thinkers will ask questions such as "Why?" or "What are the advantages of X over Y?" so that they can understand the very essence of what is being discussed. They also pose questions that will help others to see the idea from a different, and usually elevated, perspective. They will ask, "What if?" or "If we were to do X instead of Y, what would be the result?" Their questions are intended to stimulate thought and provoke discussion that will enable the idea that is being presented to become sounder and more worthwhile.

They ask thoughtful questions in an unapologetic manner because they know these questions are being raised in an objective spirit and with the intended outcome of improving the significance of what is discussed. For these reasons, we call this dimension of reasoning's external cognitive process that of a *resolute questioner*.

We began this section by stating that individuals who very often or often engage in the behaviors described in these items as thinking they are being good citizens of an organization when they act in these ways. We then noted in relation to item 21 how the mere recording of what you hear is not conducive to analytical thinking. While at first glance, items 34 ("When I attend a meeting and become confused about what is said, I will remain silent in the hope that I will eventually comprehend what is being said") and 48 ("When I am hearing a presentation in a meeting and I do not comprehend what is being presented, I wait for others to ask questions") seem like proper courses of action, they are not.

To remain silent in the hope that you will eventually comprehend the idea under discussion is as likely to occur as your beating Tiger Woods in a round of golf. When your mind becomes confused, you will in all likelihood become even more befuddled as the discussion continues unless you ask the requisite question(s) to rid your mind of the source of it.

In item 48, we forget that the questions that others ask are their questions, not our questions. Since their prior knowledge and experiences are different from ours, the probability that they will clarify our confusion is remote. By waiting for these individuals to shed light on the source of your confusion, what is much more likely to happen is that you will go through the entire meeting trying to comprehend some part of its content.

Power thinkers act in a dramatically different way. When they become confused, they do not hope that someone else will inquire about the source of their misunderstanding; rather, they themselves seek to clarify their confusion. In meetings, they will unabashedly utter a sentence such as: "You have stated that it is essential that X precede Y. In order for me to understand why we must take this action, could you state, so that I will be clear in my mind, the reasons that X must precede Y?" If after their initial question is responded to they remain confused, they will ask a follow-up query.

You will note that they do not apologize for their confusion. Their question is not one of support or opposition. It is intended to clarify their lack of comprehension, thus enabling their mind to move from a low level of cognition (understanding) to a higher one (critical analysis).

There is another difference between resolute questioners and leaders who are less able in this segment of reasoning. Because the less able group is waiting to understand what is being presented, they are unable to make meaningful comments relative to it. By asking a question to gain comprehension, power thinkers then are able to contribute to elevating the level of the ensuing discussion. They resolutely ask questions because they know that if they are dealing with the mere understanding of what is being presented, they cannot critically assess an idea because they will instead be at a decidedly lower level of cognition.

When we developed the outline of this book, we sometimes had different persons in mind to convey the various subskill processes in each thinking domain. When the area of resolute questioner was discussed, we both immediately uttered the same name.

An Exemplary Resolute Questioner: Karen Courtney Burke

Karen Courtney Burke is one of our country's foremost educational leaders. She is the assistant superintendent of Maine School Administrative District Six, a position that she has held since 1999. Burke's accomplishments have taken place far beyond the confines of her school's boundaries as she has developed and implemented statewide, regional, and national initiatives.

Although her abilities stretch across several areas, she is exceptionally competent in being able to work in teaming situations. And when she does, she asks questions in order to get the most out of other members of the group as well herself.

When a problem or an idea is being discussed at a meeting, Burke regularly does two things to establish what she terms connectedness. First, she asks herself, *Am I focused on what the person is saying?* If her response is anything other than yes, she attempts to discern why she answered as she did.

If it is because she has ambiguity in her mind, she will ask clarifying questions such as: "Here's what I heard. Is this what you're trying to say?" or, "I am confused by Y. Would you please explain it further?" Burke believes it is essential that she understand something clearly. Then she can connect it to what she already knows so that she can be a contributor to the problem's solution or the idea's development.

The second way that Burke establishes connectedness is through asking three types of questions: probing, big picture, and elevating. Burke asks *probing questions* after she has heard a presentation. She asks them for two reasons: to understand better what is being discussed or to apply what she has heard to the situation facing the group. In asking these questions, Burke seeks to draw an inference about something that was not stated so that she can connect it to a direction to which it seems to be pointing.

Big picture questions foster an analysis of what has been presented. She also raises such questions in order to connect this content to important organizational issues. For example, she will ask, "How is this a step toward achieving our master plan's objectives?"

Synthesis is the reason for Burke's asking *elevating questions*. She will raise "what-if?" questions to help a group brainstorm ideas after they have heard an idea in order to go beyond the thoughts expressed by the presenter.

Burke tactically asks questions of herself and those with whom she is working. What she does is cognitively sound and produces very positive outcomes. You would do well to emulate the strategies that she regularly employs.

Strategies for Becoming a Resolute Questioner

Certainly, we all can ask questions, but asking questions of the caliber of those Burke asks does not always come easily. If it does not for you, we recommend that you take actions that will enable your external cognitive process to kick in. We start with understanding when you should begin to ask questions of yourself or others.

In essence, you should consciously and deliberately use the stop-caution-go approach to reason (as a precursor to asking questions) when something does not feel right, you have not yet verified new information, or you feel uncomfortable with the direction your thoughts are taking (see Figure 5.1) about that which you are hearing. Stop (step 1) entails thinking beyond merely whether you agree or disagree with an issue being discussed.

The stop-caution-go approach to reasoning enables you to move beyond an immediate reaction and become objective. You therefore do not simply agree or disagree with other people; rather, you reason about which parts of this new information and other points of view expressed about it are strong and which can be improved. The following strategies will enable you to do this:

Stop strategy 1. Grant yourself permission to move beyond merely agreeing or disagreeing with others by creating a weighted characteristics test or list of positive and less positive features of a proposal as it is being discussed.

Stop strategy 2. Look up and away from a discussion and ask yourself, *What do I really want to say or do to help us move forward?*

Figure 5.1. Stop-Caution-Go Approach to Reasoning

Caution strategy. Collect additional information before you take a position, and suggest how this information can be obtained.

Go strategy. Ask questions.

GRANT YOURSELF PERMISSION. When you use stop-caution-go reasoning you are assuming more responsibility as a member of a team or leader than to merely decide whether you agree or disagree with others. As a result, many dimensions of resolute questioning and action occur. Your response to ideas also changes. Instead of merely reacting to others' ideas, you first consider the validity and value of your own preferences, biases, and facts, which are based on past (and often outdated) experiences. This pondering limits the potential negative effects of voicing your immediate gut reaction to support or reject an idea. We encourage you to promise yourself that you will think about the pros and cons of new ideas and use any additional new information you have gathered before you voice your response.

Weighing the pros and cons of new ideas is an example of proactive thinking, which is thinking before acting. Proactive thinking enables you to anticipate the positive course your words can create in a situation. Conversely, when you react without a proper amount of thought, you immediately land in the middle of a situation you have not thought through thoroughly. Reflecting before you speak makes your actions more powerful because you ignite thought processes first and delay your response until you have a considered position. Your actions with others then have a more solid footing. This kind of forethought also places the momentum that subsequent actions generate more directly under your control.

A game of chess is a good analogy for proactive thinking. A novice player reacts to his or her opponent's most recent move by taking whatever action seems immediately beneficial. By contrast, a champion player thinks several moves ahead, mentally playing out each possible course of action and the opponent's probable responses, to see what course of action will ultimately prove strongest. That is the essence of proactive reasoning.

In summary, stopping to reason through and challenge your first thoughts about an issue allows you to do more than merely agree or disagree with existing ideas. It provides time for you to become more analytical about the issue, reflect to develop a sense of its context, become proactive, and establish the pros and cons of possible positions until a positive course of action emerges.

LOOK UP AND AWAY. One way to help yourself stop and reason is to pause momentarily and look up and away from the issue at hand. Ask yourself questions such as, "What do I really want to say?" or "What can I do to make this idea create greater results for our organization?" or "What could happen if it isn't enacted? If it is enacted? If it is altered to build on our unique niche in the marketplace?" Using this process will draw on your unique talents and enable you to reason at a higher level of thought.

COLLECT INFORMATION. Access to information on practically any topic has never been so readily available as it is today. Using communication technologies and electronic encyclopedic stores of facts, theories, processes, and divergent philosophies will widen your perspective on a pending decision or action. There is no reason to rely on limited information.

ASK QUESTIONS. In the words of American philosopher Anthony Jay, "The uncreative mind can spot wrong answers, but it takes a creative mind to spot wrong questions" (Jay, 1991, p. 403). Before asking a question, however, check your reasons for asking it. Is the question an attempt to understand others, or are you trying to push your own ideas? If it is an attempt to achieve understanding, people will sense your collaborative intent and engage in freer, more honest exchanges. By considering in advance how your questions can condition and change the environment to achieve a more positive purpose, you ensure that your inquiries will not be self-centered and self-serving. Moreover, your questions will increase people's trust in you. With increased trust, you will receive additional, valuable information on which to base subsequent actions. Taking the time to ask questions will increase the likelihood that you will discover a wider variety of potential outcomes before you reach a decision. For example, a hospital administrator frequently says to people who bring him problems, "I sincerely want to know how your experience can assist our hospital in not making this mistake again. What do you think we can do to avoid this difficulty in the future?"

Equally important, when you get in the habit of asking questions, people will not spend time trying to convince you that their beliefs are factual. They know that you will ask questions like "Why?" or "How do you know?" if they try to clothe opinion as fact. Because they know you will ask them for verification, they will speak more objectively.

You can also use questioning to encourage more powerful thinking in meetings. The more powerful questions you ask in a group, the more productive the group's work becomes. When negative statements and questions are presented in a meeting, the less effective that meeting will be. Exhibit 5.1 lists questions that resolute questioners use to elicit powerful thinking in groups.

Asking questions can be difficult. Many people do not like to be questioned because they think some inquiries are designed to dissuade them from their beliefs. Generally, they do not want their beliefs challenged, regardless of whether those beliefs are reasonable, and many people quickly become defensive when questioned. Moreover, people tend to fear questions that they cannot answer with facts or reasoned judgments. If you fear being questioned, use the strategies already set out to ensure the accuracy of your answers before you speak. If you fear asking questions, check the accuracy of your information to build your confidence, and you will no longer be concerned about asking the "wrong" or "tough" questions. Instead, you will ask questions like those in Exhibit 5.1 to avoid rhetoric and more rapidly uncover important issues.

One strategy for using powerful tough questions is to allow several minutes at the end of a meeting for responses to the following question: "What question should I [we] have asked that I [we] didn't?" When you ask this question, you stimulate an integrative review of the

Exhibit 5.1. Powerful Questions for Resolute Questioners

- Why?
- Is the most important point _____ or _____ ?
- What do you mean by _____ ?
- If I understand you correctly, you mean _____ ? Is that correct?
- Where will the point you are making *not* apply? How does _____ relate to _____ ?
- If your idea is accepted, what is the greatest change that will occur?
- Would you say more about _____ ?
- What is the difference between _____ and _____ ?
- Would _____ be an example?
- Is it possible that _____ ? What else could we do?
- If _____ happened, what would be the result?

thinking that occurred during the meeting. You also focus the participants on thinking proactively for the next meeting, and you build springboards for not only your own power thinking but also for that of others. This proactive focus will help additional important issues to emerge.

PLANNING IMPLEMENTER

Planning in many organizations has the same appeal as the bubonic plague. The mere mention of the term causes even the most reticent of people to tell about instances where "miscarriages of justice" occurred under the aegis of it. It is no surprise that planning is held in such low esteem because many of the individuals who spearheaded these efforts used flawed thinking processes. As a consequence, what stemmed from their efforts was of no real import to the organization.

Of the various segments in which we studied power thinkers, there is the greatest disparity between them and professionals of lesser skill in this dimension of reasoning. The three pertinent YAT items—36, 56, and 68—amplify some of the reasons that this significant difference in skill strength exists. They also provide significant information as to the manner in which our conscious mind operates during the external cognitive process of reasoning.

We chose to label this facet of power thinking as that of a planning implementer. The two terms, planning and implementer, each describe elements of power thinkers' actions that are important to their success as leaders.

Such leaders certainly plan, and what results from their efforts is not merely filed in a binder and forgotten. Rather, their efforts are evident in subsequent actions. Accordingly, planning represents a blueprint for what, when, and how organizational action will occur. It is this linkage between planning and the strategic implementation of these desired outcomes that distinguishes power thinkers from their less able counterparts.

Understanding the Planning Implementer

Items 36, 56, and 68 of the Yale Assessment of Thinking assess the degree to which you are a planning implementer. Fill out the Planning Implementer Item Cluster Graph, entering your scores for these items from Chapter Two. If your total score was 5 or under, write as the YAT

Item Cluster Graph.   Planning Implementer Item Cluster Graph

YAT Items	Your Response
36	_____
56	_____
68	_____
Total	_____
YAT score interpretation	

score interpretation "highly skilled." If your total score was 6 or 7, write "average ability." If your total score was 8 or higher, write "need for improvement."

If you responded "very often" or "often" to item 36 ("When I plan, I find it difficult to concurrently analyze multiple courses of action"), you are not alone. Our research has found that many leaders become befuddled when confronted by a complex situation. These individuals will consider it for a period of time, and when they are unable to find a single course of action that will effectively remedy all parts of it, they pronounce the condition to be "insurmountable." After affixing it with that label, they then lower their intended outcomes relative to it.

Power thinkers recognize that a situation can be complicated and therefore understand it is highly unlikely that "one size will fit all" of it. Therefore, they devise a plan that will address each component of the condition. By "dividing" it, they are able to "conquer" it. At no time in their conceptualization does a planning implementer consider lowering an intended outcome merely because a matter requires multiple courses of action to be taken.

The perception about people relative to the planning process (item 56—"I do not know how to plan so that productive interactions occur among people") is another area where planning implementers and non–power thinkers differ. Less skilled thinkers typically view people as obstacles when planning. They ask themselves questions such as, "How can I get person Z not to oppose this?" "How can I state provision X so that the group will approve it?"

Power thinkers plan with a different outlook. They see people as resources with different knowledge bases, experiences, and talents on whom they can draw in order to advance the idea being considered. Thus, they encourage interactions rather than seeking ways to circumvent them, as less skilled thinkers do. They think, "Person Y is knowledgeable about Z. How can I best interact with her to get her enthused about this so that she will improve this part of it?"

We also found that planning implementers and non–power thinkers had significantly different levels of expertise relative to the implementation of plans (item 68—"I am better at conceptualizing ideas than in planning the steps necessary to implement them"). Frequently the ingredients of plans developed by less skilled thinkers were based on incorrect assumptions. As such, they were abandoned prior to their implementation. Or if they were initiated, they fell short of their intended objective.

A second reason that these leaders have difficulty in implementing their ideas is their perception of planning. They see planning and implementation as islands unto themselves; first they plan, and then they implement.

Planning implementers use reasoning's external cognitive process quite differently. As they and their colleagues consider possible courses of action, they discuss what steps will be needed in order to successfully implement them, such as the backward-reasoning strategy presented previously in this chapter. Power thinkers plan to implement ideas that will make their organization better. The development of a plan is not their objective. Its successful implementation is the benchmark by which they judge their success.

An Exemplary Planning Implementer: Lloyd G. Trotter

Lloyd G. Trotter is a leader who is unafraid of complex problems and uses reasoning strategies that will make his organization better. He gained international fame for a matrix. While other individuals before and after him have developed these devices, it was how Trotter used it that was so exemplary.

When he was named to the position of vice president and general manager of manufacturing for General Electric in 1990, he faced a formidable challenge: improving GE's manufacturing system and integration process of production facilities throughout the world.

His efforts culminated into what is now known as the Trotter matrix. The left-hand side of the matrix contained the practices needed to make a factory effective. Each facility manager was asked to use a rating scale of 1 to 5 (high) relative to the degree to which each criterion was being met at his or her factory.

Trotter's matrix was more than a "rate the record" instrument, however. He used it as a best practices teaching tool. For example, each manager who scored a 5 on a facet of the matrix was required to explain precisely how his or her factory got to that level of performance. It was the responsibility of managers whose facilities scored less than a 5 to learn from their colleagues and to copy what they did where feasible.

Trotter's matrix worked. In these forty plants, the operating margins went from 1.2 in 1994 to 5.9 in 1996 and 13.8 in 2000.

Today, Trotter is the president and chief executive officer of GE Industrial Systems, a $6 billion global business that employs forty thousand people. GE Industrial Systems is one of the major businesses of the GE Company, the world's largest diversified manufacturing, technology, and services company. In addition to the role that he plays within GE, he provides a superb model as to how a highly skilled planning implementer acts.

The development of planning goals is not merely an exercise for Trotter and his colleagues. Goals are a vital part of Trotter's leadership style. He believes in setting bold goals that will "shock" his colleagues "from their comfort zones." Trotter believes that by establishing these lofty goals, his organization will become significantly better even if the goals are not met. He says that planning should focus on "blazing new trails," and the content of such endeavors should be one of where "if you can dream it, you can do it." Trotter and his colleagues work feverishly toward the attainment of established goals.

As they do, he operates with three credos. First, Trotter is a teacher. He believes that by sharing best practices information between and among his managers, institutional learning will occur that will be beneficial not merely to the existing plan but also for future ones. Second, he is unafraid of mistakes—his own or those of others. Trotter uses "aggressive patience" as he and his cohorts engage in trial and error in striving, for example, to move a best practice of Plant A to other plants. Third, as plans are initiated, he concurrently expects them to be measured and have reports written as to their progress as they are implemented. Trotter states, "You get what you measure." In interactions with others, it is process and results about which they converse: defining what is to be changed, how far it has moved from the onset of the plan, and how quickly its implementation steps are to occur.

Strategies for Becoming a Planning Implementer

Lloyd Trotter's strategies are an invaluable resource as you seek to become more skilled as a planning implementer. To become more able in this aspect of reasoning, we recommend that you examine why you are not proficient in planning. Is it because you lack the confidence in your colleagues to develop important goals? Are you unsure about your capability to lead such an undertaking? Does the fear of failure keep you from planning meaningful endeavors? Or is it . . . something else?

We invite you to think about these questions with the depth that this important matter should receive. We recommend that you block out a sufficient segment of time—free from calls, e-mails, faxes, and interruptions—to identify the reasons for this belief to exist within you.

By identifying them, you can read this book more prescriptively as you come across strategies that will aid you in addressing these areas in which you are not highly skilled. You may also find workshops and professional articles that focus on the segment of planning in which you are seeking to gain additional expertise.

Just as we asked you to raise questions about aspects of your beliefs relative to planning, if you have difficulty in successfully implementing that which you have established as a goal, we recommend that you use a comparable process. Think about an effort in which a planned action fell short of its goal. Was it because subordinates lacked the skills to achieve it? Or did *you* lack them? Did you inaccurately predict the resources required to achieve the goal? What obstacles blocked your progress? Did you make faulty assumptions as you carried out your plan?

Think about these issues as you did when examining planning to discern the precise reasons for your shortcomings in this area. It will be time well spent because it can enable you to pinpoint what actions you can subsequently take that will enrich your level of skill in this important facet of reasoning. Rethink Trotter's use of matrices, and study Lee Iacocca's matrix in Exhibit 5.2, which was used to revitalize the depressed American automobile industry in the 1990s. How can visual thinking tools assist you and your colleagues to reason creatively?

Exhibit 5.2. Lee Iacocca's Matrix

Dimension 1: The American Economy

Dimension 2: The Automobile Industry	Fluctuating	Based on supply and gross national product	Gaining or losing strength internationally	Influenced by many different sectors of society	All people depend on its strength
Is highly competitive	Make cars in a more varied price range	Find a new population to buy cars	Gain large market share in Canada	Incentives to Chrysler employees to buy from Chrysler	Fluctuate loan payments based on inflation
Employs a lot of people	Tenure guaranteed	Employees make things besides cars	Open dealerships internationally	Hire from all socioeconomic levels	Barter with employees
Touches each person's life	Planned carhood	Increase need for three-car families	Increase need/value of one-car families internationally	Make buses	Add entertainment features inside car
Uses products from many other industries	Work on producing products more cheaply	Buy our own steel and plastics companies	Find cheapest suppliers	Build new plants near cheapest suppliers	Diversify our suppliers to hedge for losses
Is characterized by rapidly changing technology	Use technology that aids economy	Locate easy-to-operate technology	Best technology from most stable companies	Teach people how to use new technology in cars	Make instructions simple
Is influenced by government	Federal auto laws change according to economy	Identify new markets that will improve GNP, be protected by government regulations	Purchase equipment in countries with strongest currency	Market to sectors of population working in government	Lobby to pass lower taxes on cars for people at low socioeconomic levels
Projections based on speculations of public demand	Make parts that can be interchanged to update cars	Increase unique "want" factors built into our cars	Survey for needs of public in each nation	Make our high-profit cars more attractive to the public	Donate a percentage of every sale to a charity that people in America value

Source: Created from information described in Iacocca, L. (1989). *Talking Straight.* NY: Bantam Books.

SUMMARY

In Chapters Four and Five, we have discussed reasoning, which is based in your conscious mind and is the mind's way of taking thought-filled actions. Reasoning is one of the three domains in which power thinkers are highly skilled. In this chapter, we have presented strategies intended to help you become more adept in the external reasoning processes of:

- Establishing overarching goals, undertaking goals with tenacity, and using the backward-reasoning strategy (bold pioneer)

- Making your statements productive; having your point clear in your mind before you speak; using specific, concrete nouns and precise verbs; avoiding generalizations; not prefacing your comments with disclaimers; and learning to assert, illustrate, and stop (provocative communicator)

- Using the stop-caution-go approach in reasoning by granting yourself permission to do more than merely agreeing or disagreeing with a new idea, looking up and away, collecting information, and asking questions (resolute questioner)

- Using matrices or comparable devices when facing complex situations, identifying the factors that limit your ability to plan, delineating what conditions go awry when you seek to implement plans, and using writing strategies such as the Trotter matrix and backward reasoning (planning implementer)

On the next two pages, we have provided you space in which to write your reflections as to steps that you plan to take in order to become more proficient in each of the segments of the external reasoning processes in cognition.

REASONING EXTERNAL COGNITIVE
PROCESS THINKING ENHANCEMENT

Bold Pioneer

Provocative Communicator

Resolute Questioner

Planning Implementer

CHAPTER SIX

Insight

Internal Cognitive Process

T his chapter and the next one examine insight, which is an individual's ability to know and act without prior conscious thought being given to an issue. This chapter discusses the internal cognitive processes that power thinkers use mentally to reach decisions, solve problems, and think creatively.

Our research found that the internal insight facet of cognition has three subskill components. Because it has fewer segments than reasoning, you should not infer that it is of lesser importance than reasoning, which has four subskill component areas in both internal and external cognitive processes. All of the cognitive process areas are of equal significance. There are three components in this dimension because that is the number of skills that our research found were exhibited by power thinkers relative to this facet of insight. We classified these three areas to be that of a ready decider, distressless performer, and spirited producer.

READY DECIDER

Items 27, 54, and 58 of the Yale Assessment of Thinking assess the degree to which you are a *ready decider*. Ready decider is an apt descriptor for this facet of insight because each word embodies what power thinkers do. These individuals make a decision not when others tell them it is time to do so but when they are satisfied that they have the requisite information for effectively reaching one. And because they wait until their internal cognitive process tells them they are ready to reach a decision, what they decide to do is usually the correct course of action.

Understanding the Ready Decider

Items 27, 54, and 58 of the Yale Assessment of Thinking assess the degree to which you are a ready decider. Fill out the Ready Decider Item Cluster Graph, entering your scores for these items from Chapter Two. If your total score was 5 or under, write as the YAT score interpretation "highly skilled." If your total score was 6 or 7, write "average ability." If your total score was 8 or higher, write "need for improvement."

In our research on ready deciders, we found that it was they, not others or external events, who dictated when they were prepared to reach a decision. Once all of their internal thought mechanisms had been engaged and were satisfied that the decision they had formulated was the correct one, power thinkers embarked on a course of action consistent with it.

Persons who lacked skill in this area use a markedly different approach to reach decisions. In item 27 ("I know it is time to make a decision when people express displeasure with me for not making the decision"), if you responded "very often" or "often," it is others who are determining when you reach a decision.

Item Cluster Graph. **Ready Decider Item Cluster Graph**

YAT Items	Your Response
27	_____
54	_____
58	_____
Total	_____
YAT score interpretation	_____

Few would argue that individual differences exist among humans. Because of it, the knowledge and experiences possessed by people vary. Therefore, Person A may want you to reach a decision sooner than you are ready to do so. Does this mean that because he is ready for you to reach a decision about a matter, you should do so? Of course not.

It is *you* who has not made a decision because *your* subconscious, which acts as an internal alarm, is saying to you that you are not ready to reach one. While reaching a decision to avoid incurring the wrath of others may seem to be a wise thing to do, it is not. Precipitous decisions about which your subconscious is conveying that you are not ready to take action are typically bad ones. Ready deciders know it is wrong to ignore such a cognitive signal and therefore do not do it. Their less skilled colleagues fall victim to it.

Item 54 ("I make a decision when I am unwilling to devote any more time or energy to the matter") is similar to item 27 in that it is premised on a condition that negates, rather than positively uses, insight's internal cognition process. In item 27, it was others who were causing you to reach a decision before you were ready to do so. In item 54, it is you who is the culprit.

Some decisions are easy to reach and require little time. Many are not.

When we reach a decision because we are unwilling to devote any more time or energy to it, we are engaging in an erroneous type of thinking. You would do well to remember that this form of thought rarely results in good decisions.

By using time and energy to tell you when to reach a decision, you are acquiescing to an arbitrary standard. This self-imposed time clock really represents a quasi, rather than a comprehensive, decision-making process for you. When we employ such measures, our mind is in a decidedly less prepared phase of the internal cognitive process than when we are genuinely ready to reach a decision.

Ready deciders understand that when their concerns about a decision have been adequately addressed, they are ready to move forward. They know too that when they are uneasy about what course of action to take, their subconscious is warning them that they are not ready to decide because of some known, or at that time unknown, factor.

The signals of discomfort or uneasiness with a decision you are about to reach are important messages that your mind is giving to you as you engage in thought. Frequently, our subconscious has unearthed a segment of a possible decision that is ill founded. By allowing the internal cognitive process to fully occur, you will become more precisely aware of what your insight is signaling to you. If you short-circuit this system from completion by deciding that you are unwilling to devote any additional time or energy to the matter, then you are in all likelihood making a decision that will not represent your best thinking.

Item 58 ("I am forced to reach decisions before I am ready to make them") is an all-too-common reason cited in organizations today. In the fast-paced environment in which businesses and other organizations operate, decisions must be made often and rapidly. Previously in this book, we spoke about how many leaders believe they are being decisive because they reach decisions quickly. What separates less skilled leaders from ready deciders is how they use their time when a decision must be reached quickly.

Leaders who are less skilled in this aspect of insight do not differentiate between decisions that must be reached as soon as possible from ones requiring immediate action. For example, if you were standing on a highway and a tractor trailer was within twenty-five feet of you, you should immediately take action to get out of its path.

Many leaders when told to make a decision ASAP (as soon as possible) erroneously reach an immediate decision. In doing so, they are depriving themselves of an important dimension of the subconscious internal cognitive process: the mind's ability to generate insightful information to reach decisions.

Ready deciders act quite differently when making decisions under the constraint of a tight deadline: they tell the person that they will get back to them later in the day rather than reaching an immediate decision. They then isolate themselves from telephone calls, conversations with colleagues, e-mails, and other usual interruptions and think about the decision, using one, or at times two, strategies to consider its pros and cons. For example, they may employ the weighted characteristics test or allow their minds to brainstorm about elements of the issue before them. Then they make a decision.

This process need not occur over a long period of time. The manner in which a ready decider reaches a decision is better than that of less skilled thinkers. A ready decider is acting in a manner consistent with research about thinking when he or she grants himself or herself permission to think about an issue. First, when individuals consider a matter for a period of time (and it can be as little as thirty minutes), the decisions that they reach are appreciably better than ones made immediately. Also, freeing their mind from other distractions enables analytical as well as creative thinking to more readily occur relative to the matter at hand.

An Exemplary Ready Decider: Mark F. Santia

Mark F. Santia is a leader whose internal cognitive processes convey what it means to think like a ready decider. Santia is a senior vice president for investments at Smith Barney. In addition to excelling in his position, Santia serves as a member of the corporation's prestigious Chairman's Council. He also has been invited to speak on multiple occasions to Smith Barney's entire brokerage network about strategies that he developed and has used successfully to increase his performance as a leader.

Decision making is the essence of what Santia does each day. He must make decisions on behalf of investors and for his Smith Barney staff and associates. When Santia reaches a decision, it is because *he* is ready to reach one. He will not make a decision because other people express displeasure with him because he has not reached a decision or because he is unwilling to devote any more time or energy to a matter.

Santia's approach to decision making is straightforward and effective. He begins the process by asking, "What must I know so that I will feel comfortable about the decision I reach?" For example, if the matter pertains to a stock, he will use Charles Dow's Point and Figure charting to guide his thinking. If it is a management issue, he will establish comparable criteria.

As he is engaged in this process, Santia realizes that not all of the answers to his criteria are clear. When they are not, he relies heavily on his insight, which he says acts as a "checks and balance" relative to the item at issue. He will listen to what his gut feelings are telling him relative to whether a criterion has been met. When he has an uneasy feeling about a course of action, he will probe his thinking to identify the reason for it. When he does, Santia is then able to decide if his discomfort can be placated by thinking about the matter differently (and getting attendant data) or if his decision should be no.

Santia's approach to decision making is undergirded by a strong belief as to how he is to act during this process. He says, "You've got to see your methodology through if you are going to represent your clients in the most professional manner that you can. There are no shortcuts to making a quality decision. You have to continue searching until criteria that you have established through your successful experiences have solid answers to them."

Santia is regarded by colleagues and throughout his industry as a terrific leader. His approach to decision making has proven to be highly effective to both him and his clients. If you implement his ideas about decision making, you will become more proficient in this important thinking skill.

Strategies for Becoming a Ready Decider

If you would like to gain additional proficiency in the skills associated with being a ready decider, you must first understand and use the concept of breaking away.

Breaking away from others (and distractions) is among the most important power thinking tools that develop insight. Your subconscious signals the need to break away when worry taints your thinking. By breaking away during the onset of such occurrences, instead of continuing to experience anxiety, insight's internal cognitive processes can unite with reasoning to develop effective, novel solutions to the challenge at hand. Many leaders believe that breaking away is merely throwing your hands up in frustration or walking away for a while to avoid having to take action on a matter before them. It is not. Nor is it "stopping and smelling the roses along the way." Rose smelling is a fine thing to do, but that alone will not help you become a ready decider.

For ready deciders, breaking away is not used to delay action when they are under stress, but a purposeful choice they make to reflect alone. They use four strategies to do so: reverie, finding your own approach, bracketing, and awaiting your good indicators. These actions involve proactive thought. They initiate insight's external cognitive process because they eliminate fatigue; clear the mind for a few minutes; uplift one's mood and emotions; provide new scenery, sounds, or tactile stimuli; and vary the rate of blood circulation in your body (for instance, if you have been seated for a long period of time, "breaking away" will be more productive if you do so while standing, walking, or moving to a new location).

Breaking away strategies are also effective when you become frustrated. Frustration is a sign that you have reached the point where your rational mind, searching laboriously for a solution, has failed and asks for the assistance of insight and self-knowledge. For instance, recent scientific evidence has proven that physical activities can remove tension and provide more oxygen to the brain and muscles, thus stimulating creative thought (Comer, 2003).

In our research, we have watched how ready deciders effectively break away. When an individual spends long hours on a new task, anguish and frustration often set in. If that person continues on the task, mistakes frequently occur and tension mounts. Ready deciders, in contrast, slow down or break away from the task so that all the reasoning that had been invested in this project can integrate with insight's external cognitive processes. For most ready deciders, breaking away creates a smarter plan of action.

Here we look at the four strategies for breaking away.

REVERIE. Reverie involves consciously requiring yourself to think of nothing in particular. It can be an extended pause for several minutes or only a momentary pause. During it, your eyes and mind do not focus on the task at hand. Reverie has gained an acceptance of sorts in businesses and other organizations because it has proven to be an effective strategy for producing insightful solutions to problems.

For example, a manager at a Fortune 500 company was showing a visitor through the new corporate headquarters. The visitor was surprised to see the operations team leader seated with his feet on his desk, staring into space. Why, she asked, did the company keep this man and presumably pay him well "just to do nothing"? The manager answered, "Last year, an idea that he had and his team created earned the company several million dollars. And when the idea occurred to him, he was doing exactly what he's doing now!"

If breaking away is difficult for you at first, we recommend that you regularly schedule moments for reverie—to think of nothing in particular. You need set aside only a few moments each day. Even this limited amount of time can significantly increase the power of your insight.

BRACKETING. Bracketing is a method of scheduling time at an established time each day, or as individual needs arise, to think about a challenge that confronts you. Through this strategy, you can greatly reduce the amount of anxiety that you experience. This occurs because whenever you experience a disappointment or face a difficult challenge, your subconscious and rational mind have to recover from the initial feelings of shock, disillusionment, confusion, or loss. This takes time, and bracketing helps you not to rush the bouncing-back process.

It enables you to rid yourself of these negative emotions before you act. If used properly, it will help you to maintain a positive perspective before and during stressful projects.

Bracketing is also effective when your mind wanders to a prior disappointment while you are working on another priority. Ready deciders use bracketing as soon as their minds wander from the task at hand. To master this tool, you can look at your watch and allow yourself one, five, or even fifteen minutes to think about thoughts that are distracting you. Then promise yourself to return to the challenge (and be sure to do so) when your work at hand has been completed. If the bracketed time was insufficient, give yourself an additional period after your current project is finished. These bracketing periods enable you to discover new information related to the problem. Similarly, by disciplining yourself to think about the problem for only a set amount of time, you reduce the likelihood that your thinking will turn to negative thoughts at other moments throughout the day or that your quandary will affect other challenges that lay at hand.

FINDING YOUR OWN APPROACH. Breaking away to find your own approach increases insight and positively focuses your subconscious on problem situations. Because every person is different, it is important that you find your own approach to breaking away. To do so, think about past activities in which your mind constructed a highly effective plan in a very short span of time. What were the actions you took in that situation that enabled you to break away? Then, in future anxiety-filled experiences, use similar actions to take momentary or extended breaks away.

AWAITING YOUR GOOD INDICATORS. Awaiting your good indicators is insight's internal cognitive processes' means of communicating that your newly created idea is the correct one. When you wait for good indicators to develop within you, your energy can be targeted toward more productive ends. Because of these positive feelings, your conviction and commitment are strengthened, enabling the idea generated to become significantly better than one developed by those who did not await for their good indicators to kick in.

One way to develop your ability to await good indications is to identify your most recent decision that turned out well. It should be one in which you were in charge of the steps necessary to implement it. Analyze and write down the qualities of the actions taken that fostered good indicators to occur within you. If you cannot instantly recall those qualities, the following questions may help you to identify them:

- Was it the interaction with new people that inspired you most?
- Was it solving a difficult problem and watching the organization (or yourself) benefit from it?
- Was it causing others to think about something in a new way?
- Was it creating something new to help the organization?
- Was it gaining recognition, appreciation, or rewards for difficult or innovative work?
- Was it leading the people who report to you to reach a significant goal?

Another way to add to your level of conviction is to think of something you do not want to do that has been scheduled for the near future. Break away for a moment to think about its tasks. Then commit to this endeavor by adding a component that motivates you or alter one of its existing elements so you can use more of your talents to complete it. Take a moment to do Exercise 6.1 and reflect on your talents.

In essence, to create within you the mind-set that you need to make highly effective decisions, you must identify and await your good indicators. Incorporating them into your decision-making strategies will benefit you, those whom you lead, and the organization. In addition, by awaiting your good indicators and incorporating your talents into your decision making, you can more easily use flow experiences, which we describe in Chapter Seven.

DISTRESSLESS PERFORMER

Distress is a part of the human condition. We all worry about things and are troubled when we experience misfortune.

There is a fundamental difference between power thinkers and persons who are less skilled in the internal aspect of insight. Certainly, power thinkers worry about things, but their level of worry is moderate. It is not the predominant emotion that they experience, and it is balanced by the confidence that they have in themselves and in what they are about to do.

〜〜 Exercise 6.1

CONQUER CHALLENGING TASKS BY COMBINING TALENTS

Write below the three talents that come instantly to mind in relation to an upcoming task that you do not want to do:

1. _____

2. _____

3. _____

How can these talents be combined to reduce the difficulty within the challenging task?

_____

_____

We called this facet of their skill that of a *distressless performer* because that is precisely how they think. Fear, anxiety, and worry are kept to minimal levels as they think about future events and actions. Such an attitude is important to both the quality and outcomes of their thinking. The previously stated emotions, when they exist at high levels within us, significantly curb the ability of our subconscious to generate positive or creative thoughts. As a consequence, this important aspect of internal cognition is seriously curtailed, and the quality of our thoughts concurrently suffers.

The outcomes of our thinking are adversely affected in another way. Thoughts that are generated by adverse emotions set up a cycle of negativity within us. If you think about what can go wrong, your mind will create other possible occurrences, which will all be negative. We then will come to accept that which we imagined as being quite probable.

In summary, a distressless performer does worry and have fears and anxieties. But they are kept to minimum in that these individuals allow their subconscious to operate as they think about future courses of action. As a result, they devise sound plans—ones that they subsequently, confidently, and successfully enact. These positive outcomes reinforce their belief in themselves and keep their levels of distress at bay.

Understanding the Distressless Performer

Items 17, 37, and 43 of the Yale Assessment of Thinking assess the degree to which you are a distressless performer. Fill out the Distressless Performer Item Cluster Graph, entering your scores for these items from Chapter Two. If your total score was 5 or under, write as the YAT score interpretation "highly skilled." If your total score was 6 or 7, write "average ability." If your total score was 8 or higher, write "need for improvement."

Items 17, 37, and 43 have one thing in common. If you responded "very often" or "often" to any of them, you are self-imposing limitations on your ability to use insight effectively in the thinking process. As a result, your skill in problem solving, decision making, and creative thinking suffers.

Item 17 ("The fear of failure limits me when I am planning future actions") adversely affects us in two additional ways. First, focusing your thinking on failing sends negative thoughts to your mind. Instead of your cognitive process being concentrated on how you can make an intended action successfully take place, your subconscious dwells on what can go amiss. Thus, the mind acts as a magnet not for things that will enrich your decision but for negative dimensions of possible future actions.

Second, when we are planning a future action, that which we fear is typically the worst thing that can happen. Our subconscious, being

Item Cluster Graph.   Distressless Performer Item Cluster Graph

YAT Items	Your Response
17	_____
37	_____
43	_____
Total	_____
YAT score interpretation	_____

the nurturing device that it is, will dissuade us from the intended action because it wishes nothing hurtful to happen to us. What in essence occurs is that our subconscious justifies our fears. Here is how it takes place. If you are concerned that X aspect of a future plan will cause you to fail, your subconscious will confirm your fear and justify your not taking an action. You will be deprived of your insight's internal cognitive process objectively weighing the pros and cons of it. In addition, no creative thoughts will emanate from your subconscious. Instead, it will assume a role of justification, giving credence to the fears that you injected into it.

Item 37 ("Before a major event, my anxiety is higher than that of others") addresses anxiety, another source of distress. A good way to think of anxiety is to remember that as it rises, the insight capacity of your thinking falls. The overloads of nervous energy caused by anxiety have an effect on an individual's internal cognitive process comparable to that of a power surge on an electrical outlet. Just as what is plugged into them shuts down, so too does your subconscious when you become overly anxious.

Distressless performers use anxiety in a decidedly different manner. They understand the difference between having *some* anxiety and too much of it. We have already noted the adverse effects that too much anxiety has on performance. A distressless performer knows that having some anxiety can serve a beneficial purpose: it can be a source of motivation that stimulates our subconscious to develop positive thoughts and creative ideas. For professionals who are strong in this aspect of internal cognition, anxiety is a catalyst for effective action. For their less skilled counterparts, it is a negative force that produces cataclysmic results.

Item 43 ("I consider myself to be a 'worrier'") deals with worry and its effect on thinking. As was the case with anxiety, caution must be taken to ensure that too much of it is not interjected into our thought process. To understand how worry affects us, it is important to understand its genesis. Typically, we worry when we think that a desired condition or level may not be attained. A condition would be a fear that it might rain on the day of your daughter's wedding. This form of worry concerns a condition over which your have no real control.

When we worry about a level of performance, it generally involves a self-perceived shortcoming. For example, you may worry that you will not make a very good presentation to a group because you consider yourself to be a dull speaker. Or you worry that a team that you are leading will not meet a deadline because you have been unable to establish a spirit of cohesiveness among its members. The greater our amount of worry is, particularly if it focuses on our shortcomings, the more difficult it is for our insight to function. In essence, it drowns our ability to use this thinking skill because our subconscious is not free to engage in positive thought; rather, it focuses on this possible gap between a desired level of performance and one's perceived shortcomings.

An Exemplary Distressless Performer: Ruth Wood Mustard

Anyone who knows or who has ever worked with Ruth Wood Mustard will readily agree that she can aptly be termed a distressless performer. Mustard began her career as a nurse in Kansas and today serves as the associate director for patient care and nursing services at the William Jennings Bryan Dorn Veterans Administration Medical Center in Columbia, South Carolina. She is very knowledgeable about nursing practices and is a superb leader. For example, in 1999, she was named as the Federal Woman of the Year in the clinical category. The University of South Carolina also selected her as an Amy V. Cockcroft Leadership Fellow.

Mustard engages in several actions that establish her credentials as a distressless performer. Her attitudes about failure and anxiety are ones that can serve other persons well.

When Mustard is considering taking an action, fear of failure is not a factor she ever considers. Rather, she asks if what she is mulling over is consistent with the overarching goal that she has established for her organization: Will the action enable patients to receive better care? If her answer is no, she does not enact the initiative before her. If her response is yes, she pursues it with purposeful determination.

After she makes a decision to undertake something, failure is not something she fears. When she has decided to become involved in something because it will move her closer toward attaining her overarching goal, Mustard contends that only one of two things can occur, and both of them are beneficial:

1. Her decision will prove to be correct. If this is the case, the project will be successful, and Mustard will have made progress toward enabling patients to receive better care.

2. What she has decided to do will fail. Mustard says that even an undertaking that falls short of its objective still provides two positive outcomes. Whatever good was realized from its imple-

mentation is another step toward her organizational goal of providing better patient care. In addition, sometimes what she learns from failure is just as important as what benefits come from her successes.

How does Mustard deal with her anxiety before a major effort is to occur? She believes that there is an inverse relationship between preparation and anxiety. Before beginning something important, Mustard prepares a comprehensive list of what must be done before it can be implemented successfully. Next to each item, she describes the actions that must be taken for her to place a check next to it as a sign that it has been completed. In essence, with each check that Mustard places next to an item, her anxiety is kept to a low level because she has done what is necessary to succeed.

Ruth Mustard is an excellent model as to how a distressless performer approaches the many and diverse challenges which seemingly confront a leader.

Strategies for Becoming a Distressless Performer

Two strategies can enhance your skill in becoming a distressless performer.

USING THE COMMITMENT ANALYZER FOR OVERCOMING OBSTACLES. Whenever you become frustrated, talk negatively about yourself, or have self-doubts, you would benefit from completing the commitment analyzer in Exercise 6.2. Complete each of the statements by writing how you break away to commit. For example, for item 1 of this measure, which addresses the need to overcome procrastination, a possible answer you could give is: *breaking the task into one-hour segments and completing the first hour today.* As you reflect and write answers to the subsequent questions, we suggest that you write the date in the blank that precedes each statement. In this way, you can keep track of your growth in overcoming causes of noncommitment.

STRENGTHENING YOUR COMMITMENT AND POSITIVE PERFORMANCE. We realize that some strategies in this chapter may be difficult to master. The first attempt to overcome a personal deficit can become so frustrating that some people give up. We urge you not to develop such a mind-set because staying the course and working through your

―∿― Exercise 6.2

COMMITMENT ANALYZER FOR OVERCOMING OBSTACLES

1. If I'm confused or overwhelmed, I procrastinate. In the future, when I start to procrastinate, I will overcome it through the use of the "breaking-away" strategy. Here's how I can implement this strategy:

   _____

   _____

2. I have a tendency to exhibit ambivalence instead of speaking up to advance my ideas. In the future when I want to advance an idea, I will break away to accomplish this end by doing the following:

   _____

   _____

3. I tend to talk negatively about myself. In the future when this behavior surfaces, I will break away to develop a plan that will eliminate this specific negative self-talk. I will break away by:

   _____

   _____

4. I minimize my ability to take positive actions when a problem arises because I feel I must wait for something to turn up to solve it for me. In the future when I think in this way, I will break away to develop a plan for positive action by:

   _____

   _____

5. I tend to be impulsive. In the future before I exhibit this behavior, I will break away to reflect and formulate a strategy to avoid my impulsivity by:

   _____

   _____

6. I defer decisions to others because I believe that they are better able to make them. I then later blame them or become angry because

they did not act as I expected. In the future when this deference begins, I will break away to decide if I should make or delegate the decision by:

_____

_____

7. I often go against the grain unnecessarily. I voice a position of opposition before I have really decided that my stance is correct. In the future before I do this, I will break away by:

_____

_____

8. I tend to straddle the fence by saying positive things about both sides of an issue, so that others really do not know where I stand on issues of pertinence to our organization. In the future, when I am tempted to hedge like this, I will break away by:

_____

_____

9. I often do not follow through on things that I say I will do. In the future to increase the frequency with which I fulfill my commitments, I will break away by:

_____

_____

frustration will yield powerful, life-long benefits. A city manager once told us: "How vividly I recall twenty years ago when the book *When I Say No I Feel Guilty* was published. Eager to improve in this area, I pounced into the first chapter. After the third page, the words were so vital to my improvement, but so hard to read! By page four, however, anger began, and I closed the book indignantly. Such facts could not be true about me! Three weeks later, and only through the use of power thinking strategies, did I return to the book and profit from its content."

In the event that something in this book provokes your strong negative emotions or a refusal to engage in a recommended strategy, we encourage you to reassess your decision, just as that city manager did.

The diagram in Figure 6.1 shows the three reasons that decisions you make, even if they are successful, may not be optimally effective. You can also use this diagram to assess which decision-making strategies will most improve your own abilities to become a distressless performer.

If you are not aware of the reasons that your decisions are not as good as you want them to be, then the strategies in this chapter will add to your repertoire. The use of ovals A, B, C, and D of Figure 6.2 can aid you in improving your skill in this area.

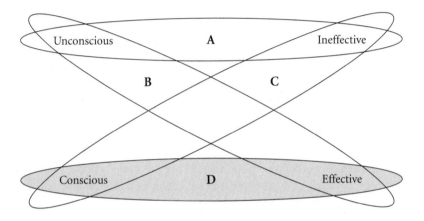

The goal is to make conscious and effective decisions—the ones that result from creative power thinking (oval D). But your decisions may fall more often in ovals A, B, or C.

- In oval A, if you make decisions that are not as effective as you want but you truly cannot identify the reasons for their ineffectiveness, strategies to strengthen your basic reasoning abilities (see Chapters 4 and 5) will be valuable—such as double thinking, the weighted characteristics test, and eliminating excuses.
- In oval B, if you succeed at times but really are not sure why some decisions work better than others, strategies that strengthen self-knowledge are needed—such as overcoming negative tendencies of human nature, saying yes and no more effectively, and monitoring your self-respect (see Chapters 8 and 9).
- In oval C, if you are reasoning well, but your decisions are less successful than you desire, we recommend that you master strategies in Chapters 6 and 7 that strengthen your insight—such as asking more questions, building stronger commitment, adding personal motivators, awaiting good indicators before making a decision, and using proactive repair (e.g., overcoming a misunderstanding by apologizing and offering a positive action to avoid similar miscommunications in the future).

Figure 6.1. Making Powerful Decisions

SPIRITED PRODUCER

Our research revealed that leaders who are animated and full of energy and courage produce success both individually and in the organizational initiatives that they lead. We call them *spirited producers.*

Understanding the Spirited Producer

Items 4, 46, and 62 of the Yale Assessment of Thinking assess the degree to which you are a spirited producer. Fill out the Spirited Producer Item Cluster Graph, entering your scores for these items from Chapter Two. If your total score was 5 or under, write as the YAT score interpretation "highly skilled." If your total score was 6 or 7, write "average ability." If your total score was 8 or higher, write "need for improvement."

Items 4, 46, and 62 on the YAT that focus on this dimension of insight clearly delineate between leaders who are and are not spirited producers. Talking negatively about one's self (item 4—"I talk negatively about myself") may seem like a positive action on the surface. After all, to do so is an act of humility, and should not a leader be humble? The answer, of course, is yes. But the frequency with which it takes place is what differentiates whether it is a positive or negative action. If on the YAT you gave a response of "very often" or "often," the action described in the item is negatively affecting you in two ways.

First, you would do well to remember that your subconscious unequivocally accepts that which you say as being completely true. The more frequently you state something, the more deeply it becomes entrenched within your subconscious. Thus, if you often refer to yourself as "stupid," "boring," or some other negative term,

Item Cluster Graph.   Spirited Producer Item Cluster Graph

YAT Items	Your Response
4	_____
46	_____
62	_____
Total	_____
YAT score interpretation	_____

your subconscious will come to accept this assessment as reality. When you subsequently attempt to reach solutions or solve problems, your subconscious will dissuade you from actions that it believes you cannot realistically complete because you are "stupid," "boring," or whatever other negative term you have repeatedly ingrained in it.

The second way in which frequently talking negatively about yourself has an impact on your effectiveness is the perception that others form about you. Let us suppose that you often refer to yourself as "inept" in the presence of others. One of two detrimental impressions will result from this course of action. If others feel that you are uttering this self-description not because you truly believe it but to feign a sense of humbleness, they will think that you are not being truthful and will judge you as untrustworthy. Clearly, this type of label will hinder your ability to function effectively as a leader. Or they could believe that you are being honest and that you "very often" or "often" act in an inept fashion. Once again, you are ill served by such a mind-set being developed on the part of others. If they believe you are lacking in skill, then ideas that you advance are more likely to be greeted with skepticism or rejected outright by others. The reason is that these individuals too have a subconscious, and the association of you and ineptness will become embedded in it.

A spirited producer operates quite differently. When this person errs or falls short of an intended objective, he or she will admit that fact and explain the actual reason for its occurrence. Those who are skilled in this internal cognitive process do not engage in self-deprecation because they are aware that it is wrong for the reasons we have stated. They engender trust on the part of others because they are honest in assessing themselves and in describing situations.

Item 46 ("I have missed opportunities because of self-doubts that I might be unsuccessful in performing these tasks") also deals with the subconscious. If you frequently have self-doubts as to your ability to perform tasks, there can be many reasons for these beliefs. The factor most customarily responsible for its manifestation in individuals is their unwillingness to make positive commitments to attaining a goal.

With these individuals, a counterproductive cycle exists. When obstacles occur, they do not persevere, and as a consequence, they fail. When a new opportunity presents itself, they have self-doubt because they remember their prior misfortunes. If they reluctantly agree to pursue the new initiative, they will do so without a high level of conviction and will abandon it once they encounter an obstacle. They will justify taking this action (perhaps by saying, "I'm just being practical") by recalling prior incidents where goals were not attained. They will repeat this cycle every time a comparable situation presents itself.

Literary history is replete with stories about authors who faced adversity. We have heard how many of their initial attempts to have their books published were met with rejection. But they made a positive commitment to what they wanted to accomplish, they persevered, and we, the readers of their books, are the beneficiaries.

A spirited producer certainly will have self-doubts at times. Although these instances are rare, when they do occur, the person will use a strategy similar to one presented in this book (such as the ladder strategy or backward reasoning) to think about positive solutions to troubling aspects of it. Once they are satisfied that these concerns have been adequately addressed, they make a strong commitment to themselves and, where warranted, to others that the objective will be realized. They do not abandon it when obstacles arise. They confidently work through them until their objective is met. They exhibit tenacity because they are committed to achieving the end that they established. Also, they are free of doubt that they will eventually attain it.

Item 62 ("When compared to people my age, I become more frustrated than they do when things aren't going right") describes the attitudes that individuals exhibit as they encounter obstacles. Our research found a very different internal cognitive process on the part of leaders who are less skilled in this aspect of insight and individuals found to be spirited performers.

People commonly feel frustrated when things are not going as planned. It is insight's way of telling us that we are not achieving that of which we are capable of attaining. When less skilled thinkers become frustrated, they initially direct it at the situation. They will ask questions such as: "Why did this have to happen?" "Why didn't Person X foresee it?" and "How much longer will this condition last?"

Then their venting will become much more pointed, and the source of it will be directed at themselves. They will say things like: "Why did I even try this?" "Don't I ever learn from my mistakes?" "I tried Y and failed, and now I am going to fail at this," and "This project is unrealistic. I had to be a fool to even attempt it."

This self-flagellation serves no positive purpose. Instead, it disparages the leader and his or her associates, and it also does nothing toward getting the endeavor back on the right track.

When spirited producers are in a comparable situation, they direct their insight quite differently. They ascertain the causes as to why something is not going correctly. Then they devise strategies for rectifying the condition.

Remember that they are *spirited*. They tackle tasks with energy and enthusiasm, and they are positively reinforced when they accomplish their planned actions. Although they may exhibit frustration, it is quite brief and then replaced with thoughts designed to attain the end to which they made a commitment.

An Exemplary Spirited Producer: Bill Walsh

Bill Walsh was a great coach. He led Stanford University to football prominence and later the San Francisco 49ers professional team to three Super Bowls. Walsh, nicknamed "The Genius," transformed the 49ers from a poor football team into a winning one. His impact on the sport is immense. Many teams have copied Walsh's ideas, such as the "West Coast offense," and use them today.

He had success as a coach not merely because of his knowledge about football. Walsh knows what motivates people to win and is acutely aware how an environment can be created that accepts innovation. The strategies that he used as a coach are ones that he believes are germane to organizational success. Although there are many reasons that he was a winning coach, Walsh believes one of the primary factors was that his team respected him. He states: "You have to have a history of being an expert in a given area. The single factor the players responded to was the fact that I was very good at what I did, managing the game under stress" (Cyr, 1999, p. 34).

Walsh did not talk negatively about himself, and even when he became frustrated, he rarely openly criticized individual players. He operated with a can-do attitude both personally and with his team. He wanted his players to believe that they would attain greatness. Walsh's words about what it takes to produce winning teams exemplify what we term a spirited producer.

Strategies for Becoming a Spirited Producer

The strategies examined so far provide a framework for you to enhance your skill as a spirited producer. Following are four additional strategies that we found in our research that power thinkers used to employ their internal cognitive process of insight to the fullest:

WILL I LEARN? Whenever you become worried or anxious or fear failure, this strategy can help you overcome these three negative inhibitors to insight. Essentially, the strategy entails asking yourself a key question: "Will I learn from the situation I am about to undertake?" If the answer is yes, then the decision you are about to make is likely a correct one. This answer will enable your insight to focus on the positive aspects of the new challenge and eliminate or greatly reduce the amount of worry, anxiety, or fear of failure that you have regarding it.

You can employ the strategy of asking "Will I learn?" whenever you begin to feel worry, anxiety, or fear of failure creeping into your mind as you face a new challenge or opportunity. To a large extent, the degree to which your insight can assist in your power thinking in new situations is dependent on whether you would like to learn from the challenge and the people involved in this activity. For example, a young attorney, Jeff, had to make a decision whether to accept a job with a new firm. He used this strategy of "Will I learn?" and in doing so was able to engage his insight in weighing the positive and negative features of the job rather than his mind merely dwelling on the worries about potential aspects of it.

VISION VERSUS DAYDREAMS. "A vision without preparation, planning, and performance is just another daydream" (Donnie and Linkie, 2000, p. 101). An important strategy that has proven to be effective in overcoming your negative emotions is to be cognizant that such feelings will trigger self-limiting thoughts. Worrying and fears are like putting on a pair of glasses that magnify every possible failure. These two emotions not only make things look worse but also reduce your ability to use insight productively.

The first step in confronting fear or worry is to take stock of yourself. Break away long enough to become aware of the different sensations that you are feeling, examine your thoughts, and ask why you are afraid. Substitute the feelings of failure with thoughts of times when your decisions and actions were successful and made you a winner. By recalling when you felt good about something similar that you did in the past, these positively engendered emotions will help you to critically examine and creatively infuse new ideas to address the challenge that faces you.

WHEN YOU BECOME ANXIOUS, ADD SOMETHING THAT MOTIVATES YOU. A decision or implementation plan that incorporates qualities that inspire and motivate you indicates that the decision is one that you will be able to complete successfully. If the plan does not generate your good indicators, you may want to reconsider the entire decision or plan, or elements of it.

Another way to make insight a more integral part of your decision-making process is to think of a project you do not want to do that has been scheduled for the near future. Break away for a moment to think about its tasks. Then commit to the project by adding a task that motivates you or including an element that enhances what *you* want to *achieve for yourself* or *the organization.* Before you read the next paragraph, pause for a moment and write such a motivational element on a sheet of paper.

If you wrote down something that you truly value, you will notice a positive elevation in your attitude about undertaking the project. This is the feeling you are striving to possess as you approach all projects about which you are not initially motivated to tackle. Moreover, by identifying what motivates you—your good indicators—and incorporating them into either your decisions or implementation plans, you can move more easily into flow experiences (described in Chapter Seven), which increase your chances for success.

To know what motivates you, you can analyze different traits of your personality as described in Figure 6.2. Under each of these traits are specific strengths that you can use when you are facing a new challenge. By studying Figure 6.2, you can better understand how you can take a negative thought that is encroaching on your insight and rephrase it into a positive strength. When this transformation takes place, you can use that strength, which you now possess, to enable you to go forward to reach new goals.

In sum, we all can fall victim to internally generated negative emotions or limitations that we feel we have. By adding something that motivates us to face new challenges in a positive way, our brains can turn this potentially negative outlook into a positive one.

USING FORESIGHT WHEN THINKING ABOUT THE FUTURE. Foresight is the ability to make decisions about the future. Distressless performers have good foresight, and as a result, they are skilled in making good decisions because they are careful observers, capable problem solvers, good data collectors, and they understand the nature of change and reasons to think positively about it.

People who use their foresight strategically are able to recognize and use changes productively. If you are not yet skilled in the area of

Creating/Performing

Strengths	Limitations
Spontaneous	Unpredictable
Entertaining	Superficial
Unconventional	Irresponsible
Inventive	Irrational
Flexible	Aimless
Adaptable	Inconsistent
Socially skillful	Manipulative
Enthusiastic	Unrealistic
Charming	Insincere
Dramatic	Melodramatic
Youthful	Immature
Witty	Indiscreet
Versatile	Scattered

Promoting/Leading

Strengths	Limitations
Forceful	Domineering
Self-confident	Egotistical
Assertive	Intimidating
Influential	Arrogant
Decisive	Impatient
Expressive	Argumentative
Competitive	Ruthless
Ambitious	Power oriented
Confrontive	Demanding
Persuasive	Exploitive
Practical	Insensitive
Self-reliant	Uncaring
Direct	Invasive

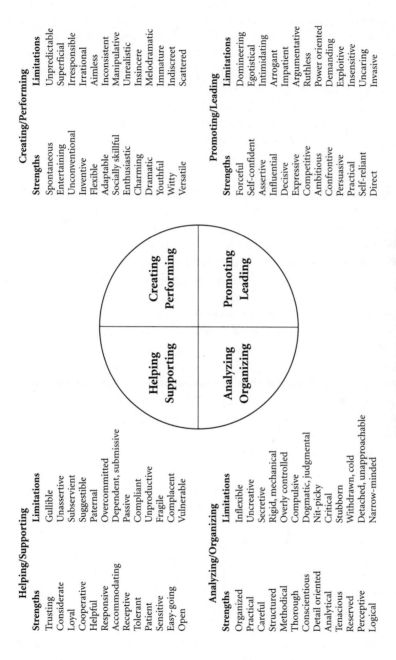

Helping/Supporting

Strengths	Limitations
Trusting	Gullible
Considerate	Unassertive
Loyal	Subservient
Cooperative	Suggestible
Helpful	Paternal
Responsive	Overcommitted
Accommodating	Dependent, submissive
Receptive	Passive
Tolerant	Compliant
Patient	Unproductive
Sensitive	Fragile
Easy-going	Complacent
Open	Vulnerable

Analyzing/Organizing

Strengths	Limitations
Organized	Inflexible
Practical	Uncreative
Careful	Secretive
Structured	Rigid, mechanical
Methodical	Overly controlled
Thorough	Compulsive
Conscientious	Dogmatic, judgmental
Detail oriented	Nit-picky
Analytical	Critical
Tenacious	Stubborn
Reserved	Withdrawn, cold
Perceptive	Detached, unapproachable
Logical	Narrow-minded

Figure 6.2. Components of Personality

foresight, you can begin to plan ahead better and to conceive courses of actions that produce more productive ends as you develop your prowess. With this newly found skill, you will then predict appreciably more accurately events that will occur, and you will be better able to respond positively to unanticipated ones. To become more proficient in foresight, four steps are necessary.

Foresight begins as we become more acutely aware of changes (step 1). We can become more cognizant of them by paying closer attention to new concepts, ideas, or things that others are beginning to value. As you practice identifying these new entities, you will notice that you begin increasingly to ask yourself the reasons that people value these new things. You will find that the reasons customarily relate to the way these entities do one or more of the following: make their life happier, easier, more productive, or more organized. As you identify reasons for this success, which is new to you, your sensitivity and observation skills will expand. As this growth occurs, you will notice you can predict which events and changes in your life will be significant. Our research has shown that when leaders can predict emerging changes that will become important, they are less often led astray simply because they become enamored with that which is new.

Step 2 of foresight involves a person's ability to forecast problems that could emanate from new ideas and creations. Isaac Asimov stated, "The power in predicting the future is not to forecast that the automobile will be built, but to foresee that once it is built, there will be parking problems" (cited in Block and Mangieri, 1996, p. 27). By putting seemingly unrelated ideas together in order to predict and avoid potential future difficulties, distressless producers are able to imagine ideas being used alone or in a group.

Step 3 of the forecasting strategy entails the ability to seek many different types of information before enacting a new idea. Leaders who are quite adept at foresight use many of the strategies that have been previously described in this book to create, store, organize, and use new information and knowledge. For example, powerful leaders who use foresight test ideas out in their own mind, ask others what they think, and create small implementations of ideas a few times before suggesting them for larger settings. They are aware of how people feel about new ideas, how they use them, how fast an idea is being accepted, and how people and themselves can affect an idea's success. People who collect this kind of information are often considered perceptive.

Step 4 of the forecasting strategy is having the ability to view change as a promise of good things to come. Distressless performers have this capability because they envision two positive options that can result from every new event that enters their lives. For example, when something changes unexpectedly, power thinkers typically ask themselves to think of two positive results that such a change could have. By taking this approach, they are able to face the new challenges created by that change and respond proactively to it with one or both of the two positive solutions that are already clearly formulated in their minds.

SUMMARY

In this chapter, we introduced insight, which is an individual's ability to know and act without prior conscious thought being given to an issue. Like reasoning, the subject of Chapters Four and Five, insight is one of the three domains in which power thinkers are highly skilled. In this chapter, we presented eleven strategies and devices intended to help you become more adept in insight's internal cognitive process:

1. Breaking away to commit
2. Reverie
3. Bracketing
4. Finding your own approach
5. Awaiting your good indicators
6. Using the commitment analyzer for overcoming obstacles
7. Strengthening your commitment and positive performance
8. Will I learn?
9. Vision versus daydreams
10. When you become anxious, adding something that motivates you
11. Using foresight when thinking about the future

In addition, we shared the strategies as well as the philosophies of three leaders who are highly skilled in insight's internal cognitive processes: Mark F. Santia, Ruth Wood Mustard, and Bill Walsh.

Finally, we described the three subcomponent skills that constitute the internal cognitive process of insight: ready decider, distressless performer, and spirited producer. On the next two pages, we have provided space in which you may write your reflections on steps that you plan to take in order to become more proficient in each of these segments of internal cognition.

INSIGHT INTERNAL COGNITIVE PROCESS THINKING ENHANCEMENT

Ready Decider

Distressless Performer

Spirited Producer

CHAPTER SEVEN

Insight
External Cognitive Process

T his chapter explores the other half of insight: its external cognitive process. As you may recall from Chapter Five, external cognition pertains to the actions taken by the mind as a consequence of the decisions, solutions, and creative thoughts generated by it.

We discuss the four dimensions of insight's external cognitive processes in which we found power thinkers to be particularly adept: intrepid committer, punctual generator, peaceful winner, and electric creator. As was the case in prior chapters, you can also learn how you stack up as compared to these individuals relative to the subskills of this aspect of insight by filling in the item cluster graphs at the beginning of each section.

INTREPID COMMITTER

On the wall in the office of the Center for Leadership and Personnel Development hangs a sign that reads: "Lead, Follow, or Get Out of the Way." It is an appropriate summary of what our research found relative to the *intrepid committer* facet of insight. The sign's words convey that a decision must be made by a person as to whether he or she intends to lead, follow, or get out of the way.

Understanding the Intrepid Committer

Items 16, 24, and 60 of the Yale Assessment of Thinking assess the degree to which you are an intrepid committer. Fill out the Intrepid Committer Item Cluster Graph, entering your scores for these items from Chapter Two. If your total score was 5 or under, write as the YAT score interpretation "highly skilled." If your total score was 6 or 7, write "average ability." If your total score was 8 or higher, write "need for improvement."

Item 16 ("I make decisions about matters in the order in which they are called to my attention by others") pertains to reaching decisions. Courage is often needed when reaching decisions that may be unpopular (such as deciding not to lead a project). Courage too is frequently required to say no (item 24—"When asked to perform tasks I'd rather not do, I find it difficult to say 'no' to people") when asked to perform such tasks. Power thinkers do not casually commit to do something: once they make a commitment (for example, to lead an effort to its successful completion), they will do it.

Our research found that leaders who were highly skilled in this domain of thinking met the criteria of being intrepid. They had the fortitude to complete that which they had made a decision to undertake regardless of the number and complexity of obstacles encountered.

Item Cluster Graph. Intrepid Committer Item Cluster Graph

YAT Items	Your Response
16	_____
24	_____
60	_____
Total	_____
YAT score interpretation	_____

Hence, *intrepid committer* is a fitting description of this aspect of power thinking.

For individuals who responded "very often" or "often" to item 16, making decisions about matters in the order in which they are called to their attention by others may seem like a sound practice. It is not. When you respond in this manner, others are setting your priorities. You are acting on matters not as to their organizational importance but rather in response to squeaky wheels. You are also establishing an informal operating principle that is negative, will reinforce itself, and will occur with greater frequency in the future. Subordinates will soon realize that when they clamor for a decision, you respond. Therefore, they will clamor more regularly.

An intrepid committer acts differently. When a matter is called to an intrepid committer's attention, this person will respond that she or he is not ready to make a decision about it. The individual may also say when she or he anticipates reaching a decision but will not customarily act on it immediately merely to appease the person raising the issue.

Their action may seem as though it is an unnecessary exercise of power. In fact, it is establishing actions according to what is important and an adherence to that prioritization.

You may be wondering why this skill falls under insight rather than reasoning. Less skilled leaders, who acquiesce to the calls for actions of others, often justify these responses in some way. They fail to understand that their subconscious, which wants tranquility for them, will create a rationalization for what they did. Intrepid committers stay the course and act on matters according to the importance they attached to them and in the order in which they planned to deal with them.

Our subconscious too plays a role in saying no to people when we are asked to perform tasks we would rather not do. In this instance, intrepid committers correctly listen to it. Their less skilled counterparts do not.

Typically, we seek to avoid doing things for which we have little aptitude or that do not challenge us. If we agree to do something in an area where we lack skill, completing it will likely require a great deal of time on our part, and the end product will usually be mediocre.

If we think the task is boring, two negative consequences usually occur. First, we will procrastinate, which is the way that our subconscious keeps us from engaging in the unpleasant. (We say more about procrastination in the next section of this chapter.) Second, our attitude of malaise will spill over to other things in which we are engaged prior to doing this task. As a result, our mind will not give its focused attention to the matters that occur before the dreaded task is completed.

Intrepid committers do not want to perform functions that they will do poorly and do not want to be labeled a procrastinator. As a consequence, they say no when asked to perform tasks they would rather not do. They do not make up lies to justify such a stance. They say no confidently and with conviction because they know that they and the organization are better served by their doing so.

The crux of item 60 ("In the past, when I sought to change certain behaviors, I found my efforts were basically a waste of time") is akin to that of a New Year's resolution. The content of this type of list is sealed by good intentions, but they rarely are attained. As a consequence, the lowering of our cholesterol, becoming a better spouse, showing greater patience, or whatever else we resolve to do usually is abandoned by February and goes unmet. While we justify the nonrealization of these goals in many ways, the truth of the matter is that although we called them resolutions, we did not pursue them very resolutely.

The same holds true with the many change initiatives that we seek to undertake. We did not attain their desired end because we sought to realize them with the same degree of noncommitment we made to our New Year's resolutions.

Our research found a very different attitude and rate of success between intrepid committers and persons less skilled in this segment of insight. Intrepid committers were decidedly more selective about what they made a commitment to change. Once they initiated actions to attain it, they relentlessly pursued it. With such an attitude, is it any wonder that they had a much higher rate of success in attaining behavioral change?

These individuals refuse to listen to the justifications and alibis offered by their subconscious as reasons that they should cease in their efforts to change. Instead, they consciously remind themselves of the benefits that they will realize from making the intended change. When they face adversity, they will make this reminder be even more pronounced so that they can drown out the voice of their subconscious, which is telling them that it is okay to abandon their efforts.

For these leaders, making a commitment to change something means to them that they will accomplish it. This can-do credo manifests itself in the way they act as leaders. It is an important reason that they are outstanding in the level of success that they realize in these roles.

An Exemplary Intrepid Committer:
William J. McKim

William J. McKim serves as a wonderful example of how an intrepid committer acts in the workplace. He has been the assistant general counsel for the United States Steel Corporation for approximately five years. Prior to assuming this role, he had been a distinguished attorney for over twenty-five years. After completing law school, he served in positions of increasing responsibility, including that of law clerk for a senior judge of the U.S. Court of Appeals for the Third Circuit. Despite maintaining a demanding schedule at the United States Steel Corporation, McKim has regularly taught a legal ethics course at Duquesne University Law School for a number of years.

Making decisions and delivering legal strategies for problems that either United States Steel or its leaders face is the crux of McKim's responsibilities. Time is an important commodity to McKim. Often he must provide legal advice quickly in response to an emerging situation. Also, because United States Steel is a large corporation, the matters sent to him are complex and numerous.

Does McKim make decisions about matters in the order in which they are called to his attention by others (item 16)? Absolutely not. He believes that to operate in such a fashion would mean that someone else was deciding his priorities, and by acting this way, he would be doing a disservice to his organization and professional responsibilities within it.

McKim uses a two-step process to establish his priorities. First, he asks if the matter before him is important to the organization. If it is not, he will inform the person who called it to his attention that it is not a matter on which he will take action. If it is important to the organization, McKim will affix a priority status to it, determining its degree of importance (for example, highly important, important, or something else) to the organization and its management.

It is by using this process, and not responding to the clamors of associates, that McKim establishes priorities. Once he has agreed to consider an issue, colleagues know that he will act on it and in a timely manner.

McKim frequently says no to tasks that people ask him to perform (item 24). If another person seeks to engage him in activities outside his area of expertise, McKim asks two questions of himself before agreeing to participate in them: Do I have the skill to do this task well? and Do I like doing it? If the answer to either question is no, that will be his response to the request.

McKim says this about turning down tasks he would rather not do: "As a result of other job responsibilities, you can easily make commitments for that which you cannot do when you promise to do them. If you don't fulfill a commitment that you've agreed to, others will be more disappointed that you didn't finish something, than if you had initially said no to the request."

Thus far, we have discussed McKim's commitments to others. What about those that he makes to himself? McKim readily accepts the inevitability of change. He believes that a person has to embrace new developments and assess things from a fresh perspective. Often, in order to do so, an individual needs to change rather than hold on to prior thinking. McKim states, "No one should be a finished product until they're dead."

When he needs to change a facet of his performance, McKim devises a concrete plan to achieve this objective. After this occurs, he, like the Nike company advocates, "just does it" by implementing the planned actions. McKim boldly engages in change because he is a firm believer that people should challenge themselves to become better and not accept limitations within themselves.

McKim is intrepid in the performance of his responsibilities as a leader. The commitments that he makes to others and to himself are the products of careful thought. And when he gives his word to others or to himself, McKim will follow through on time and well. He provides an excellent example of what an intrepid committer is, as well as how one acts.

Strategies for Becoming an Intrepid Committer

In order to help you to become as proficient in this segment of insight as McKim is, we provide some strategies. Unlike the discussions presented previously in this book, you should do these strategies that increase your abilities to become an intrepid committer in the order we present them.

Because they have not developed the skills that we describe next, non–power thinkers tend to respond to the most recent request made of them, regardless of whether it demands, improves, or increases their areas of talents and enhances their corporation's success. The strategies that you can master to become an intrepid committer are (1) knowing how to say no effectively, (2) valuing the truth in your felt senses, (3) developing the habit of saying, "Tell me more," when challenged, and (4) engaging the insights of subordinates when you are uncertain of the correct course of action.

KNOWING HOW TO SAY NO EFFECTIVELY. The ability to say no (when that is the most effective answer to give) enables intrepid committers to decline requests that are not most important to their organizations or require their most outstanding skills and talents as a leader. Many leaders have not developed this ability. Learning to say no is not an easy skill. Intrepid committers are equally capable of declining invitations that are not within their company's mission as they are of accepting those requests that maximize their talent. Without this skill, you will continuously assume responsibilities that do not build power thinking. In *Henry VIII*, Shakespeare summarized the need for knowing how to say no well:

> Over commitment is like a circle in the water
> Which never ceaseth to enlarge itself,
> Till by broad spreading it disperses to naught.

To develop the ability to say yes and no effectively, you should say yes only to tasks that stretch your abilities or actualize the ideals which you want to achieve as a leader. The most important strategy for developing such skill is learning to identify why you want to say yes before you reflexively respond. To develop this habit, practice answering requests with a sentence that begins: "The reason I tend to want to say yes is because _____."
When this statement becomes habitual, you will be less likely to respond impulsively to the emotion of the moment. Then realize that four psychological reasons create the difficulty in saying no. Exercise 7.1 can identify which of these four reasons are restricting your ability to become an intrepid committer.

The next sections explore some reasons why saying no is so difficult and describe the power thinking strategies that enable you to decline unnecessary commitments. For each of the two statements that you marked as 1 and 2 in Exercise 7.1, read the related discussion that follows:

Answer A: *The needs of others are more important than my own.* Intrepid committers know that the priorities that they establish for themselves are just as important as those that other people want them

---

—⁓— Exercise 7.1

DETERMINING WHY IT IS DIFFICULT FOR YOU TO SAY NO

1. Think of a person to whom [or a situation in which] it is difficult for you to say no. Write down that person's name [or a description of the situation] here: _____ . Why do you have difficulty saying no to that person or when placed in that situation? _____ . Describe the reasons or conditions that lead you to say yes when a no response is warranted

_____ .

2. Which of the following reasons best explain why you do not respond as you truly feel to this individual or in the situation you described? Place a 1 before the statement that best describes your reasons and a 2 beside the one that describes your second-best reason:

  ____   A. The needs of others are more important than my own.
  ____   B. I say yes to most of the requests made of me.
  ____   C. Most of the time, I would rather work as a team rather than alone.
  ____   D. When I have made a commitment that is more taxing than I had anticipated, I stick to it regardless of the time and energy required to complete it.

---

to pursue. You can increase your decision-making power by prioritizing actions that contribute to your skill as a leader. One way to realize this goal is to do something for self-improvement every day. Bettering yourself helps you formulate higher-quality thoughts and decisions to share with others. Such increases in your external cognitive insights processes lead to strengthened self-reliance and decreased expectations that other people will meet your needs. Giving more time and resources to yourself also increases the number of initiatives you can lead because you are not saying yes to too many requests during the detail-laden implementation stage.

To increase your resolve to value your priorities further, consider the following. If someone wants you to do something that he or she actually should (and needs to) do, you can assist that person to take charge of his or her own problems if you say no. Thus, saying no to inappropriate requests helps others identify power-thinking abilities within themselves. Furthermore, when you say yes and take action to alleviate another person's anxiety, you diminish his or her own abilities to identify and solve the causes of his or her problems. Another negative ramification of your inability to say no effectively is that because you choose to say yes to solve problems that are not within your responsibilities, your actions are likely to be based on incomplete information. Your naive solutions could create complications that actually increase the problem.

In reality, there is only one response you should give to friends and colleagues when they face difficulties that they need to handle themselves: sincerely listen and ask questions to help them discover their own reasons, insights, and self-knowledge. The moment you cross the line from listening to that person to becoming the person who takes action, you have said yes inappropriately and diminished that person's potential for growth.

If this pattern reoccurs frequently in the future, evaluate such requests by asking yourself, "Does this request fall within the context of my responsibilities as a leader? If not, do I have the unique skills to meet this person's need?" Saying yes or no selectively allows you to focus your energies within your areas of talent, thereby improving your results, your efficiency, and the contributions that your power thinking can make to the people whom you lead. To say no in such situations, use some or all of the following actions and power thinking strategies:

- Refer the person to appropriate resources or someone else, and explain why you feel you are not the best person to meet the request.

- Think to yourself, "Others will determine priorities for me if I don't expend effort toward attaining the goals that I have established for myself and the organization." Listen to the person, and ask questions until that colleague's insight, reasoning, and self-knowledge lead him or her to a correct course of action.

- Have in mind one important objective you want to accomplish each day. In this way, when someone makes a request, you can respond by saying that this objective is a priority and preceded his or her request.

- Ask yourself, "Have I helped others or myself overcome this problem before?" If so, and if doing so will (a) take limited time on your part, (b) have a multiplicative effect by developing several people's skills, and (c) be easily accomplished, yes can be the correct answer.

- Ask yourself, "Does this person need to be mentored before he or she can independently contribute success in this area to the organization?" If so, you will receive an extra reward from saying, "Yes, I'll do it with you as a mentor," because by strengthening this person, you also strengthen the company.

In summary, if you tend to value the needs of others above your priorities, each time you want to reach out to help someone who should learn how to solve *independently* the difficulty under their responsibility, say to yourself, "I tend to want to say yes to this request because _____ ." Then, either (1) refer the person to appropriate resources or another person, (2) listen to the problem and ask questions until that person feels capable of correcting the difficulty, (3) state your priority and why it takes precedence over that person's request at this time, (4) say yes if it has the multiplicative benefits of expanding many colleagues' skills and can be done easily in a limited amount of time, or (5) ask yourself if the organization would benefit by you mentoring this person and completing the task with him or her.

Answer B: *I say yes to most of the requests made of me.* If you placed a 1 or 2 before this sentence, it is likely that you are saying yes so frequently because you do not maximize the reasoning strategies (described in Chapters Four and Five) before you answer. Every request should have a 50 percent chance of receiving a no answer from you. The following strategies will help you reason more powerfully so that you no longer pursue every squeaky wheel that beckons.

- If you want to say no but feel you cannot, stop for a few seconds and say nothing, even silently counting to ten before saying yes. When you do this, other people are likely to detect your hesitance, and they will help you decline. They realize that it would not be in your best interests to say yes.

- If you cannot identify reasons to say yes, you may be saying yes inappropriately merely to satisfy your ego needs or because you assume that acquiescing will increase others' respect for you as a leader. A test of whether these are the true reasons that you tend to say yes too frequently is to ask yourself whether you sometimes feel used by others or if others do not reciprocate in ways you desire. If so, you could be sacrificing and impulsively responding yes too quickly. Wait for one full day before you answer a request that you judge to be outside your talents and your company's priorities. In addition, if you say yes to a request that conflicts with your internal beliefs and values, you will likely promise an unrealistically successful performance.

• If you take on so many responsibilities that you cannot deliver on your promises or are unable to function optimally as a leader, others may subsequently judge you to be untrustworthy or inept. You then will lose the respect you hoped to achieve by saying yes. Ask yourself when you could realistically turn your attention to this request and if it is too late for the person, suggest some other way that he or she could address their needs.

Answer C: *Most of the time, I would rather work on a team than alone.* As you are aware, group work is best for many tasks. However, some leaders say yes to requests from others merely to avoid working alone. The problem of being in groups too often is that you lose the reflectivity time necessary to develop your own unique talents, insights, and ideas. Also, you could become so much of a group member that you lose sight of who you are. Too many group-focused tasks also limit the number of opportunities you could have to experience different aspects of yourself and actualize your leadership potential.

Instead, when you no longer say yes to every request, you will cease to be the first person to whom people turn to complete every undesirable or difficult job that no one else wants to do. By becoming more discerning, you project an image of a leader who has many interests and commitments, and you attract more people to work with you who are capable of assuming their own responsibility. As a result, your company's productivity increases exponentially.

You may be surprised to know that intrepid committers spend more than 50 percent of their time alone and that most of their close interactions involve only a few people. To make more effective decisions about saying yes and no effectively if you tend to work more as a team member, you can:

- Establish a time each week when you will work alone or with only one other person to develop a new idea, project, or activity for your company. This change also will increase your self-confidence relative to your skill as a leader.
- Set aside time to develop a leadership skill your company needs.

Answer D: *When I have made a commitment that is more taxing than I had anticipated, I stick to it regardless of the time and energy required to complete it.* No one can judge perfectly the amount of time and effort that challenging new tasks take. Experience performing the same task increases your accuracy in allocating time priorities. The following strategies can assist you when a task proves to be more taxing than originally planned:

- Ask other people for help.
- Ask for an extension of time.
- Share the completed portions with the people to whom you gave your commitment, and ask them to suggest what could be done to meet the deadline.
- Use the Do It Better the Second Time Around strategy, which we will describe later in this chapter, with some component of the new task so you save time when working on that aspect of the project.

VALUING THE TRUTH IN YOUR FELT SENSES. The second step in developing the ability to become an intrepid committer involves pattern recognition. By identifying conditions common to your greatest successes, you can cultivate a "felt sense" about which talents most contribute to your success. "Felt sense" means trusting the ability of your external insight's cognitive processes to know something will work even though you cannot articulate how it will. To develop this ability, complete Exercise 7.2.

Through this analysis, you have identified the talents through which you have greatest success and are most automatic for you. In the future, rely on this felt sense in your areas of talent to move your company forward. As an example of how valuable a strong felt sense can be for a leader, we turn to Michael Jordan. In spite of his enormous athletic gifts, he was not strong enough in his felt sense to know

—ᴡᴡ— Exercise 7.2

DEVELOPING YOUR FELT SENSE ABILITY

List on the lines that follow the three most recent and largest successes you have had as a leader. Beside each one, identify the single thought, action, skill, or talent that you initiated in response to an external condition that was crucial to the success of that project. Then identify the common talents and attributes that characterize your successes.

1. _____

_____

_____

2. _____

_____

_____

3. _____

_____

_____

Common talents were:

_____

_____

Common attributes were:

_____

_____

that his talents as a basketball star would not translate well to baseball. For this reason, he was a less successful leader when he was outside his areas of talent.

In summary, by following felt sense, you will become a more intrepid committer, and your ability to overcome procrastination will increase.

DEVELOPING THE HABIT OF SAYING "TELL ME MORE" WHEN CHALLENGED. The third step in increasing your skills as an intrepid committer is to learn how to reply to people who challenge you or your company rather than to delay action because they disagree with your course of action. Most often when opposition occurs, less effective leaders respond by saying: "I don't think your idea will work because . . ." and then give all the reasons that the person who proposed the alternative action should pursue your course of action. You might think that responding to opposition by championing your own ideas is a successful strategy. It is not. You are digging yourself in to defend your actions rather than allowing yourself to move forward and lead.

Instead, when someone opposes your plan of action, reply by saying, "Tell me more." Possibly the opposer will provide insight into a potential roadblock that could occur ahead and propose actions to avoid it. Because you receive these suggested alternative plans, your foresight will increase in arenas outside your talents, and you can also enlarge your support network so you will know to whom you can turn whenever similar projected difficulties occur.

Every leader has areas of weakness. An intrepid committer recognizes possible blind spots to his vision as he begins, so that he can identify people who can assist him. This strategy also builds intrepid committers' ability to build first-rate multitalented teams.

ENGAGING THE INSIGHTS OF COLLEAGUES WHEN THE CORRECT COURSE OF ACTION IS UNCLEAR. The last strategy to become a more intrepid committer is to hold highly effective meetings whenever you are uncertain as to the next step to take. Some power thinkers who are not intrepid committers face challenges beyond their areas of talent by procrastinating. They tend to commission a study, develop a task force, or set up a committee to study a problem that they cannot solve. Although these actions are appropriate at times, if you are not clear as to the exact problem, we recommend that you try to engage a discussion before you assign the problem to a task force committee. This discussion should vary each time a problem occurs so that fresh thinking occurs.

There are three prompts that vary such discussions. They will ensure that you initiate creative thinking and approach new challenges from a fresh perspective. The first prompt is to put the problem in a story about a hero that everyone in your group knows and is a hero you particularly admire. In this story, you will create events in which the hero takes actions to solve the uncertainty that faces your company. In the process, you will analyze why the hero took the action she did and why it worked. (The explanation as to why you should choose a hero that everyone admires will be given to you in Chapter Eight.)

The reverse failure team prompt, the second prompt, is to ask your team to imagine that the uncertainty that your company faces completely eliminated all profits and positive gains of the project that was initiated. Ask yourself and your team what went wrong that caused such a failure. As you complete this discussion, you will list each of the actions that took place. In doing so, you are likely to come across a plan that can circumvent such a failure.

The last prompt is to use the backward-reasoning strategy. Describe the ultimate goal in great detail to the group, and then discuss all that would have occurred right before the ultimate goal was achieved. Continue listing all steps until you reach the problem at hand. In this way, when you reach the problem situation, you will have identified courses of action that you can take to overcome the difficulty.

PUNCTUAL GENERATOR

A great deal has been written and said about time. Among other things, we have been told that it is "a precious commodity" and "money." Songs such as "Get Me to the Church on Time" and "Time in a Bottle" have been written about it.

If time is something that is valued in our society, why do some individuals squander it? Why are their reports seemingly always late? Why do they perpetually miss deadlines? Items 6, 35, and 50 from the Yale Assessment of Thinking deal with procrastination. They can help us to understand why some individuals are punctual about completing assignments—they are *punctual generators*—and others are not.

Understanding the Punctual Generator

Items 6, 35, and 50 of the Yale Assessment of Thinking assess the degree to which you are a punctual generator. Fill out the Punctual Generator Item Cluster Graph, entering your scores for these items from Chapter Two. If your total score was 5 or under, write as the YAT score interpretation "highly skilled." If your total score was 6 or 7, write "average ability." If your total score was 8 or higher, write "need for improvement."

Item 6 ("When I am confused or feel overwhelmed, I procrastinate") provides a clear differentiation between the actions of power thinkers and less skilled counterparts when feelings of confusion or being overwhelmed occur. In the midst of such a condition, those who are overwhelmed typically cease their efforts.

Their rationale is that since what they were attempting was not working, it would be futile to continue now. They say that they will try it again in a few days. Their logic for this approach is that "things may change" due to an external event or "I may get a brainstorm."

This action differs from the breaking-away strategy discussed in Chapter Six because during this interval, they give little thought to the matter. When they do, it is superficial, and they quickly abandon their thinking because they remain confused about it. Eventually, after being cajoled by a third party (perhaps a supervisor), they will complete the task in a desultory manner, though usually this occurs after the initial deadline has passed. If the task does not involve others and there is no accountability for its completion, it will be abandoned with a justification that it will be reinitiated "when things change."

Item Cluster Graph. **Punctual Generator Item Cluster Graph**

YAT Items	Your Response
6	_____
35	_____
50	_____
Total	_____
YAT score interpretation	_____

Contrast this scenario with that of a punctual generator. At times, they too experience confusion or feelings of being overwhelmed, but how they act in response is quite different. When adversity occurs, a punctual generator will not abandon what is before him or her. Rather, this person's thought is directed toward analyzing what is needed to turn the existing situation in a positive direction. Punctual generators use their minds to brainstorm possible solutions to the problem before them.

When punctual generators see negative feelings begin to manifest within themselves, they understand that this is a signal of sorts from their insight's external cognitive processing. What they are being told is that the approach that they are using is not effective. But unlike their less skilled counterparts, they do not abandon what they are working on. They made a commitment to others or themselves that it would be done, and getting things done in accordance with deadlines (being punctual) is important to them.

They turn their less-than-fruitful efforts into successful ones by analyzing what is lacking in what they are doing. For example, they may substitute a new component for one of its ingredients. Or maybe all of the components are fine, but something needs to be done to supplement them. Conversely, they may decide to use a new approach to get the task completed.

Item 50 ("I procrastinate when a problem arises") too deals with procrastination in the face of adversity. Item 35 describes how some people deal with feelings of confusion or being overwhelmed. It focuses on how individuals act when a problem arises.

As was the case with item 6, our research found that less skilled thinkers abandon the task before them in the face of adversity. Although they continue to think about the matter periodically, their cognition will be in the form of daydreaming. They will hope that the source of the problem will go away or a magical cure will manifest itself.

In contrast, punctual generators will take actions designed to deal with this type of situation. First, they will be sure that they have accurately assessed the obstacle facing them. Then they will discern which problem solution strategy (for example, backward reasoning or the ladder strategy) should be used to generate a solution to the problem.

Punctual generators proactively address problems. They do not procrastinate or wait for a miraculous solution to appear. They generate solutions because they are committed to getting the task done on time.

Item 35 ("I have trouble meeting deadlines") deals with a related but somewhat different dimension of procrastination. Items 6 and 50 focused on situations in which procrastination occurred because feelings of confusion emerged when a problem occurred. Item 35 is not situation specific but rather describes individuals who perpetually fail to meet deadlines. For some of these individuals, time commitments have little value. In addition to not meeting deadlines, they are regularly late for appointments and meetings. These actions may seem minor, but they are not. Remember that they directly or implicitly made a commitment to be somewhere at an agreed-on time. That they are chronically late is a message that the person whom they are meeting is not very important to them.

Our research revealed two reasons that the majority of individuals who responded "very often" or "often" to this item act as they do. Be mindful that one or both of these reasons can be the cause of your procrastination.

The first reason that some individuals frequently fail to meet deadlines is poor work habits. They may have inadequate time management skills and cannot effectively plan to perform task A and task B to comply with a deadline, or, for the reasons already described in this book, they do not say no to things they do not like doing. As a result, they procrastinate because they are seeking to avoid doing unpleasant assignments.

Second, our research found that individuals who have trouble meeting deadlines frequently have low morale. They view their jobs as unchallenging and their responsibilities as "same old, same old." Procrastination is the way their subconscious conveys dissatisfaction with what they do and the responsibilities that it entails.

If you responded "very often" or "often" to this item, we urge you to identify which of these causes is responsible for your procrastination. Remember that it can exist due to one or multiple factors. Make an effort to discern correctly why you act as you do. If necessary, enlist the assistance of others so that you can accurately pinpoint the causes of your actions.

After you have done this, we urge you to address the source of your procrastination. Procrastination is not merely a matter of lateness: it affects how you think, how others regard you, and the quality of your work.

An Exemplary Intrepid Committer: Richard Robinson

Richard Robinson, chairman of the board, president, and chief executive officer of the Scholastic Corporation, provides an excellent example of a leader who is a punctual generator.

Under Robinson's leadership, Scholastic has become the world's largest publisher and distributor of children's books in the English language. The company's annual revenues are $2 billion, and it has over ten thousand employees with operations in over fifteen countries around the world. In 2000, Scholastic acquired Grolier, a leader in print and on-line library reference publishing and books for parents of children from birth to age six. In 2001, Scholastic purchased Tom Snyder Productions, a leading developer and publisher of interactive educational software.

Robinson has received many honors for his work, including, in 2001, the Ed Press Hall of Fame Award, the educational publishing industry's highest honor. Many factors are attributable to Robinson's being a superb leader, but his personal and organizational approach to deadlines is particularly noteworthy.

In the publishing industry, setting and meeting deadlines is crucial to success. If one facet of the company misses a targeted date, it affects the entire schedule. Under Robinson's leadership, Scholastic simply does not miss deadlines.

For every major endeavor, the company posts the deadlines by which each segment of the undertaking must be done. Robinson has established an ethos, which employees and managers are keenly aware of, that if their units fail to accomplish a task by an established date, they have let Scholastic down. They also know that they will be looked at unfavorably by the other units involved in the project that expected them to finish their work in a timely manner. The unit is reminded as well that its tardiness affects the children and teachers who would use the product.

With human nature being what it is, how does Robinson deal with procrastination in addition to posting schedules? With each important challenge that faces Scholastic, he identifies what segment of it people will want to do the least. Robinson states: "The best thing for a writer to do in order to start on a book is to put a piece of paper in a typewriter. The best thing for a company is to get started doing what they want to put off doing."

Robinson also employs another strategy that is beneficial to him as a leader: setting important goals. To ensure that he is not procrastinating in his efforts toward their attainment, he regularly asks himself: Am I doing the right things to accomplish my goals? If he believes that he is not, he scrutinizes his actions and makes the changes necessary for him to get back on track. Robinson calls this his "recalibration process."

Strategies for Becoming a Punctual Generator

Richard Robinson is a gifted leader who does his utmost to combat procrastination within himself and the company he leads. He also uses strategies to ensure that deadlines are viewed as important to the company's well-being and are met. In addition to the strategies that Robinson uses, our research found that power thinkers frequently employ five other strategies in their roles as punctual generators: (1) begin but not at the beginning, (2) increase commitment and creative thinking, (3) create a better method the second time around, (4) establish effective deadlines, and (5) make assembly lines. These strategies can assist you in avoiding procrastination when you feel overwhelmed or confused so that this confusion will never delay your positive actions.

BEGIN BUT NOT AT THE BEGINNING. The first power thinking strategy that assists when you feel overwhelmed is to begin your project as soon as it is assigned. It is not necessary to do its requisite tasks in sequential order. Dealing with the difficulty through a task that you can complete right now, rather than starting at a complex section, is the first step in overcoming procrastination when you are confused. Addressing a problem from its outer extensions, which will be some distance from its most challenging core, is the best procedure when you lead an initiative with many challenges.

By beginning with simple tasks you do well, you can reach the central challenge more rapidly. Just as the main knot in a densely knotted ball of yarn cannot be seen at the outset but will be found only at its core, the central issues of new and large challenges often become more visible only after the easier, external knots have been untied.

To use this strategy, as soon as a problem emerges, take an action to improve one aspect of the situation immediately. Then analyze the effects of the action you took, and turn your thinking toward a second aspect of the challenge.

As you methodically work to rectify each smaller dimension, the web of the problem will likely unravel. Moreover, by continuing to make minor corrections, so that you succeed with each small step, you will keep less complicated dimensions of the situation from becoming more entangled. Also, your actions will make positive changes in the conceptual and behavioral patterns that underlie the central issue.

Alternatively, if you try to establish an ill-conceived grand solution before you have first-hand experience with the challenge, you are likely to create more knots in your problematic ball of yarn. These knots will make the central problem worse because people's feelings are usually hurt when they are not consulted in such unilateral decisions, and your actions will set in motion such detrimental processes, whether real or perceived. Moreover, such decisions encourage some people to oppose the actions you have initiated (the pendulum swing effect) or to dig in their heels by championing the status quo or neutralizing their power to contribute positively to the solution through protests. In addition, beginning now but not at the core enables you to find opportunities that others may miss.

INCREASE COMMITMENT AND CREATIVE THINKING. Have you noticed that when you commit to a project, the work becomes easier? The reason is that commitment focuses your rational energy and inspires you to persevere toward a clearly identified target. Moreover, once you commit, your subconscious no longer has to consider different directions simultaneously (for example, "If I do A, then B will happen, but if I do X, then Y will happen"). Instead, it can focus all its energy toward a single plan of action. Also, after commitment engages, momentum builds, and power thinking can expand. Thus, you can develop the ability to become a punctual generator, and your momentum can increase because you have begun a project instead of waiting until you can solve the project without action.

Creativity is the ability to bring something into existence—to make something out of nothing and to not do everything exactly as it was done in the past or as others do it. The four methods of enhancing creativity are to (1) create win-win situations, (2) engage what-if thinking, (3) accept, connect, and join ideas, and (4) stay loose until rigor counts. These methods are described next.

- *Win-win situations.* In these situations, you lead so that both sides of an issue advance in a positive direction as the result of creative thinking, which must occur if both sides are to grow. Win-win situations enhance creativity more than incidents in which only one side wins, because two dissimilar goals must unite if two dissimilar objectives are to be reached. This union often establishes innovations that could not have been achieved if only one goal was reached. The win-win principle should be engaged whenever you are in difficult situations involving other people.

- *What-if thinking.* What-if thinking is the second strategy that eliminates blocks to creativity. It means you will use the group members' imaginations to solve a complication. You ask, "What if we could or did . . . ?" What-if thinking eliminates blocks because it reduces the temptation to label problems as difficult and causes you to think of previously successful experiences with similar complications. This recall stimulates creativity because you will not be tempted to exactly replicate a solution you used previously. Instead, you will engage creative thinking to improve on all prior decisions relative to the issue facing you now so that all your experiences since you last faced similar challenges can add to the quality of your plan of action. Therefore, when you face a problem, ask yourself, "What if I could or did . . . ?" Then write and discuss the thoughts that occurred as a result of using this strategy.

- *Accepting, connecting, and joining ideas.* By using this strategy, you learn how to hold in reserve the best from another person's perspective until you can connect it to the best from your point of view to increase the quality of a decision. Holding in reserve the best from another person's perspective until you can connect it to the best in their point of view will create a new outlook. These ideas unite to create a strategy that eliminates blocks to creativity. Leaders who learn to accept others' perspectives, even if these points of view are very different from their own, will be more creative and reach better solutions. By learning to accept others' outlooks and connecting your goals to your company's projects and products, you can also address more people's needs.

- *Staying loose until rigor counts.* "Staying loose" means continuously seeking new ideas and noticing new possibilities. This type of thinking eliminates blocks to creativity because it enables your mind to explore many alternatives as you fashion new projects and ideas. Adding rigor is equally important. To have maximum creative thinking, perpetual generators have also learned how to change their mindsets near the end of projects, rigorously testing their final decisions, and becoming as critical of their ideas as possible right before their final products are produced.

The second component of this strategy is to use your commitment and momentum to eliminate barriers to your creative thinking. Three barriers to creative thinking and methods for overcoming these barriers follow:

• *Fault finding.* Most things in this world can be improved, but listening to people who constantly find fault with others will eventually diminish your commitment and creative thinking. Perpetual generators overcome this barrier by performing the following external cognitive process. Whenever someone is criticizing, they accept that person's perspective long enough to identify good points in the position and then join only those points (and not the entire series of critiques) to the goal they are seeking. Most important, these power thinkers know that using critiques to improve ideas requires that they maintain a high level of self-esteem and confidence (using strategies described in Chapter Eight).

• *Impatience.* Impatience limits creativity because it leads nonperpetual generators to invest energy in implementing ill-conceived plans rather than using more time at the beginning of their thinking to derive a more creative and effective plan. Power thinkers sense that they are becoming impatient, and they use the strategies set out in Chapter Six to increase their insight before they act.

• *Stereotyping and not seeing new possibilities.* This limits creativity because it handicaps leaders' abilities to see unique features in each new idea, challenge, or project. Each time perpetual generators view a unique feature, they have established a competitive advantage over their non–power thinking peers.

A summary of these methods appears in Figure 7.1, which can be tailored to your company, and shared with colleagues for brainstorming, problem solving, and creative planning meetings.

CREATE A BETTER METHOD THE SECOND TIME AROUND. Whenever you have to complete an action for a second, third, fourth, or fifth time, your insight increases when you create a better method to do that single activity with each repeated use of it. Perpetual generators who repeat the same action taken in the very first encounter with a specific task find that the second implementation becomes more successful

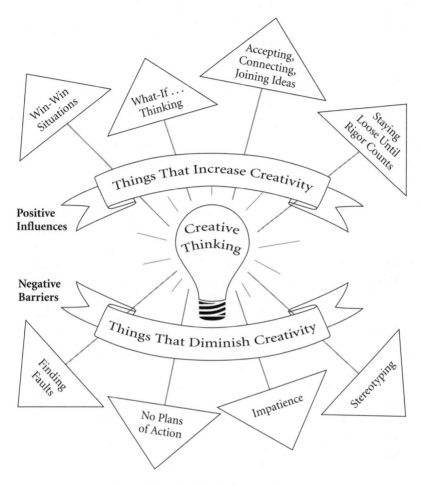

Figure 7.1. Positive Influences on and
Negative Barriers to Creative Thinking

because they add something creative the second time that they implement that same action.

For example, a power leader who is to do a keynote address for the first time plans extensively. The second time, this leader will not follow the same notes, but instead will alter and add new knowledge gained since the last address. Also, when power leaders have to complete something that is routine (such as returning calls), they find a way to make that routine less of a drudgery, sometimes accomplishing two things at once. For example, many power thinkers return calls while they are performing something that they enjoy. One leader reported to us that he returns calls at the end of the afternoon while he is in the hot tub relaxing.

In summary, doing something better the second time around can be defined as doing it in less time, doing it with higher quality, adding creativity to it so it accomplishes a greater good, or inventing a new dimension that can enhance the productivity of the action. This ability enables perpetual generators to continuously increase their skills.

ESTABLISH EFFECTIVE DEADLINES. Whenever a problem nags to be addressed, you feel guilty for not having solved a challenge, or you tend to procrastinate, set a deadline. Because deadlines set a time at which a product will be delivered, you will commit to the project more rapidly and work more diligently toward its success. You do so to save face, avoid disappointing others, and demonstrate your competence as a leader. Before you use this approach, however, you would benefit from examining your existing positive and negative beliefs about deadlines. Non–power thinkers do not respond well to the pressure that self-imposed deadlines create.

To identify your beliefs about establishing deadlines, you will benefit from completing the self-analysis in Exercise 7.1. Then you can compare your answers to those of an insurance executive set out in Exhibit 7.1.

When the insurance executive completed this analysis, he realized that his response to deadlines was more positive than he had anticipated. Before he completed this personal analysis, he believed that he worked best by establishing as few deadlines as possible. Now he uses them frequently to attack problems, and he has fewer problems as a leader. He also discovered that in the future, he wants to add the following power thinking strategies to increase his ability to set more effective deadlines:

- Focusing his priorities in areas of his talent
- Taking more frequent, but earned, breaks to maintain his personal health
- Saying no to low-priority activities
- Channeling solutions into his areas of talent to better enjoy the rewards of meeting deadlines

---

—〰— Exercise 7.3

YOUR RESPONSE TO DEADLINES

1. Recall a recent deadline that you set for yourself on a personal or professional task.

   _____

   _____

2. List your beliefs about the positive outcomes you experienced from setting that deadline.

   _____

   _____

3. List your negative beliefs about and responses to that deadline.

   _____

   _____

4. Review your lists. What insights did you gain about the value of deadlines for you?

   _____

   _____

Exhibit 7.1 shows a sample response to this exercise.

MAKE AN ASSEMBLY LINE. The final strategy to assist you here is to make the tasks that are necessary to overcome a problem into an assembly line. An assembly line enables your company to master separate sections for similar tasks together. This power thinking strategy involves grouping similar aspects of a problem together and completing them together. The repetitive actions develop a rhythm and increase the speed of completion.

Completing an entire group of tasks at one time and then moving consecutively to the next set until you reach a solution increases

Exhibit 7.1. Sample Insurance Executive's
Self-Analysis of Responses to Deadlines

POSITIVE FEELINGS AND BEHAVIORS

1. When I reach my deadline, I feel satisfied—as though a weight is lifted from my shoulders.
2. When I impose a deadline, I do higher-quality work because I concentrate more, and I force myself to use my most intense, highest levels of thinking uninterrupted.
3. With a deadline, I stick to the task at hand instead of frequently changing my focus. This saves me the time of having to reorient myself to the task; my time is spent in advancing rather than merely trying to recapture former thoughts, so I accomplish more.
4. With a deadline, the results of my work are timelier.
5. When I set a deadline, I do not overkill an idea as I tend to do when I allow myself unlimited time to work on something.

NEGATIVE FEELINGS AND BEHAVIORS

1. I do not eat healthily, and I interrupt my sleeping schedule.
2. When I underestimate the time it will take to reach a deadline, I fall behind on other projects.
3. I have more difficulty engaging in reverie to strengthen my insight.
4. I need to improve my creative ability to maintain my important, normal routines and still meet deadlines without as much self-imposed pressure.
5. The intensity that I have to use to meet a deadline needs to be counterbalanced so that I do not lose sight of other important aspects of my life.

your efficiency because you gradually refine your approach to each task and are less likely to overlook or forget important elements in each task. This procedure can be especially useful when a problem involves several people. When you approach each person in turn, you can be sure to cover all the issues relating to that person individually before addressing the unique elements related to another person's similar situation.

For example, the CEO of a financial planning corporation said that when it came time to downsize his company, instead of completely eliminating a full division or a specific rank of employee, he used the assembly line procedure. He identified all the employees who would be affected by downsizing and proceeded to interview each one. In the interviews, he asked the employees questions about actions that the company was taking, and the employees offered a wealth of information about what could be done more effectively and about existing actions that worked and those that failed. They made suggestions for innovative and profitable initiatives. Each successive interview became increasingly refined and valuable in pinpointing a solution. As a result, many of his employees' talents were rechanneled, and the company identified a unique market niche to pursue.

The cartoon character Dagwood Bumstead is daily portrayed as a buffoon who is late for his carpool. His boss, Mr. Dithers, constantly chides him for missing deadlines. His colleagues regard Dagwood as someone who is concerned about the unimportant. Do you want to be the Dagwood Bumstead of your organization? If not, then take the steps that we have presented in this section, and do something to reduce the frequency with which you procrastinate.

PEACEFUL WINNER

Most readers of this book are familiar with the song "Let There Be Peace on Earth." This song, whose title is also its first line, then contains the words, "and let it begin with me." Items 15, 19, and 45 describe situations when we do not experience peace. They also convey the manner in which we handle this turmoil.

Given how frequently negative events occur in our lives, it would be reasonable to expect that we would be accustomed to them and that they would not unduly affect us. For some individuals, that is indeed true. With others, it is not.

How we deal with emotions like hurt and anger is certainly important to our psychological well-being. What is often overlooked is its impact on our cognitive processes.

Imagine that you have just had a heated argument with your boss. This is not an optimal time for you to engage in creative thinking or to be in a meeting where a high degree of concentration is required. The emotional upheaval would block out your concentration. It would also prevent your creative juices from flowing, thus impeding your ability to brainstorm, be visionary, or be innovative.

Since turmoil is rather common, our goal when experiencing it should be to learn what precipitated this state within us so that we can lessen its frequency. Of equal importance, we must learn to rid ourselves of its after-effects as quickly as possible. Then we can think at peak capacity rather than in a diminished way. By being able to lessen the frequency of turmoil and improving our handling of it, we will experience a sense of inner peace. We will also be able to think powerfully and reach sound decisions, solve problems effectively, and think creatively. For individuals who act in this fashion, *peaceful winner* is an apt description.

Understanding the Peaceful Winner

Items 15, 19, and 45 of the Yale Assessment of Thinking assess the degree to which you are a peaceful winner. Fill out the Peaceful Winner Item Cluster Graph, entering your scores for these items from Chapter Two. If your total score was 5 or under, write as the YAT score interpretation "highly skilled." If your total score was 6 or 7, write "average ability." If your total score was 8 or higher, write "need for improvement."

The data that exist in this subskill area can provide you with important diagnostic information. You can discern from your responses to items 15, 19, and 45 the facets of thinking that you are using effectively as well as those you are not. Their content's implications can also serve as a blueprint for improving your level of skill in this area.

In item 15 ("I refrain from conveying to others the hurt that their actions have caused me"), it may seem as if you are being noble to refrain from conveying to others the hurt that their actions have caused. This restraint is, in fact, an erroneous course of action.

When individuals are not made aware that they have hurt you, you are in essence absolving them from taking responsibility for what they did. In the process, you are assuming this burden and keeping it within you. Since you did not tell them what they did that was hurtful, you are inviting a repeat of their action.

Item Cluster Graph.   Peaceful Winner Item Cluster Graph

YAT Items	Your Response		
15	_____		
19	_____		
45	_____		
Total	_____		
YAT score interpretation	_____		

By not conversing with these individuals about this matter, you are assuming responsibility for their actions. Since the cause of what prompted them to hurt you is unknown, attempts to understand the motivation for their action represent conjecture on your part. While your mind is attempting to sift and winnow through all the possibilities for their action, your ability to engage in insightful thinking is severely curtailed. It will remain in such a state during the length of time that you seek to determine why a trusted colleague hurt you or, if it was caused by a relatively unknown person, while you ask yourself, "Why me?"

As you would expect, a peaceful winner deals with this type of situation quite differently. A peaceful winner will take two actions when someone causes him or her hurt: meet with and convey to the person the hurt that was experienced by the action of that individual and find out what he or she did to elicit such an action from that person.

Peaceful winners seek closure to disruptive situations. By discussing what prompted this occurrence, they will alter their behaviors, where warranted, to prevent their reappearance in the future.

They seek to attain peace not only with the person who hurt them but also within themselves. Peaceful winners know that until they reach closure, their ability to function effectively as a leader suffers greatly. They do not waste their time in mental conjecture. Rather, they get facts from the person who hurt them and then mentally move on to more important matters for organizational success.

Item 19 ("One or more people consistently anger me") also describes a condition in which a peaceful winner and a person who is less skilled in this segment of insight act quite differently. If you responded "very often" or "often" to this item, then you are letting others control your emotions and your ability to think insightfully.

All of us experience anger. What causes it within us and how we cope with it are the two important ways that differentiate how we address it.

If someone frequently angers you, this individual has found your Achilles heel. By knowing what sets you off, that person has identified your vulnerability. By taking certain actions, he or she can turn your spirit from being positive to negative. And who gives them this Svengali-type control over you? You do. Every time their actions anger you, you have reinforced what they did. You have sent them a message: "What you did achieved its goal. I am angry. Therefore, my emotions are negative, and while I have this attitude, I will be unable to think effectively or creatively. You won!"

A peaceful winner does not act in this way. These individuals know that anger is the easiest negative emotion for them to identify at its inception. When they start to experience it, they turn their thoughts to something positive (perhaps their children) and stop the anger. As a consequence, the other person's efforts to cause them consternation failed, and the peaceful winner has inner peace and has "won" over this person who sought to anger him or her.

Item 45 ("When I become angry about the actions of others, it affects me for a longer period of time than it should") also deals with anger. Since much of what we said about item 19 also holds true for this one, our remarks will be brief.

When you remain angry, your insight is being held hostage. Anger is its central issue rather than the development of new ideas. You are allowing yourself to remain in such a negative state of mind. Why would you allow what someone else did to shut down your insight and to control your emotions?

Peaceful winners move beyond their anger quickly. When they do, they become happy once again, and the organizations that they lead are better for it.

An Exemplary Peaceful Winner: Teresa L. Ortiz

Teresa L. Ortiz thinks as a peaceful winner does. Ortiz has been acknowledged for her actions as a leader by the military and for her success as a civilian. As a member of the armed services, she was awarded the prestigious Meritorious Service Medal by the U.S. Army, which has also given her the Army Commendation Medal five times.

After leaving military service, Ortiz started a career with the Department of Defense. Her rise within that organization has been rapid. Today, she is the associate dean of the Defense Acquisition University South Region. While working for this department, she has been recognized for her record of accomplishment. Ortiz was given the Armament, Munitions, and Chemical Command Commanding General's Service Award for Exemplary Service.

Has Ortiz endured hurt in her career? Has she ever been angry with others? Has Ortiz been successful as a leader? The answers to these three questions are yes.

When a person does something that causes Ortiz hurt, she uses what she calls her "1, 2 strategy" immediately. In using step 1 of this strategy, she withdraws to be by herself. She examines her own actions and comments in order to determine if she was responsible for the other person's vitriolic attitude toward her. After considering whether she was at fault for the incident, Ortiz initiates step 2. If her answer is yes (she was responsible for the misunderstanding), Ortiz will meet with the person and apologize. If her response is no, Ortiz asks herself: "Was the basis of this person's actions an intellectual difference of opinion or was it with me personally?" After considering which of these two options it was, Ortiz meets with the individual and is quite direct. She says words to the effect, "You said [or did] X. It has caused me concern because. . . . I would like to discuss this matter with you."

Ortiz employs this strategy for two reasons. First, it enables her to achieve closure personally relative to an incident. Second, it helps her to resolve the matter with the other person. Ortiz believes the first reason helps her to get back on track as quickly as possible. By discussing it with the other person, Ortiz hopes to identify (rather than engage in conjecture) what caused the incident and to clarify its source so that additional similar ones will not occur in the future.

For individuals who have angered Ortiz and will likely try to do so again, Ortiz formulates a strategy to neutralize what they do. She will say to herself: "When person X says or does action Y, I will not become angry. I will avoid becoming angry by doing. . . ." By forewarning herself that a person may try to anger her and planning an action that will offset what this individual says or does, Ortiz is able to diffuse its possible impact on her.

With regard to instances where anger-generating events seem to pop up from unanticipated persons or events, she offers an insightful perspective: "People at my level have strong beliefs about leadership and management. They have strong personalities too. So it's inevitable that conflicts will sometimes occur. When they do happen under these circumstances, a leader has to personally get over her anger quickly. After she does, she has to go to the source and resolve the conflict with that person. Long-term anger or resentment keeps a leader from thinking clearly, and it keeps an organization from being as productive as it can be."

Strategies for Becoming a Peaceful Winner

The actions that Teresa Ortiz takes are an integral part of her success as a leader. Being a peaceful winner entails dealing positively with the negative emotions induced by others or ourselves. Following are additional strategies to help you acquire increased competence in this important aspect of insight's external cognitive process.

MAINTAINING POSITIVE SPIRITS. Peaceful winners understand the importance of nurturing positive emotions. Their external insightful cognitive processes are powerful, so they can spot the nucleus of negative emotions in others and harness their own negative energy to more beneficial purposes. Because emotions, like hope and joy, guide peaceful winners through many difficulties, it is critical that you develop the ability to recognize what truly brings these emotions into your life. Manifestations of emotional knowledge such as character, patience, and integrity are built through conscious nurturing of positive emotions.

This cultivation requires an appreciation of what a given experience means to you and to others. It also includes the ability to appreciate that each person's perceived reality and emotional responses to events are likely to be unique. Figure 7.2 depicts the levels of emotion in order of their importance in powerful thinking. The order of emotional states reflects the closeness of each state to the surface of one's insight. For example, anger is the most assertive negative emotion and the easiest to elicit. Moving up the emotional scale, the feelings of hurt and fear are more difficult to elicit and to detect in yourself and others.

Although negative emotional energies can ignite instantly, higher and more positive energies (such as satisfaction from assuming

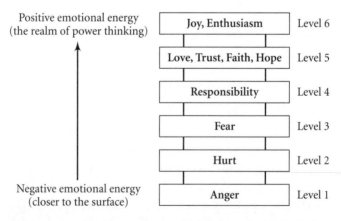

Figure 7.2. Maintaining Positive Spirits: The Emotional Scale

responsibility, hope, and enthusiasm) require more time to emerge and be identified. As you become a more powerful peaceful winner, your emotional level will dwell more consistently at the top three levels of the emotional scale. We encourage you to refer frequently to Figure 7.2 so that you can understand where your negative and positive feelings fall on the scale.

A first step in recognizing and nurturing your positive emotions is to identify what lowers your mood and emotions. After you read each level, write the first three words that come to mind: people, actions, or events that stimulate that emotion most consistently in you. This exercise will sensitize your insight to overcome these negative triggers to your emotional state more rapidly, or to place yourself in the company of those persons or situations that reinforce your positive emotions more frequently. First, we will look at the negative emotions:

• *Level 1: Anger.* Anger cannot be destroyed or forgotten; it has to be converted. Anger is the easiest emotion to display because society has convinced us, especially men, that it is acceptable to express anger but inappropriate to express hurt or fear. Anger is insight's first reaction to something that interferes with your ability to accomplish goals or solve problems. If it is not converted to more positive energy through use of the reasoning strategies in Chapters Four and Five, anger can expand to become unjust blame, resentment, envy, jealousy, or hate. In its most advanced form, anger becomes a permanent emotional state in which negative biases about a specific event or people consume your life, contaminate your reasoning and insight about other issues, and frequently affect other facets of your performance as a leader. People who have difficulty converting anger to more positive gains may direct it back onto themselves, and depression results.

The most effective method of moving beyond anger to higher levels of positive emotion is to write or reflect on which obstacle is impeding your goal achievement and determine how to remove it. This approach usually generates an insight about a blind spot in your reasoning and insight cognitive processes that you can use to eliminate the circumstances that elicited your anger. For example, a peaceful winner who becomes angry at incompetent actions by an employee can write down the specific incident that angered him or her, identify the possible paths of action in a circle around it, and list reasons for pursuing each action on lines drawn between the incident and the potential resolutions. This drawing may lead a peaceful winner to discover a weakness in his or her leadership style (perhaps unclear task expectations or an invalid reward structure) that created a climate in which this type of incompetence would be tolerated.

• *Level 2: Hurt.* Hurt is the second-easiest emotion to feel. Because hurtful feelings are so painful, you might quickly repress them through denial. Non-peaceful winners tend to pretend that they do not feel the hurtful emotions that engulf them. The most effective method of moving beyond hurt is to acknowledge your pain to those who hurt you. Voicing the hurt lets you jump to level 4 of positive emotional energy: the satisfaction of assuming responsibility. In this case, by taking positive action to overcome the hurt, you have to overcome fear, and in the process you will attain the lowest level of positive productive emotions. Without this action, you may consciously or subconsciously intensify your pain and hurt until it becomes self-pity, sadness, disappointment, martyrdom, or depression.

• *Level 3: Fear.* The third easiest emotion to feel is fear. Fear can be a positive as well as a negative emotion. In its positive form, your external cognitive insightful processes protect you from harm. Protecting yourself from imaginary dangers, however, is detrimental to powerful thinking. For example, no matter what the arena, the anxiety (a form of fear) that builds in anticipation of an event exaggerates fantasies of failure and catastrophe, which can affect the likelihood of success for that event. Fear of failure is another good example. This type of fear can loom so large that you delay action. Ironically, because you delay actions to correct a situation, it is the delay (created by inadequate power thinking strategies to overcome negative fears) that leads to your failure.

An irrational fear of failure in the workplace can emerge subtly. For example, you may say to yourself: "If I bring up this new idea, and it flops, then I'll make a fool of myself at the meeting. My subordinates will see me as incompetent." So you sit back and say nothing and tell yourself, "Better safe than sorry," and you hide in your comfort zone. Because of your own inaction, you do not lead this new project. Your own experience probably can show you that when you face whatever it is that you fear, you discover that it is much less fearful a situation than you imagined it to be before you tackled it. Unchecked irrational fear decreases your positive energy and can manifest itself as paranoia, distrust, selfishness, shock, and detachment from others.

To overcome these negative emotions, remember that other people do not control your emotions. When someone else's action stimulates negative emotions in you, it is because that action shook an aspect of your emotions or thoughts over which you have not yet gained self-control. Power thinking means recognizing when a person has activated one of those sensitive areas. So, for example, instead of saying to someone else, "You make me so mad!" realize that the person has simply activated a sensitive area of your emotions or thoughts. Say to yourself, "I am angry. I am hurt, and I wonder if I misinterpreted. I'm afraid, and I'll do something to gain more information so I can transform this fear into a positive emotional state such as drive and determination." Responding to people or situations that stimulate negative emotions in you with statements similar to these and that begin with the word *I* instead of the word *you* is your first step in overcoming negative emotions. This response allows you to take responsibility for your emotions and avoids escalating a negatively charged environment into a damaging conflict.

Self-control also can come through the strength of an effective support group of family, friends, or coworkers with whom you can share your thoughts. When you know someone really cares about you, negative emotions—toward that person as well as others—are more difficult to stimulate and sustain.

You can transform anger, hurt, and irrational fears into stronger, more positive emotional powers, as poet and philosopher Kahlil Gibran described in *The Prophet:* "When you are sorrowful, look again in your heart, and you shall see that, in truth, you are weeping for that which has been your delight." When a negative emotion arises, it frequently results from a responsibility, or a source of positive emotion has often been taken from you. Thus, positive emotional levels can become more permanent states in your life when you can sustain insight, reasoning, and self-knowledge to fill voids in your well-being. Positive emotions are like individual wires that fuse into a single cable. They encase your power thinking in a protective, impermeable covering like the rubber that protects electrical currents. When these positive emotional cords multiply, they strengthen the web of positive emotional states, insights, and reasoning that can become a permanent aspect of your demeanor. The following descriptions of these positive emotions include actions you can take to achieve each positive state:

• *Level 4: Satisfaction from assuming responsibility.* This emotional level encompasses feelings of control, accomplishment, contentment, and persistence. Peaceful winners reach this level because they take action to overcome remorse and regret for wrongs done to them. Level 4 also occurs when they initiate positive endeavors for their organizations.

• *Level 5: Drive and courage fueled by trust and hope.* This emotional level is manifested in a desire to create and sustain positive purposes for yourself and others. One way to know that you have reached this state is when you believe in something so deeply that you are willing to sacrifice something of yourself for it.

• *Level 6: Joy and enthusiasm.* This level of positive emotions begins when you express understanding, forgiveness, or appreciation. Joy and enthusiasm stem from care and concern for others, which evolve through less self-centeredness and more concern for others' well-being. When you become a peaceful winner, you use the strategies in this book to manage the stresses and savor the joys that loved ones and treasured professional goals bring into your life. As a result, your ability to sustain high spirits increases.

LOOKING AT DIFFERENT POINTS OF VIEW. The second method of becoming a peaceful winner is to develop the ability to look at different points of view more consistently. There are four steps in developing this ability:

• Step 1: Put yourself in another's shoes. When a perspective is difficult to understand, put yourself in that person's shoes. Pretend you are the person talking. Ask: "How would I feel if I were that person, and how would my feeling contribute to the meaning I was trying to convey?" "What would I think about . . . ?"

• Step 2: Use details. Read or listen for details, opinions, and values that suggest a person's specific points of view, and then use those details.

• Step 3: Try to understand the other person's point of view. To understand others, you may have to view an opposite perspective of items under discussion.

• Step 4: Transform social conditions. Peaceful winners look for spaces where performances interrupt authority. These disruptions are the open spaces where social conditions and power relations can be transformed. Interruption of social and interpretive power often occurs during discussions. Thus, when you pay close attention to discussions when someone makes a proposal to change a social condition or a power relationship, you can lead your company's goals forward most effectively by being the first to propose an effective option for change. By making these suggestions before the person who suggested that a change was needed, you can lead others to become peaceful winners. Another way to build positive emotions in a group setting is to change a ritual that exists in your business. Such ritual changes enable people to invest their emotional energies toward creating new initiatives rather than investing negative feelings into a ritual that no longer addresses their needs. When a company sustains an existing ritual, people tend to find problems with it and transfer negative emotions toward other company rituals.

ELECTRIC CREATOR

Andrea del Sarto, a sixteenth-century Italian painter, once said, "Man's reach must exceed his grasp, or what's a heaven for?" Although his quotation does not mention women, what del Sarto said several centuries ago still holds true today for all individuals.

Items 20, 22, and 53 all pertain to stretching our abilities as we seek and respond to new challenges. In our research, we found that leaders who were highly skilled in this area were dynamic individuals—hence, the "electric" descriptor. Also, they were constantly seeking to develop new challenges for themselves and the organizations they lead. This trait causes us to also think of them as being a "creator."

Understanding the Electric Creator

Items 20, 22, and 53 of the Yale Assessment of Thinking assess the degree to which you are an electric creator. Fill out the Electric Creator Item Cluster Graph, entering your scores for these items from Chapter Two. If your total score was 5 or under, write as the YAT score interpretation "highly skilled." If your total score was 6 or 7, write "average ability." If your total score was 8 or higher, write "need for improvement."

The first of the three YAT items in this subskill of insight is item 20 ("I seek to be involved in initiatives in which my ability exceeds the challenge itself"). If this attitude—that you should not seek to be involved in an activity in which your ability does not exceed a challenge—frequently describes you, it will be helpful to understand why it does.

Our subconscious is multidimensional. It can work toward positive ends such as creative thought generation. Conversely, there are times when it can serve us disingenuously. The content of item 20 is

Item Cluster Graph.   Electric Creator Item Cluster Graph

YAT Items	Your Response
20	_____
22	_____
53	_____
Total	_____
YAT score interpretation	_____

this type of situation. One of the functions that our subconscious performs is that of an internal source of nurturing. When functioning in this mode, it identifies potential pitfalls for us and then cautions us about pursuing actions in which we would experience failure.

This process can adversely affect us if we do not adequately understand it. The belief that you are not up to challenging tasks was not put into your subconscious by you but by others. Hence, this self-imposed limitation is not based on what your abilities truly dictate but on the comments and perceptions of others. These individuals may or may not be friends, and they certainly do not have your best interest in mind.

Challenges are the very essence of what motivates an electric creator. These individuals know what they can do and are confident in their ability to respond to what is seemingly the undoable. Why are they successful?

An electric creator uses his or her subconscious not to harbor negative thoughts intended to dissuade him or her from new endeavors but rather to think in creative ways about challenges ahead. As a result, instead of being limited in vision by the doubts instilled by others into their subconscious, this type of leader uses it forcefully and effectively to tackle that which is new, exciting, and different.

How do they develop this type of viewpoint? They have a correct perspective about failure. Even when they fall short of their intended objective, these individuals believe that good came from the effort. What they did accomplish is a positive end that it will make the organization better. In addition, they know that what they learned from the experience will be beneficial to future leadership attempts.

In item 22 ("I would rather perform routine tasks than think about complex problems"), our research revealed an important difference between electric creators and less skilled thinkers: talent identification. If electric creators were asked to name what they could do superbly, adequately, and not so well, they could quickly and accurately develop such a list. In contrast, this was an onerous task for their less skilled counterparts. What they did identify was incomplete and had several errors as well.

This research has added significance when its relationship to performance is considered. Less skilled thinkers in this area prefer to perform routine tasks because to them, work is work. Thus, it does not matter whether what they do is challenging, stimulating, and creative or boring, repetitive, and trite.

Electric creators enjoy dealing with complex problems, which they find to be stimulating. Often their involvement in these types of situations spurs their creativity and causes them to develop innovative ideas in different but related areas.

If you responded "very often" or "often" to item 53 ("Because I am aware of my levels of competence in various areas, I avoid activities in which my skills are overly challenged"), beware: you may be one of the persons about whom Laurence J. Peter wrote in his classical book, *The Peter Principle* (Peter and Hull, 1969). The premise of the Peter Principle is that employees within organizations advance to their highest level of competence and then are promoted to, and remain at, a level where they are incompetent.

While very few individuals would openly admit to being at their level of incompetence, by avoiding activities in which their skills would be challenged, that is precisely what they are conveying. They are viewing themselves as a finished product, and as a consequence, they are avoiding challenges because they do not desire to learn anything else or stretch their talents or acquire new skills.

An electric creator acts like a work in progress. These individuals want to enhance their abilities. They see challenges as a way to learn new things, perform different tasks, and become a better leader. More often than not, they are successful in what they attempt.

Electric creators are exciting people to have within an organization. They create a sense of synergy for those with whom they work. The units that they lead are successful and the catalysts for much of what is new and positive within an organization. Would you rather have an electric creator or a Peter Principle devotee as your leader?

An Exemplary Electric Creator: Walt Disney

The person who embodies what it means to be an electric creator is deceased. Walt Disney nevertheless remains a household name, and his impact on our culture and the entertainment industry has been monumental.

When we speak of Disneyland, Disney World, the Disney Channel, or the movies and products made by his company, we think of this icon of creativity. We also associate his name with quality and success. Disney was not always rich or famous. In fact, it was his humble beginnings that provided the spark for what was to become his initial triumph.

Disney started his career as a graphic artist. While working in a filthy, disheveled basement, mice often ran over his feet, around the room, and across his work table. Instead of becoming depressed about this dismal environment, Disney envisioned a creative challenge: he would train a mouse to stay within a circle that he had drawn on his paper. Failure after failure ensued, and despite some not-so-gentle comments from coworkers, he persevered, and eventually the mouse began to stay in the circle! Disney then developed a greater challenge for the mouse: to stand on its hind feet while in the circle and hold a toothpick. It was when that mouse learned not only to hold a toothpick but to pass it from paw to paw that another mouse was created in Disney's mind.

After Mickey Mouse was created, Disney's rise to fame was meteoric. As he created animation and initiated other ventures throughout his career, he always asked of himself and those with whom he worked to think not of what exists but "what could it be?" It was this relentless quest to envision the new and the different that made Disney the premier creator that he was. His enthusiasm was the spark that drove him and his organization.

Strategies for Becoming an Electric Creator

Would your colleagues characterize you as a creator? Do you continuously challenge them to develop new endeavors? Is the organization you lead an exciting place in which to work? If you answered no to one or several of these questions, consider the strategies that we next review.

CREATING FLOW EXPERIENCES. When you avoid complex problems, it is an indication that insight's external cognitive processes are not influencing your thinking. To increase it, you need to create more opportunities in which the use of your talents can lead to "flow experiences." In the book *Flow* (1990), psychologist Mihalyi Csikszentmihalyi defined *flow* as optimal thinking experiences that occur in this way:

> When we feel in control of our actions, [we feel ourselves to be] masters of our own fate and we feel a sense of exhilaration, a deep sense of enjoyment that is long cherished and that becomes a landmark in our memory for what life should be like. Moments like these, the best moments in our lives, are not the passive, receptive, relaxing time but usually occur when a person's body or mind is stretched to its limits in a voluntary effort to accomplish something difficult and worthwhile. It is something that we make happen! Flow is the state in which we are so involved in an activity that nothing else seems to matter; the experience itself is so enjoyable that people will do it at great cost, for the sheer sake of doing it [p. 3].

Total engagement, or flow, is an experience that electric creators achieve by balancing the challenge before them with their ability to master that responsibility. When this situation occurs, such power thinkers create opportunities while pursuing the challenge to grow incrementally and receive information with which to continuously measure their professional skill improvements. With each new challenge, they learn strategies that enable them to take on new and greater challenges. This expanded professional capability in turn sustains electric creators' high levels of internal motivation. The resultant high levels of motivation and accomplishment provide satisfaction and positive feedback so that complex tasks in turn become more valued.

When non–power thinkers face challenges beyond their skills, their frustration often leads to worry and anxiety; their solution is to seek tasks beneath their existing skill level. But when professional skills exceed the challenge of the task, boredom occurs. Thus, neither simple nor complex tasks provide job satisfaction, motivation, or professional growth. Procrastination and daily hassles obstruct flow because they distract consciousness with minor commitments that were not completed. Such loose ends and other daily tasks inhibit the complete mental immersion necessary for flow experiences. This is the reason that reverie, breaking away, and making appointments with yourself are so important to becoming an electric creator.

When athletes accomplish flow in the course of the game, they call it "being in the zone." Everything they do when in this state of insightful external cognitive processing is successful, and opposition is stifled. Flow can occur for you both personally and professionally when you become more aware of the conditions that place you at the edge of your competence. When you are there, your confidence, competence, and drive can increase simultaneously.

If flow experiences are not a regular occurrence in your professional day, pause in your reading and complete Exercise 7.4. This activity can strengthen insight's external cognitive processes and your ability to succeed in challenging situations.

To review, flow more readily occurs when you manage conditions so that complex challenge can draw on your talents; elicit your drive, courage, and enthusiasm; and provide continuous feedback to increase your motivation and professional abilities. After you complete monumental tasks, reflect on the positive emotions and insights that assisted your work. Also determine what other conditions were present. Did you need to take frequent breaks and tell a few jokes before really engaging in a task? Did you need to be alone in a room? Did you need to know that minor difficulties were delegated properly? Did you need to have completed your personal exercise program? Whatever the conditions were that preceded your most recent flow experiences, however insignificant they may appear, those are the ones that should be present as much as possible when you face large challenges. Building those conditions into your leadership style creates a situation where flow can begin. When it does, you will outperform those

---

─⚘─ Exercise 7.4

DEVELOPING FLOW EXPERIENCES

Recall a recent accomplishment that elicited your pride. This act must have involved the use of one or more of the power thinking strategies described in this book, as well as a challenge you had not previously faced at so high a level. When you have this accomplishment in mind, recall what special actions you took or special conditions that contributed to reaching your goal. Those actions or conditions should be present in your life on a more regular basis so that you can experience more flow states.

who are attempting the same challenge without the support of flow and insight's external cognitive processes.

SUMMARY

This chapter has focused on the outcomes generated from insightful external cognition. We discussed the four dimensions of this important element of insight: intrepid committer, punctual generator, peaceful winner, and electric creator. The strategies that we presented, although many and diverse, all have one common ingredient: thinking effectiveness. We urge you to review this chapter and decide which strategies you wish to add to your thinking repertoire:

1. Knowing how to say no effectively
2. Valuing the truth in your felt senses
3. Developing the habit of saying "tell me more" when challenged
4. Engaging the insights of subordinates when you are uncertain of the correct course of action
5. Begin but not "at the beginning"
6. Increasing commitment and creative thinking
7. Learning to establish effective deadlines
8. Making assembly lines
9. Maintaining positive spirits
10. Creating flow experiences

On the next two pages, we provided space in which you may write your reflections on steps that you plan to take in order to become more proficient in each of these segments of external cognition.

INSIGHT EXTERNAL COGNITIVE PROCESS THINKING ENHANCEMENT

Intrepid Committer

Punctual Generator

Peaceful Winner

Electric Creator

CHAPTER EIGHT

Self-Knowledge
Internal Cognitive Process

A lthough we are presenting each domain singularly, none of the three is an island unto itself. They work interdependently as well as independently as your mind engages daily with many diverse matters.

Self-knowledge, the subject of this and the next chapter, is the most interwoven of the three thinking domains. The Venn diagram in Figure 8.1 illustrates the degree to which its relationships to reasoning and insight occur.

In this chapter, we discuss the internal cognitive process of self-knowledge that powerful thinkers use when they reach decisions, solve problems, and think creatively. Our research found that individuals who are highly skilled in this aspect of thinking were particularly proficient in the following four areas of it: valid viewer, receptive realist, confident keystone, and successful failer.

VALID VIEWER

Our research found that the perceptions of power thinkers relative to their abilities were accurate: they knew what they did well and what they did less ably. In addition to having a valid view of their areas of

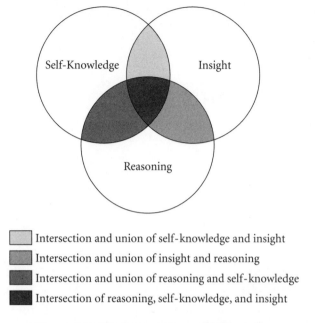

Intersection and union of self-knowledge and insight

Intersection and union of insight and reasoning

Intersection and union of reasoning and self-knowledge

Intersection of reasoning, self-knowledge, and insight

**Figure 8.1. The Intersection and Union of
Self-Knowledge, Reasoning, and Insight**

skill, they had an equally valid view of themselves as persons. Their facility in correctly assessing their abilities and themselves is why we term an individual who possesses this skill a *valid viewer*.

Understanding the Valid Viewer

Items 44, 47, and 67 of the Yale Assessment of Thinking assess the degree to which you are a valid viewer. Fill out the Valid Viewer Item Cluster Graph, entering your scores for these items from Chapter Two. If your total score was 5 or under, write as the YAT score interpretation "highly skilled." If your total score was 6 or 7, write "average ability." If your total score was 8 or higher, write "need for improvement."

If you responded "very often" or "often" to item 44 ("People have a higher regard for my abilities than I do"), it is quite probable that you do not understand your abilities. Your lower estimation of your abilities than that held by others likely exists because of a mind-set trap into which you inadvertently fell. Here's how it operates.

Item Cluster Graph.   **Valid Viewer Item Cluster Graph**

YAT Items	Your Response
44	_____
47	_____
67	_____
Total	_____
YAT score interpretation	_____

Some individuals believe that they should be uniformly strong in all aspects of behavior. With this type of mind-set, they use their areas of strength as benchmarks for what their skill levels should be in each area. When they fail to meet such standards in those in which they are weaker, these people erroneously adopt a uniformly low regard for all of their abilities.

A valid viewer has a very different attitude about his or her abilities. Valid viewers identify those areas in which they are strong and those in which they are not as able. They certainly seek to improve the latter, but while they are working toward that objective, they do not demean their abilities across the board.

There is another way in which valid viewers and persons less skilled in this facet of self-knowledge differ. Valid viewers will develop a plan of action to supplement their areas of weakness whenever they have to use that behavior. For example, they will build a team that includes persons with strong abilities in the areas in which they themselves lack proficiency.

Individuals who responded "very often" or "often" to this item typically treat the use of skills in which they lack ability as a litmus test of sorts. They will not delegate tasks requiring these skills to others but rather believe they must do the task alone in order to prove to themselves that they have ability. When they fail, they assume an "I told you so" attitude relative to the low abilities that they possess in this area.

Our research revealed that individuals who responded "very often" or "often" to item 44 also gave a similar response to item 47 ("My level of self-esteem is lower than it should be"). Persons who believe that their abilities are minimal also have a comparable view of themselves. They reason that since they are not very skilled, their human worth should not be very high. This flawed self-view plays itself out in how they act as leaders.

Individuals with low self-esteem tend to avoid challenges. They believe that since they have less-than-average ability, they will fail if they tackle something difficult for them. Hence, their units are usually boring ones in which to work; these are low-performing, uncreative sites where change is shunned in favor of the tried-and-true.

Valid viewers are not egocentric. They do, however, have a positive self-esteem. These individuals have confidence in their own abilities as well as in their capacity to bring about success. The units that they lead are high performing, and within them, there is a sense of excitement that what is being done is important. Valid viewers are typically considered to be the stars of an organization. Their units are the ones to which references are made as how other divisions of the organization should "be like them."

Your response to item 67 ("I berate my abilities") can tell you a great deal about yourself. If you responded "very often" or "often" to this item, you should ask yourself: "Why do I frequently berate my abilities?" If you engage in this self-mockery because you truly believe that your ability levels are problematic, then you should find out if your assessment is correct. Consult evaluations of your performance, discuss the areas of concern with valued colleagues, take assessment measures, or do whatever else will give you accurate information as to your strengths in these areas. If you are indeed deficient in certain facets of performance, do not beat up on yourself. That will not improve your performance at all. Instead, embark on a plan designed to improve your ability in the area of concern.

If you berate your abilities in order to serve as a sense of motivation for yourself, your insight will take you at your word and record in your subconscious that you are a person of limited ability. Then when you face a challenging situation, your internal self-knowledge will kick in and dissuade you from pursuing it. In essence, you will be limiting yourself from developing as a professional by taking on new tasks. You will also implant within yourself a negative self-esteem, which is delimiting to your effectiveness as a leader.

Valid reviewers rarely, if ever, berate their abilities. They know that self-criticism does not build skills. If they believe their skills are lacking in an area, they seek to improve them. While this process is occurring, they take actions (described in the discussion of item 44) to act as stopgap measures to increase their likelihood of success. Successful performance is what power thinkers are all about. Their less skilled colleagues engage in actions such as berating their abilities for unfounded and incorrect reasons.

An Exemplary Valid Viewer: Joyce Brothers

Joyce Brothers has experienced great success as a result of being a valid viewer. Most adults would be hard-pressed to remember when she was not part of the American scene. Often referred to as the dean of American psychologists, Brothers's words have been heeded by audiences for over thirty years.

Countless Americans read her newspaper column, published in more than 175 newspapers. Her many books are immensely popular, as is her daily broadcast on the NBC Radio Network. The accolades that she has received are numerous and impressive. She has been listed in George Gallup's Poll of the most admired women, named by a United Press International Poll as one of the ten most influential American women, and was ranked in another poll by *Good Housekeeping* magazine as one of the "Women in the World Most Admired." How she attained her fame is instructive.

Brothers had to quit her teaching job to raise her daughter. With her husband and child, she was living on fifty dollars a month when she came up with an idea. Her plan had nothing to do with psychology (she had received her Ph.D. in psychology from Columbia University), involving instead an area in which her knowledge hardly qualified her as an expert.

At the time (mid-twentieth century), there was an immensely popular television quiz show, *The $64,000 Question,* and Brothers decided to compete on it. The contestants were often unusual men and women: a shoemaker who was an expert in opera, a U.S. Marine who enjoyed gourmet cooking. Brothers felt that she would enhance her chance to be selected to compete if she became an expert in something that seemed incongruent with her persona, so the diminutive intellectual learned about boxing. Some friends and family members told her the idea was ridiculous and her efforts were a waste of time. They urged her to abandon her "silly" idea because she could never learn enough information about boxing to compete successfully on the show. They told Brothers that it was unlikely that she would ever get selected as a contestant, and if she did, she would make a fool of herself on national television by incorrectly answering an easy question. But Brothers persevered, and she was chosen to become a contestant.

On the weekly program, contestants who answered questions correctly were given the opportunity to quit and keep the money they had already won or risk their winnings by taking more difficult questions with a higher payoff. When Brothers answered the $8,000 question correctly, despite urgings from many persons to take the money and leave while she was a success, she risked it all three more times, winning $16,000, $32,000, and finally the grand prize of $64,000.

Her confidence never faltered, and as a result, she won a lot of money. She also achieved a degree of fame that she was able to parlay into the international figure she is today.

In some respects, the possibilities in your future parallel the ones that Brothers faced when she was preparing to be what she hoped would be a contestant on a game show. When others told her that she lacked the ability to be selected for this television program, she could have listened and given up studying about boxing. Or she could have heeded their assessments of her knowledge about boxing and stopped after correctly answering the $8,000 or $16,000 question. But she had a positive concept of her capability, and she was confident that she would attain her objective. She persevered and kept on going. Brothers launched her noteworthy career because she has prowess as a valid viewer.

Strategies for Becoming a Valid Viewer

Valid viewers overcome low self-esteem by identifying their core beliefs, analyzing their level of self-esteem, "keeping score," eliminating self-imposed limitations by rephrasing negative self-talk, and strengthening their self-concept and self-efficacy. If your skills in these areas are lacking, the following actions can strengthen your internal self-knowledge cognitive processes tremendously. Leading psychologists and leadership therapists have found that

> almost all human problems stem from low self-esteem, from not liking ourselves very much. Fears of failure, poverty, rejection, criticism, and loss are all a result of low self-esteem. When you genuinely like and respect yourself as a valuable and worthwhile person, the less you fear failure, because you realize your failures are not you. The less you fear rejection, the less you are concerned with what people like or dislike about you, and the more willing you are to reach out to fulfill your full potential [Dyer, 1998, p. 177].

IDENTIFYING CORE BELIEFS AND VALUES. Most people think that living in the lap of luxury produces happiness, but researchers have proven otherwise. A study from the University of Missouri-Columbia demonstrated that the keys to satisfaction are those that we present in this book: the freedom and skill to choose what you do, being an effective leader, having close relationships, and owning self-esteem (Sheldon, 2002). Lead author Kennon Sheldon discovered that these four components determine leadership success worldwide.

In another study, John A. Clausen, at the University of California at Berkeley, determined why some people have a considerably better chance of succeeding in adulthood than others. He tracked the development of three hundred people (beginning at ages five to seven) for a period of fifty years. His data showed that children who possessed self-confidence, intellectual curiosity, and dependability by age eleven had reasonably assured chances for success (Clausen, 2002). The exercises in this chapter can strengthen your self-confidence, intellectual curiosity, and dependability.

Core beliefs are the foundation for all of the experiences that have positively or negatively affected you. They are a result of the influence of those who reared you, friends, people in your institutions, and contemporaries who made an impression on your sense of self (self-knowledge's internal cognitive processes).

By knowing your core beliefs, you can use more components within your self-esteem to contribute to your success. These separate dimensions motivate you, mobilize your passion, and increase the energy you place into effective leadership. After you complete an assessment of your core beliefs, you will rise to function at your highest levels of talent. These benefits result because high self-esteem ignites a passion for what you want to accomplish. This passion will drive you over obstacles. Moreover, the gap between skill level and performance level can be closed when you accurately assess your core beliefs. It can move skill level (representing potential) to performance level (representing production).

For most power thinkers, successful levels of self-esteem have evolved through positive experiences built one on another. As a result, they become valid viewers because they have had numerous opportunities to assess very specific talents they (and others) contributed to effective accomplishments. If you desire to increase your self-esteem, we ask you to complete Exercise 8.1.

—◦◦◦— Exercise 8.1

INCREASING YOUR SELF-ESTEEM

Rank-order the following core beliefs and values by placing a number in the *left blank* preceding every item, with 1 denoting your most important belief and 36 your least important belief. We encourage you to thoughtfully complete each ranking, as every order will have importance in the next step of this self-assessment.

CORE BELIEFS, RESPONSIBILITIES, AND VALUES

___ Achievement ___   ___ Kindness ___

___ Money/high earnings ___   ___ Competition ___

___ Recognition ___   ___ Cleanliness ___

___ Independence ___   ___ Fame/recognition ___

___ Loyalty ___   ___ Orderliness/precision work___

___ Adventure/excitement ___   ___ Productivity ___

___ Structure ___   ___ Power and authority ___

___ Punctuality ___   ___ Independence/flexibility ___

___ Security/stability ___   ___ Affiliation ___

___ Solitude ___   ___ Security ___

___ Appreciation ___   ___ Job tranquility ___

___ Health ___   ___ Challenging problems ___

___ Creativity ___   ___Customer interaction and service ___

___ Knowledge ___   ___ Quality ___

___ Change and variety ___   ___ Aesthetics ___

___ Personal development/   ___ Independence ___

competence ___   ___ Fast or slow pace ___

___ Self-respect ___   ___Family happiness___

___Friendships ___

(Continued)

Exercise 8.1 (Continued)

Now examine the rankings you gave. Select two or three that you would like to increase in its value for you. Check the right blank of those items. Those are the items that you can develop further. In addition, circle the one core belief and value that is taking a larger proportion of your time than it deserves according to its importance in your life. On the following line, write an action you can take to eliminate the time relegated to this belief or value:

_____

_____

Finally, write a sentence in which you can use a strategy that you have read about thus far in this book that can increase the amount of time that you use three of the your top fifteen rankings in your daily schedule and interactions to increase the influence of self-knowledge's internal cognitive processes in your thinking as a leader:

1. _____

   _____

2. _____

   _____

3. _____

   _____

ANALYZING YOUR LEVEL OF SELF-ESTEEM. To become a valid viewer, strong reasoning and insight are not enough. You have to work continuously to understand yourself (self-knowledge) and build a positive, passionate self-esteem to drive your actions. As Horace said, "He who has confidence in himself will lead the rest." Exercise 8.2 assesses your level of self-esteem. We suggest that you answer each of the questions in the exercise regardless of how strong you perceive your level of self-esteem to be. We will explain why we want you to write your analysis in the next section of this chapter.

⟋ᜠ⟍ Exercise 8.2

ASSESSING YOUR LEVEL
OF SELF-ESTEEM

1. Write down the three words that most accurately describe you as a leader.

   _____ , _____ , _____ .

2. Write down what you say to yourself when you must do something with which you have had little previous experience.

   _____ .

3. Compared with your peers, would you call yourself a risk taker?
   ____ Yes, I judge myself to be a risk taker, because _____ .
   ____ No, I do not judge myself to take as many risks as my peers because _____ .

4. Do you think that others respect your abilities as much as you do?
   ____ Yes
   ____ No

5. Which of the following comments do you receive most often?
   ____ Others tell me I could do more.
   ____ Others compliment me on things that I do that I value.
   ____ Others do not realize what my capabilities are.
   ____ Others compliment me on things I do that I do not necessarily value that much.

6. Recall two situations in which you were timid in the past. Identify what specifically decreased your courage in each situation.

   (a) _____

   _____

   _____

   (b) _____

   _____

   _____

(Continued)

Exercise 8.2 (Continued)

7. List two situations, and the conditions that surrounded them, in which you took an action that required a lot of courage on your part. What was it about these situations that enabled you to overcome your timidity?

(a) _____

_____

_____

(b) _____

_____

_____

8. In the past, have you mastered most of the tasks and goals you established for yourself, or did you cease efforts before a goal was attained?

____ I master most goals I set.

____ I give up on goals more frequently than I desire.

____ I finish tasks that are easy and within my talent range, but not those that lie outside my areas of strength.

What do you believe the answer that you checked above indicates about you? _____

9. Do you consider yourself a success?

____ Yes

____ No

Why or why not? _____

In what area(s) do you want to succeed to a larger degree?

_____

10. Tell why achieving greater success in the areas you listed in question 9 is important to you at this time. _____

11. What effect does continual criticism or steady indifference have on you? _____

What emotions does it elicit? _____

What question(s) does such an environment cause you to question about yourself? _____

12. Think of the last time you had self-doubt or felt insecure. What people were involved, and what were the circumstances?

   _____

   What does this example demonstrate about your present level of self-esteem that can be used to strengthen your self-knowledge?

   _____

13. Thinking about all the above answers, what causes you self-doubt or insecurity?

   _____

14. How would you rate your self-esteem?

   ___ As strong as I expected

   ___ Neither strong nor weak

   ___ Weaker than I desire

15. In questions 1–14 to which you responded positively, what is the pattern that is emerging among your answers? For example, were you self-determined in successful situations? Did you use humor effectively? Was your self-esteem raised because you cooperated well with others? _____ .

16. In the answers in which you related weaknesses, what was the common thread among your responses? For example, what was similar in situations when your confidence fell? Were you involved in activities that you did not value as highly as others? Did you not have a role model to follow? Did you lack enthusiasm? Were your beliefs challenged? _____

   _____

17. Rate the level of self-confidence you feel at this moment from 1 to 10, with 5 being equal to average_____

   How do you think you can use your reasoning, insight, and core beliefs more frequently to raise your self-confidence, self-knowledge, and levels of leadership success? _____

   _____

   _____

Questions 1 through 3 of Exercise 8.2 assess your self-efficacy (the belief that you can overcome adversity). Our research concluded that people with the strongest self-esteem more frequently take risks. They seek to improve themselves, others, and situations by leading improvements (within their range of talents) without being asked to do so. These people's answers to questions 1 and 2 would be positive, and they express confidence in their ability to learn and discover. If you answer questions 1 through 3 with any sense of trepidation, you can increase your self-efficacy by identifying and developing more of your talents. We present methods to do this in Chapter Nine. Question 3 also assesses your internal locus of control (defined as the degree to which you believe you cause positive events to occur in your life). If you answer that you are a risk taker, one of your core beliefs is that you have a high level of personal control and positive power over events and that your effort is valuable. If you answer that you are not a risk taker, your sense of personal control may be less positive. It could be that you attribute too much of your personal success to luck, circumstances, or the input of others.

Questions 4 and 5 assess how well you communicate your talents, self-esteem, and self-knowledge to others. If you answer yes to question 4, you will waste fewer moments explaining your actions to others than will peers who feel others do not give them the respect that they deserve. If you wish to increase the amount of respect you command, the first step is to demonstrate qualities that you respect more frequently. For example, if you respect your generous nature, give to others often. In doing so, be aware that some may try to persuade you that your strength is actually a weakness (for example, when they observe your generosity, they might say, "You are a pushover" or "Others will take advantage of you if you don't look out for number one").

Being true to your core beliefs, regardless of others' interpretations, allows you to attract more people to your organization who value these same qualities. The synergy that develops in the work accomplished together will result in higher levels of success—even more success than was possible without this shared belief system between you and your colleagues. You will become more personally fulfilled. Question 5 assesses whether you are working within your areas of talent. If you choose the second option ("Others compliment me on the things that I do that I value"), you are projecting the talents that you value. Most people should understand your personality and how it is reflected in your leadership actions.

Questions 6 and 7 identify situations that do not make use of your talents. These circumstances may even require core beliefs that hold low priority for you. By rereading your answer to question 6, you can reflect on the validity or invalidity of the underlying value or belief that requires your courage to act. Because life may place you in situations demanding daring performances more frequently than you desire, you can review the motive you wrote in question 7 to build your self-esteem in such settings.

Question 8 determines whether you do not finish cycles of effort in your life. If you answer that you "give up on goals more frequently" than you desire, your insight and emotions are drained frequently and unnecessarily. You most likely waste energy because you abandon thoughts, plans of action, and goals before they reach fruition. Such dissipation increases the likelihood that other future actions will remain unfinished as well. Your ability to identify priorities can increase by identifying something you left unfinished that you can complete today. With completion, you will experience a resurgence of energy for other challenges. Also, your ability to view and assess your self-esteem in a more valid way will increase with each new success.

Questions 9 and 10 analyze your self-image. If you answer yes to question 9 and identify specific areas of success, your self-esteem is contributing positively to your power thinking. Question 10 can help you identify aspects of your self-image that you value most.

Question 11 is designed to identify your level of self-confidence. The answers to the questions in item 11 also identify the most powerful conditions that lower your self-confidence.

Questions 12 and 14 are posed to identify an inner resource from which you can draw whenever self-doubt or lowered self-confidence emerge. Question 14 identifies whether you have an adequate and effective level of self-esteem.

Questions 15 through 17 assess whether a positive or negative pattern exists in your life that decreases your self-esteem. We present methods of eliminating such negative patterns in Chapter Nine.

KEEPING SCORE. Another strategy to strengthen your self-esteem is to use a scoreboard. Without keeping score, you could be winning and not know it. One way of keeping score is to set, write, and achieve goals. By writing goals, you become involved in continuous self-driven professional development, which consistently raises your self-esteem.

The Power of Positive Students (POPS) Center (1998) in Denver, Colorado, reported that only three in one hundred people write their goals. People who do so achieve at least 50 percent more than those who do not. By writing your goals, your vague dreams become more focused and concrete. Moreover, the writing process places these goals into your subconscious, closer to your insight. In this way, your mind remains more alert to new opportunities. This mental focusing does not occur as readily when you merely say goals to yourself or others.

To begin keeping score, write your goals or objectives in a predictable location, such as in a special day planner, notepad, or calendar that you reference daily. Reread them frequently. Try a practice goal writing experience in Exercise 8.3 to get you started.

An example of someone who knows how to achieve his goals is Paul, who wants to be a professional writer. He has become friends with an experienced and successful author. They meet every Saturday afternoon, and the author offers insights about writing strategies as well as professional conduct. As the demands on Paul's time have intensified, it would have been tempting to let other priorities and interruptions interfere with these regular meetings. Instead, Paul and the author "keep score": they establish goals for Paul and set a date on which they measure the results of his progress toward its attainment.

The second step in "keeping score" occurs when the deadline for your goal arrives. Analyze why you did (or did not) attain your goal. With this reflective action, you will automatically learn more about the core beliefs and values that contributed to each success, increasing the probability of future success.

By this point in the book, you have built a strong foundation for powerful thinking. You can reason to make ideas practical. You have learned to use breaking away, good indicators, and flow experiences to inspire new ideas. You have completed a personal assessment to realign your core beliefs and values and developed greater self-esteem to become a more valid viewer. You are aware that writing goals daily has the power to increase your levels of success and self-esteem. The last strategy to become a valid viewer is to eliminate self-imposed limitations.

ELIMINATING SELF-IMPOSED LIMITATIONS BY REPHRASING NEGATIVE SELF-TALK. Another strategy to strengthen your self-esteem is to eliminate limitations that you impose on yourself. Why would any of us impose a negative or self-restricting limitation on ourselves? We do it unintentionally. Because many of our self-imposed limitations are

—◢◣◤— Exercise 8.3

WRITING GOALS REGULARLY

Here is a way to develop the habit of writing goals:

1. Write a goal that you want to achieve by the end of this week now:

   _____

2. Develop an action plan for your goal by writing what you will accomplish each day and how long it will take. (Remember that your goal is just for this week.) This plan should state the reasoned, insightful, and self-knowledge-driven methods that you will use to attain this goal. This action plan will keep you from ignoring inconvenient, annoying details or from omitting small but important responsibilities.

   _____

   _____

   _____

3. Visualize how you will feel when your goal has been reached. Taking the time to picture how you will feel will contribute to greater levels of positive, passionate self-esteem, which engages more of your talents to work on that goal. And when you work with more talents, your flow experiences enable goals to become more specific. When goals are as specific as possible, it is easier to use your core beliefs and values to contribute to them. Describe your picture of the achievement of this goal:

   _____

   _____

   _____

4. State a day or time by which you want to reach your goal. This deadline makes the plan more challenging, immediate, and enjoyable.

   _____

acquired at an early age, we accept many core beliefs (including others' beliefs that we limit us) for irrational reasons. As children, we wanted to please someone we looked up to, and these people rewarded us for believing as they did. When we were young, we were not capable of discerning if their core beliefs enhanced our own unique talents and strengthened components within our strong sense of self (self-knowledge). When your core beliefs conflict with your innate set of abilities, you tend to belittle your sense of self so that your actions can fit within the limiting set of beliefs that you have assumed. To do so, you self-impose unwarranted limits on your abilities.

In a research study, people were given a list of negative qualities, such as "selfish" and "being a penny-pincher," and asked to indicate whether each item was a characteristic they possessed. If it was a trait they had, they were asked whether they had tried to change it but had failed. Next, the leadership development researchers rewrote each item in a more positive manner. They asked subjects if they *valued* that quality in themselves; for example, they recast "penny pinching" as "thrift" and asked if that was important to them. Results suggested that the negative characteristics that people tried to change in themselves (but apparently could not) were actually qualities, when phrased in positive ways, that they valued highly as a strong component in their sense of self. Therefore, many self-imposed limitations and much negative self-talk can be removed by understanding the outward action that emanates from our core beliefs.

The method we use, and ask those in our leadership seminars to follow, to eliminate negative self-talk begins as soon as one experiences negative thinking. We use the power thinking strategy of changing those negative thoughts into a question. For example, if you say to yourself, "I am so stupid!" you should immediately change that into the question: "What can I do to keep from [feeling stupid] at this moment?" The answer to this question will eliminate negative self-talk, and you will think of a positive action to take.

A second power thinking strategy to use when you are stuck in a negative pattern of self-talk is to give yourself what you want others to give you. That is, when you want someone to give you something, give something to yourself or someone else instead. This strategy does not necessarily mean that you will give the same thing you wanted to receive or that you have to give the exact something to the person from whom you wanted to receive something. By giving instead of regretting that you are not being given to, you will receive something positive from others, which will reverse your negative internal cognitive processes and self-talk.

Here is a sample situation. Deanna is the director of marketing for a clothing manufacturer. She has a boss who does not compliment her accomplishments. Deanna realized how important receiving compliments was to her, so when her subordinates achieved a meritorious goal, Deanna praised them. They reciprocated when Deanna achieved something positive. Thus, instead of allowing a difference in beliefs between herself and her boss to lower her self-concept or bemoaning the fact that her boss was "not meeting her needs," she changed her negative pattern of thoughts by giving to others what she wanted—in other words, "doing unto others as you want others to do unto you." In essence, she gave to herself by giving to others. Her self-esteem expanded because one of her strongest core values was to give to others. As a result, her employees saw deeper into Deanna's self-knowledge. An unintentional outcome for Deanna was that she now receives numerous accolades from several people, and not just one person, when she attains major goals for her company.

STRENGTHENING YOUR SELF-CONCEPT AND SELF-EFFICACY. Another valuable strategy in developing a strong self-knowledge internal cognitive process is to nurture your sense of self—what psychologists refer to as your self-concept. A positive self-concept is developed through the success that occurred in your early years of growing up, successful adult accomplishments, self-respect, belief in your own worth, and confidence that you can overcome adversities. A healthy self-concept is manifested in a clarity of purpose that elicits the admiration of others. It initiates frequent flow experiences and insights, creates more reflections, develops patience, and results in captivating speaking. It also enables you to pursue more challenging commitments because your need for fear-induced self-protection is removed.

If you have a positive self-concept, you will lead easily and naturally because you know that you have the ability to change adversity to prosperity. Moreover, our research on outstanding leaders supports the view that an optimistic sense of your ability to make positive changes also improves your psychological and physical well-being (Block and Mangieri, 1996). Data indicate that most successful failers are neither anxious nor despondent. They take an optimistic view of their personal ability to make positive things happen. This perspective enables them to exercise monumental influence over events that affect their own and others' lives.

Each time you accomplish a new and different thought or task (or a past task with greater success than you had expected), your capacity for a positive self-concept expands. Thus, in reality there is no such thing as a limited capacity. The concept you hold of yourself right now can increase in the next moment as the result of a successful experience. When you exceed a previous "best," your sense of your own potential rises and you see yourself as more capable than before.

Self-imposed limitations also can arise when you do not assess the value of your personal worth. Specifically, when you place the needs of others far above your own, you limit your capacity to strengthen your own talents and belief systems. Those self-limitations suppress the power that self-knowledge can deliver.

You can sabotage your self-concept in other ways as well. You can subconsciously create hassles and problems because you do not value your needs, talents, and beliefs. For example, our friend Frank used to get frequent parking and speeding tickets until he realized that he valued the image of himself as a good driver and that the hassles created by the tickets were too distracting to his goals. Therefore, to avoid incurring those hassles and creating a situation that decreased his self-image, he changed his driving and parking patterns. As a result, he has not received any tickets for driving violations for several years.

In power thinking, regardless of the failures and successes of the past, the present is always totally new. By using the strategies of power thinking, you use your previous thoughts to increase the strength of the next thoughts and create positive possibilities for yourself. You recognize and control your own self-imposed limitations. Thus, every time you feel a negative thought about your capabilities or reason that a self-imposed limitation is justified, you can turn to Exercise 8.4. Write the self-limiting thought in the first blank, the condition that triggered the thought in the second blank, your goal in the third blank, and the power thinking strategy from this book that you will use to reach that goal in the last blank. When you complete the last statement, your resolve to overcome obstacles by engaging your personal talents, power thinking strategies, and positive beliefs can strengthen. Such self-talk will engage your power thinking, and increasingly positive self-images, reasoning, insight, and self-knowledge will unite to overcome your self-imposed limitation. If your sense of self is not as strong as your desire, write on a notepad something you want to change about yourself. Then complete the statements presented in Exercise 8.4 relative to what you want to change.

For example, André is the director of accounting for a textile company in a large city. He also loves to play golf and agreed to play in an out-of-town golf tournament. When he returned home early Sunday evening after the tournament, he was tired and knew from experience that fatigue reduces his power thinking. As he unpacked, he began to belittle himself with a barrage of negative self-talk: "If you weren't so lazy, you'd go into your office and begin working toward your deadlines right now! You've been gone all weekend and haven't accomplished a single thing toward your professional goals. You sure are falling behind, aren't you! Boy, if you don't work constantly you'll never catch up!" And so forth. When André heard himself thinking these negative statements, he began to agree and to impose self-limitations. As his sense of self declined, he turned to Exercise 8.4 and wrote:

> I feel tired. When I chose not to go to the office tonight, I was concerned that I would fall behind in my work. But I know it won't happen because I control my deadlines; I will not only do my work but I'll do it in a quality manner; and I will have increased energy tomorrow

---

∿ Exercise 8.4

OVERCOMING SELF-IMPOSED LIMITATIONS

I feel _____[state the emotion] when I [you, it] _____[state what happened during the moment the emotion began]. I am concerned that _____ [tell what you do not want to occur in the future]. But I know it will not happen because I _____

_____

_____

_____

---

morning to regain time toward the deadlines I have set for myself. The power thinking strategies I will use are *breaking away* and *doing it better the second time around.*

Through using Exercise 8.4 to overcome his self-limitations, André increased his positive sense of self, removed his negative thinking, and gained peace and strength from the hours that he spent unwinding after the golf outing. During that break-away time, he also mentally restructured the next day's priorities and had an insight that improved a project that he was developing. He met his deadline and created a new initiative for his bureau.

RECEPTIVE REALIST

If you are highly skilled in this segment of self-knowledge, we have termed your level of competence to be that of a *receptive realist.* This label is an appropriate one for two reasons. First, you are willing to admit that not all of your beliefs may be correct, so you keep an open mind when others point out gaps in those beliefs. You are also receptive to ideas that are offered as alternatives to them. In addition to having a realistic view that you may be wrong sometimes, you are internally consistent. Your beliefs are the engine for your thoughts. Thus, you are faithful to your beliefs when you take actions as a professional.

Understanding the Receptive Realist

Items 2, 25, and 40 of the Yale Assessment of Thinking assess the degree to which you are a receptive realist. Fill out the Receptive Realist Item Cluster Graph, entering your scores for these items from Chapter Two. If your total score was 5 or under, write as the YAT score interpretation "highly skilled." If your total score was 6 or 7, write "average ability." If your total score was 8 or higher, write "need for improvement."

Items 2 and 25 concentrate on both receptivity and fidelity to one's beliefs. If this is an area in which you lack skill, you will learn why you have this shortcoming and what you can do to address this condition.

It may seem admirable to cling to one's beliefs when information that contradicts them is presented (item 2—"When someone challenges my belief, I become even more resolved to retain it" or item 25—"When evidence contrary to my belief is presented, I test this evidence

Item Cluster Graph. Receptive Realist Item Cluster Graph

YAT Items	Your Response
2	_____
25	_____
40	_____
Total	_____
YAT score interpretation	_____

several times before I alter my belief"). It is not. It is a mind-set that will have a negative impact on your internal cognitive process.

Consider all of the people who were convinced that the earth was flat, flight was impossible, television would be a short-lived fad, or computers would never be able to send mail. The holders of these beliefs probably included educated professionals who were in positions of importance. Does this description—an educated person in an important position who holds certain beliefs—sound like you?

When you adhere to your belief when it is challenged, you are not demonstrating conviction, but rather are blindly adhering to an assumption. What you are doing is erecting a moat around yourself to keep new perspectives out of your mind. The belief to which you are clinging may be a correct one, or it may be wrong. What is important is the fairness with which you assess new ideas and how receptive you are to reconsidering a belief that you hold.

A receptive realist does not have this "I know best and I can't be wrong" mentality. Certainly, these individuals have beliefs, but they know that our world is changing greatly seemingly each minute, and so what may have been true one year ago, last month, or even last week may no longer be. They do not blindly accept every new contention as fact, nor do they refuse to consider the possibility that a belief of theirs is no longer viable.

In discussing items 2 and 25, we described how rigidly clinging to beliefs in the face of new evidence hinders your thinking skill. So too does an abandonment of your beliefs when you act as a professional, which is the essence of item 40 ("An individual's beliefs should not be evident in that person's professional actions").

Our research showed that people who answered "very often" or "often" to item 40 were frequently portrayed within their organizations as individuals who act from a sense of political correctness rather than convictions. These leaders do things like give across-the-board raises because they contend that they are being fair.

A receptive realist knows that actions like the preceding one are wrong. They understand that treating unequals as equals is an injustice. A receptive realist has beliefs, and persons who report to them are aware of what they are. Their beliefs are known because they do not abandon them in their actions as a leader. Receptive realists are authentic. They act as they really believe, not to be politically correct, but because that's how their self-knowledge leads them to think. They are remarkably consistent in that what they espouse is also reflected in their actions as leaders.

An Exemplary Receptive Realist: Hedy White Manry

Hedy White Manry is the vice president of sales leadership deployment for IBM. She has been an executive for fifteen years at IBM, and her record of accomplishment has been exemplary. In the six years in which she served as the sales executive for IBM's K–12 division, products in her area of responsibility grew from a minimal presence in the market to one of over $400 million. As a result, one of four kindergarten students in America has used her company's Writing to Read software.

Accolades for her leadership accomplishments have been many and diverse. She has received the prestigious IBM Excellence Award for outstanding achievement three times. Her alma mater, Auburn University, recently named her as one of the "Top 100 Outstanding Women" in the university's history.

Manry's thinking processes are clearly that of a receptive realist. They are manifested in a remarkably straightforward approach to leadership. What she believes, she expresses, and what she advocates is reflected in her actions.

Beliefs are an integral part of Manry's operational style. Although she has a strong set of them, Manry does not view them as absolutes. In fact, she welcomes challenges to them. It is her contention that such a philosophy serves two important purposes. First, when opposing viewpoints are conveyed, Manry uses them to examine the validity of her own belief. This introspection has been a source of many of her significant ideas. Second, she contends that her openness to new perspectives is clear to her colleagues: "I respect the thoughts and ideas of people in the organization. It encourages them to come forward with these ideas. Even if it does not, on the surface, seem like a good idea, I look beneath it for the merit that it may have."

When evidence contrary to a belief Manry holds is presented, she does not dig in her heels and resist it. If it is valid, she alters her belief. If it is not, Manry will use the "peel away its layers" strategy in order to see what facets of it can be used to improve her organization's quality or performance. Manry treats contradictions to her beliefs as beneficial because they often serve as a stimulus for her and colleagues to engage in creative thinking.

Beliefs are an integral part of Manry's operational style, and they are evident in the goals that she sets for herself and IBM. For example, she places a high degree of importance on optimizing the strengths of individuals. Therefore, she takes professional actions with the objective of giving colleagues the freedom and skill requisite to be professionally empowered. She also seeks to show respect for others, be a person of integrity, do everything with excellence, and encourage creative initiatives.

Hedy White Manry has attained much success as a leader. She has adhered to some of her beliefs throughout her career and altered others because of changing conditions. Manry's willingness to accept the new and different has encouraged an atmosphere where innovation is frequent. She provides direction to a group of individuals who are committed to highly successful performance, an expected outcome in an organization with this receptive realist as its leader.

Strategies for Becoming a Receptive Realist

Hedy White Manry provides many clear examples as to how a receptive realist thinks and acts. Within her organization, she has developed a positive ethos where there is a receptivity to new ideas. Our research has found that other power thinkers have an attitude similar to Manry's and use strategies that have the same objective as her "peel away the layers" one does. Here we look at overcoming low self-confidence and evaluating the validity of your beliefs when challenged.

OVERCOMING LOW SELF-CONFIDENCE. For a long time, we have known that there was much more to leadership than possessing a vast array of knowledge and learning a set of prescribed skills. We have seen too many individuals in leadership positions who, despite their knowledge and skill, utterly fail to inspire and truly lead. Research has affirmed that power thinkers have gone beyond a cursory examination of their beliefs to illuminate and act on their noteworthy virtues and ethical belief systems, and it is this scrutiny that elevates them to excellence (Glanz, Grant, and Monteiro, 2002).

Receptive realists possess ingenious self-knowledge cognitive processes that work in harmony. They repeatedly analyze their core beliefs, nurture them, and manifest their unique talents in positive, productive manners.

Non–power thinkers have not become receptive realists, partly because they have not developed the abilities to consistently acknowledge the contributions of others and are biased, unjust, lack the steadfastness to make tough decisions, are closed-minded, or uninspired.

Because courage comes into play when one's beliefs and attitudes are called into question, receptive realists have learned to use the strategies explored in this chapter to remain faithful to their ethical and moral principles. This is what courage is all about. On a daily basis, receptive realists exhibit more subtle forms of courage: the courage to do what others prefer not to do, the courage to confront difficult and uncomfortable situations, and, most important, the courage to remain steadfast in their most ethical and effective self-knowledge-driven talents and beliefs. They affirm their beliefs about what is most important. A courageous leader therefore should have a well-reasoned, articulated belief system that supports and affirms the rights and dignities of all people. A firm set of leadership beliefs guides their behavior. In this sense, then, courage is integral to the effectiveness of a leader.

Without courage, leaders become nothing more than custodians of their respective companies or institution. Leading involves making the right decision. Courageous leaders have developed the ability to stand behind their principles, and that ability displays their immense strength of character. Courage arises from evaluating the validity of your beliefs in each challenging situation, and if found valid, this tested conviction converts to strong drive and passionate action to move toward success. If validating your beliefs is difficult for you, the following strategy can assist you.

EVALUATING THE VALIDITY OF YOUR BELIEFS WHEN CHALLENGED. Validating your beliefs creates a conviction that certain things are true. By frequently analyzing the conviction that guides you in challenging situations (or when someone else criticizes you), you can act less frequently on the bases of ego, biases, or irrational desires. When beliefs go unexamined in challenging situations, they often limit self-knowledge because they are accepted uncritically as complete fact. If you are working in a new environment, your own beliefs may represent only a partial view of reality. When you do not know if the belief you hold is right, self-knowledge's internal cognitive processes weaken, and self-doubts emerge. Your quandary reduces your courage.

You should evaluate a belief when your conviction becomes unreasonable or does not feel right for you. For example, a food chain corporate executive firmly believed that "good managers do not hold too many meetings." Four months into his job, he felt a need to analyze this belief and did so using the strategies in this chapter. Essentially, he found that for him, it was more effective not to hold too many meetings, but as the new leader of a group that did not take on initiatives effectively, his belief was not working. Instead of clinging to his belief, which was counterproductive in a new situation, he asked himself the questions in Exercise 8.5. He modified his conviction as a result and began holding weekly meetings. The food chain soon increased its productivity above that of the competition. The manager found that his belief that "too many meetings are signs of a weak leader" was tempered. He discovered that the two concepts are not causally linked. Rather, he learned that receptive realists hold the number of meetings that are needed to improve employees' abilities.

A very common occurrence is our final example. Perhaps you have been taught that an open-door policy at the office is the best method of building a receptive and responsive corporate communication system. Such a policy can prompt people to stop by for a chat during the day. If you adhere to this unevaluated belief-based action, you may find yourself taking home more work than you desire, leaving less time for your family. Analyzing the causes of the resulting rising levels of stress caused by this conflict in values may trigger the realization that your unevaluated core belief in an open-door policy has negative consequences. You must reassess your belief in the light of this new development. Possible solutions include limiting the hours during which your door is open or being more assertive about assisting chatty visitors to assume more responsibility for solving the difficulties that they stop to tell you about.

—*w*— Exercise 8.5

EVALUATING BELIEFS, CONVICTIONS, AND COURAGEOUSNESS

1. Identify a situation that is interfering with your most pressing leadership goal. Describe that situation in one sentence here:

   _____

2. Write down the beliefs or values that motivate you to persist toward this goal:

   _____

3. Write the basis for these beliefs. Explain the likely reason you accepted this belief as true for you. For example: "My former boss held this belief and used it successfully in his interactions with me, so I determined that this belief was important for me."

   _____

   _____

   _____

   _____

4. Describe ways you can modify your beliefs so that they provide greater support to the reasoning and insights you have about the situation described in number 1 above. Why is this goal still elusive? For example: If I continue to work 18 hours a day to achieve this single goal, I may create future challenges because I am not leading other equally important goals forward. If I lead several initiatives simultaneously, I could create a synergy that my focus on a single goal would not achieve.

   _____

   _____

   _____

   _____

Receptive realists are more effective leaders because they have completed the analyses in Exercise 8.5 and understand why or how they came to develop their beliefs. This exercise also enables them to examine the limits of their beliefs.

To identify how your beliefs are influencing your success in positive and negative ways, complete Exercise 8.5. Similarly, whenever your beliefs or values are questioned, use Exercise 8.6 to reason through this aspect of your self-knowledge's internal cognitive process. Your analysis will either more firmly establish that belief as a valuable component of your working style in this specific situation, or help you modify the belief so that it can more effectively contribute to your leadership goals.

In closing this discussion, we want to emphasize that you should not exclude the beliefs of others from consideration. However, equally important, your own beliefs should not be thrown aside or hidden from subordinates to sustain a position of mysterious power or to reach a compromise. For example, a leading corporate president was advised to move his company's headquarters to another state. The move would save a considerable amount of tax dollars. Consultants pleaded and presented charts, statistics, and case histories in support of their advice. The president, however, refused to move. He reasoned through his beliefs (using Exercise 8.6) and realized that he did not want to move because living in the house where his parents and grandparents had lived was very important to him. He believed that his personal happiness was more important to the success of the company than the increased profits that would accrue from a lower tax rate. This president's belief proved superior to the more focused, reason-driven logic of the people who gave him unsolicited advice. By remaining true to his self-knowledge's internal cognitive process, this receptive realist has led his company to remain one of the most profitable in its industry.

You must choose beliefs that are most valid for you: the ones that bring you the most productivity, appreciation, results, and understanding. Start to resist the influence of others who seek to change your beliefs. Continuously analyze the beliefs you acquired in the past that are no longer valid. When you value your own beliefs, you will no longer respond to pressures to alter them and will not accept someone else's word that a belief will carry as much truth for you as it does for him or her.

Exercise 8.6

EVALUATING A CHALLENGED BELIEF

1. I believe that the following belief is true, even though someone challenged it:

   _____

2. Is this belief completely true, partially true, or invalid in this situation? Why is this the case?

   _____

   _____

3. In what ways does this belief contribute positively to my company's mission?

   _____

   _____

4. If someone challenges my belief, what three questions can I ask to make it easier for our beliefs to become compatible?

   a. _____

   b. _____

   c. _____

ANALYSIS OF ANSWERS

QUESTION 2: Does the belief that you wrote in question 1 match your leadership style and talents? If so, this belief will stimulate your motivation, build closer relationships with people, establish trust, and produce positive purposes more rapidly. How many incidents can you recall in the past week in which this belief assisted your work? Write that number here. _____. Hampered it? Write that number here. _____.

QUESTION 3: If the belief is not making a more positive than negative contribution to your organization, you will find that you could not answer question 3 easily. Reasoning will not allow you to list positive experiences unless this belief indeed contributed to those experiences.

QUESTION 4: Rather than offer a rational, insight-driven or self-knowledge-led appeal in defense of your beliefs, ask questions whenever your beliefs are challenged. For example, instead of arguing with someone about whether your beliefs are correct, ask if he or she understands how your belief could be compatible with his or her beliefs or ask what you can do to make your and his or her differing beliefs compatible.

CONFIDENT KEYSTONE

We have noted that failure can affect the confidence level of some leaders. We will now examine confidence, but here we look at individuals with a high degree of confidence who use it strategically in their actions. For these individuals, just as a keystone serves as a support for the other pieces in an arch, self-confidence performs a comparable function for a power thinker. For this reason, we called this aspect of self-knowledge the confident keystone.

Understanding the Confident Keystone

Items 5, 30, and 42 of the Yale Assessment of Thinking assess the degree to which you are a confident keystone. Fill out the Confident Keystone Item Cluster Graph, entering your scores for these items from Chapter Two. If your total score was 5 or under, write as the YAT score interpretation "highly skilled." If your total score was 6 or 7, write "average ability." If your total score was 8 or higher, write "need for improvement."

Item 5 ("My level of self-confidence is lower than it should be") focuses on having a chronically low quantity of self-confidence. If you responded "very often" or "often" to this item, two things are usually true about individuals like you. First, this low level of self-confidence is hurting your effectiveness as a leader in several ways. You probably do not establish meaningful goals and are not courageous about tackling anything new to you. You prefer "the same old" to that which is challenging when it comes to tasks. As a consequence, the organization that you lead is low performing (as compared to other units), and morale is low.

Since you have not set challenging goals for yourself or your organization, what you do is unimportant. An activity represents merely

Item Cluster Graph.   Confident Keystone Item Cluster Graph

YAT Items	Your Response
5	_____
30	_____
42	_____
Total	_____
YAT score interpretation	_____

a task to be completed, with little self-satisfaction gained at its conclusion. Your self-confidence may increase or decrease depending on the praise or lack of it given to you by others. Because what you choose to do is unimportant to you, its completion does not provide you with a sense of positive internal reinforcement. Therefore, your self-confidence will rise when you receive praise from others and plummet even lower when you do not.

Power thinkers who are confident keystones possess high levels of self-confidence and they welcome new, different, and challenging initiatives because they know they can do them. This attitude permeates the organization as well. Colleagues are stimulated by the novel assignments given to them, and as a result, employee turnover rates are low because the environment that they establish is an exciting one in which to work.

As for a confident keystone, reinforcement may come from others, but within such an individual, there is a high degree of positive internal reinforcement from accomplishing things that matter. Confident keystones do not like to fail, but when they do, they learn from it and are not dissuaded from continuing to implement other equally complex efforts.

The reaction of a confident keystone and someone less skilled in this external cognitive process is quite different in reaction to criticism (item 30—"When I am criticized, I question my abilities"). If you responded "very often" or "often" to this item, you question your competence when you are criticized. And when you do, you are acting in a manner that will lessen your ability to think powerfully.

Persons who responded in the preceding manner to this item treat all criticism as valid. Even when it is not, they will contort what was said until they can claim it was accurate. As strange as it may seem, you have created within you a mental process that goes into effect when you are criticized. It will make whatever leaps are necessary to justify whatever negative thing was said about you. Thus, your perception that you have limited abilities is reinforced within you.

Confident keystones do not assume that every criticism directed at them is deserved. Nor do they think that nothing done by them warrants negative reaction.

In the television show *Dragnet*, Sergeant Joe Friday used to ask for "just the facts." When criticized, confident keystones act in precisely this manner. They will examine the situation, the negative comment made about it, and ask, "Could I have done this task better?"

If the answer to this question is yes, they take note of this information and use it, when appropriate, in the future. If their response is no, they take solace that they performed the task well. A confident keystone will then turn attention to the person who made the critical remarks.

Unlike their less skilled counterparts, confident keystones do not accept all criticism as true. Although they know it can be valid, they also realize it may have been made because the other person does not like them. Or the individual who made the criticism may have had good intentions but be in error. With such a colleague, confident keystones will meet with the person and treat the discussion as a personnel development opportunity. They will explain how they investigated the person's criticism and, based on facts X, Y, and Z, convey why they acted as they did. They may or may not alter the other individual's viewpoint, but at least that person will know that their belief was considered.

While we were conducting the research for this book, we were the most surprised by the explanations offered by professionals who responded "very often" or "often" to item 42 ("When my hard work goes unnoticed, my self-confidence lessens"). When we questioned many of these individuals, a pattern of thought emerged. Such individuals would describe the number of hours, including nights and weekends, that they devoted to completing something. They also said that their immediate supervisor did not commend their work.

The supervisors, when we followed up, agreed that they had not commended the employee in question. The reason they gave was that the task took the individual much longer to perform than they thought it should have. And with this added amount of time, the supervisors could not consider this effort exemplary. We repeatedly heard how these individuals did tasks satisfactorily (the reason they were not terminated) but at a slower pace than confident keystones.

Our research on this facet of a confident keystone's performance was equally illuminating. Not only did they do things faster than persons who answered "very often" or "often" to this item, but the quality of work was generally much better.

We found that confident keystones work smarter rather than longer at a task. They have a plan for what they tackle, and they accomplish it before boredom sets in. Confident keystones learn from prior efforts, and they put this knowledge to use so their subsequent efforts are better and require less time on their part.

An Exemplary Confident Keystone: Ken Chenault

Ken Chenault was named CEO of American Express in 2001. He had worked at American Express for over twenty years and had held various positions within the company. Regardless of the role in which he operated, Chenault was known for his focus on performance and bottom-line results.

With such objectives, you may envision him to be a cold-hearted bureaucrat. Nothing could be further from the truth. Appraisals of Chenault over his career have consistently praised him for his honesty, finesse, and vision. He is probably most noted for the self-confident manner in which he implements change.

Chenault does not have low self-confidence (item 5) and does not question his abilities when he is criticized (item 30). When his hard work goes unnoticed, his self-confidence does not lessen (item 42). It is for these reasons, plus his exemplary performance, that we present Chenault as a model of a confident keystone.

Through his career at American Express, Chenault has been unafraid of change. He analyzes what needs to be done, and then he meets with all groups affected by the change in order to answer questions and listen to comments. After such sessions, typically the overwhelming majority of these individuals support the change that Chenault is advocating.

The confidence that he expresses for the need for a change as well as for what will take place is a leadership tool that Chenault uses masterfully. Those who hear his words leave the meeting convinced that the new action will make American Express a better company.

Chenault's self-confidence is based on honesty. He does his homework carefully, and when he knows that a change is to occur, he has carefully assessed its pluses and downsides. He states both of them in his presentations to associates.

His message is not only well delivered (because he is confident about its merit) but also honest. Associates have heard him forthrightly explain why downsizing needed to occur within American Express. Since being named CEO, he has sought to alter the corporation's culture, which he labeled as one of "arrogance." To achieve that objective, Chenault has initiated actions designed to move American Express from an elitist organization to one more designed to serve the mainstream of American culture.

Despite a weak economy, American Express has grown from having 100,000 to 500,000 merchants accept its card. The company's card also is now used at Wal-Mart, the world's largest retailer.

Through his illustrious career, Ken Chenault has been a keystone for the organization. Others have relied on him for support as they initiated change and supported these actions because of his self-confidence in the soundness of the proposed action.

Strategies for Becoming a Confident Keystone

Ken Chenault is a superb leader who carefully considers new directions and then confidently presents them to others. What he does to make American Express a better company are things that other leaders would do well to copy. If you implement his ideas about confident leadership, you will become more proficient in this important thinking skill.

If you would like to gain additional proficiency in the skills associated with being a confident keystone, you can use four important strategies that we explain: monitor your self-respect, administer proactive repair, make appointments with yourself, and turn daydreams into visions.

MONITOR YOUR SELF-RESPECT. Monitoring how much your self-respect rises and falls after each decision can become an effective gauge of the degree to which you are a confident keystone. You will know you have used power thinking during decision making if your self-respect rises when the decision is made. For example, when you have made a good decision, regardless of the self-sacrifice required or the difficulty of the task, you will experience responsibility, trust, hope, or enthusiasm (levels 4 through 6 on the emotional scale in Figure 7.2). A sense of pride will emerge as you engage in the task. When you exercise the courage to explain your decision without excuses, you will also experience increased integrity and the freedom to focus on other important decisions.

If you do not monitor the rise and fall of your self-respect, you may say yes or no unwisely when a request is made. You also may become angry with the situation, be tempted to do less than your best, or beg off having to decide by creating an excuse as to why it would not be wise to consider the issue before you at this time.

ADMINISTER PROACTIVE REPAIR. Because we all respond inappropriately at times, confident keystones monitor their self-respect with the power thinking strategy of administering proactive repair. This action has four steps that are initiated as soon as a leader's self-respect diminishes, indicating that a decision or behavior just enacted was not effective or proper.

Proactive repair consists of actions you take when your decisions are not moving toward positive ends or to correct mistakes in behaviors that you advocated. This strategy has two parts: proaction and repair.

In proaction, you (1) find out what went wrong, (2) apologize for negative outcomes that your decision or behavior caused, (3) explain why you made the decision (or took the initial, ineffective action) and why it did not achieve the results expected, and (4) state what you want to achieve in the future with a new decision or action.

If your proaction is positively received, you can break away and await your good indicators to make a more effective decision. Then you communicate this new direction by replacing excuses with explanations. If your proaction is met with resistance, you immediately turn to the repair portion of this confident keystone strategy.

Repair occurs whenever it is necessary to enact a thoughtful action to remedy the damage or ill will that a past decision or action created. Repair begins by acknowledging the negative consequences your actions caused (by saying, for example, "I am aware that my decision angered and frustrated many of you"). Then you state that you want to avoid such detrimental effects in the future. Openly ask for others to offer suggestions that can ensure that such decisions or actions will not occur again, and state an action that you are going to take to ensure that it does not.

The benefits of proactive repair apply when even the smallest decisions go awry. The president of one of the world's largest oil companies uses this strategy regularly. When he knows that he has angered a constituency, he visits that group (or colleague) and explains that his actions were not meant to be hurtful or to indicate a refutation of that group's competence. He then states the original intent of his less-than-optimal decision, why he believed that the decision was the correct course of action at the time, what he will do to avoid future errors in thinking, and ask for suggestions as to how such situations can be avoided. This president, an adept and successful confident keystone, has employees who admire him and are loyal to him and the company.

The strength in leadership that proactive repair establishes is undeniable, but the strategy can be difficult to use for the first few times. To help you practice proactive repair, we suggest that you complete Exercise 8.7.

Exercise 8.7

PRACTICING PROACTIVE REPAIR

1. Think of a situation within the past few weeks in which a decision you made may have inadvertently caused difficulty for another person or your company. Briefly describe that event.

   _____

   _____

   _____

2. Write proactive repair actions and statements that you could use to correct the negative results of that decision, ensuring that you perform all four steps in proaction and repair.

   _____

   _____

   _____

MAKE APPOINTMENTS WITH YOURSELF. To strengthen self-knowledge's external cognitive process, make appointments with yourself that cannot be cancelled, just as if you had made the appointment with a colleague. Such actions provide blocks of time in which to nurture insight, accomplish problem solving, write goals, and refine ideas. By having professional decision-making and problem-solving space, you increase the speed with which self-knowledge, insight, and reasoning can unite to establish broad and brave visions.

Internal problem-solving space is our term for psychologically setting an uninterruptible, distraction-free appointment with yourself. Regularly entering your internal problem-solving space will cause you to rethink the things you prize and set new standards for yourself. *External problem-solving space* is a portion of your home or office (even just a specific chair) that you designate as a thinking area. When you move to that location, you enter your internal problem-solving space.

When you use your time wisely, you accomplish more because your plans will be more carefully thought through. You minimize wasted time by setting unbreakable appointments, which enables you to take the time to give higher-quality time to others.

TURN DAYDREAMS INTO VISIONS. In our study, we found that excellent leaders who are confident keystones visualize successful solutions before taking action. Our research also documented that less effective thinkers visualize failure scenarios, a tactic that undermines their performance.

The power thinking strategy we encourage you to use to trigger positive visions about problematic situations is to say to yourself, "If we lived in a perfect world, what would we do? If we could create the perfect outcome, what would it be?"

The difference between visions and daydreams is that daydreams are merely illusions of receiving a desired goal without personal effort. Using the power thinking statements above can change daydreams to positive visions for the future. This is true because they channel your thoughts into specific actions and mental steps that must begin for visions to become reality.

To distinguish between visionaries and daydreamers, observe what you (and others) talk about. Visionaries describe actions they are taking to reach goals. Daydreamers talk about what others should do to reach a goal they desire, or they describe why the ideal hasn't happened yet.

SUCCESSFUL FAILER

When we think about successes and failures in our lives, we typically associate them with the event that caused them to occur and do not think much about what happened after the success or failure took place. Ironically, that about which we give little thought plays a much more crucial role in the attitude that we have relative to success and failure. Here we examine the *successful failer.* This is a person who positively addresses adversity, both the kind that springs from success and the kind that emanates from failure. Such individuals learn from these experiences and use this knowledge in positive ways.

Understanding the Successful Failer

Items 7, 12, and 31 of the Yale Assessment of Thinking assess the degree to which you are a successful failer. Fill out the Successful Failer Item Cluster Graph, entering your scores for these items from Chapter Two. If your total score was 5 or under, write as the YAT score interpretation "highly skilled." If your total score was 6 or 7, write "average ability." If your total score was 8 or higher, write "need for improvement."

For most of us, the word *success* conjures up pleasant thoughts. After all, attaining a favorable result is what leadership is all about. Who would not want to be successful? If you responded "very often" or "often" to item 7 ("Past successes have created negative events in my life, and have placed pressures on me that limit my enthusiasm for pursuing new challenges"), the answer is you.

Item Cluster Graph. Successful Failer Item Cluster Graph

YAT Items	Your Response
7	_____
12	_____
31	_____
Total	_____
YAT score interpretation	_____

As you will recall from the discussions about insight in Chapters Six and Seven, our subconscious performs many tasks. One of its foremost functions is to support us in positive ways. One of the ways that it achieves this objective is to keep negative things from happening to us.

Our subconscious recalls what happened in the past that elicited anger, disappointment, hurt, or other negative feelings. Determined to keep us from a repeat of this emotion, our subconscious will dissuade us from the experience itself and will generalize to labeling success as negative.

For example, Diane is a faculty member who wrote a successful management book. Instead of receiving praise from her colleagues, she was criticized as being a faculty member who was seldom in her office, cared more about writing the book than teaching her students, and took credit in the book for ideas that were theirs, not hers. She was stung by this criticism of her success, and when a major publisher asked her to write another book, she declined.

A successful failer would have responded to these negative events quite differently. When criticisms were leveled, he or she would have examined each one to see if it was valid.

Let us suppose Diane was indeed absent from her office a great deal while writing the book. A successful failer would agree to write another book because success is important to her. However, she would devise a strategy so that she did not repeat the error that she made before when writing a book. As a successful failer, she might decide to maintain office hours on Monday and Wednesday mornings and be in the office on Thursday afternoon. Time not spent in the office would be devoted to writing the new book.

If the criticisms leveled were not valid, a successful failer would mentally categorize them as such. She would view the criticisms as reflecting jealousy on the part of colleagues, and since for successful failers success is important, she would agree to write another book because it would generate success for her.

Items 12 ("I become despondent when I fail") and 31 ("When I fail, the confidence that I have in myself decreases") deal with the opposite of success: failure. If you are not highly skilled in this facet of self-knowledge, you would do well to adopt an attitude like that of Thomas Edison. After numerous and repeated attempts to invent the phonograph, Edison was asked about his failures. His reply was, "I didn't fail, I learned."

If you responded "very often" or "often" to item 12, you did not learn from failure. Instead, you gained an incorrect understanding of it.

It is a natural human reaction to experience sadness when our efforts fall short of our intended goal. The length of time that we maintain this feeling is crucial to our internal cognitive process. Also of importance is the manner in which we let it go.

Individuals who responded "very often" or "often" to this item harbor their negative emotions for much longer than their highly skilled counterparts do. They may say these feelings stay within them because they care deeply about their work, but their prolonged existence is due to how they handle these negative emotions.

Typically, these individuals direct their postmortem of sorts at their decision to initiate the failed action. They will ask themselves, "Why did I do this?" "What can I do so that I will never do anything like this again?" and similar other questions.

Successful failers ask different questions. They want to identify what they can learn from this failure so that they can use this newly discovered knowledge to be successful in the future. They will ask themselves, "What caused the failure to occur?" "How could I have detected it was off-track sooner?" "If I was to reinitiate this in the future, what would I do differently?"

These two groups are dissimilar not only in the length of time in which they analyze failure and the types of questions they ask but also in one other significant way: the consequences of failure.

Less skilled persons will come away from an experience in which they failed with a strong desire not to fail again. In order to realize this objective, the subconscious, being the loyal and caring instrument that it is, will rationalize the lowering of goals that they seek to achieve. When they are considering an initiative in which there is even a slight chance of failure, their subconscious will justify their nonpursuit of it or setting its benchmarks at a much safer level.

This lowering of aspirations does not occur within successful failers. They realize that no one has a 100 percent success rate and that some attempts will go awry. By focusing on not repeating errors by learning from them, these individuals continue to have high aspirations that they pursue doggedly because success is important to them as leaders.

Much of what was said about the prior item also is true for item 31. With its emphasis on self-confidence, it is slightly different. Our research on leaders who responded "very often" or "often" to this item revealed some valuable information about themselves. We found that the confidence of these persons is akin to a thermometer. It fluctuates according to the temperature and will have no memory of the prior day's weather or even that which occurred earlier in the day.

These individuals lack perspective in terms of remembering both their prior successes and failures. As a result, their emotional bank account seems to rise or fall according to each event. Clearly, this lack of an emotional anchor means that periods of despondency for them will last longer and be more pronounced after a failure.

We have advised persons who have this mind-set to begin to think differently. This change can occur rather easily. Our recommendation is to keep a written record of your successes. Next to each entry—a success you experienced—give it some type of rating: a grade (A, A–, B+) or evaluation (excellent, very good, above average). When the inevitable failure occurs, you can use this list to keep your action in perspective (by writing, for example, "I've done *six* things that have achieved success. This *one* didn't"). You can also use this list to conduct an analysis ("What did I do differently in those situations where I was successful than in this one where I failed?").

An Exemplary Successful Failer: Michael S. Dell

If you are trying to think of a contemporary leader whose thought processes are those of a successful failer, you have to look no further than Michael S. Dell, founder, chairman, and CEO of Dell Computers. His Horatio Alger–type story has been told often, and the ascendancy of the company that he founded with $1,000 into one whose sales have grown to $36.9 billion is legendary.

Dell has been honored many times for his leadership successes. These accolades include being named the Chief Executive of the Year by *Chief Executive* magazine and Entrepreneur of the Year by both *Financial World* and *Industry Week* magazines.

If you believe that a success-oriented leader like Dell would have little tolerance for failure, you are wrong. Dell (2002) has said about it, "At Dell, innovation is about taking risks and learning from failure" (p. 41). His ability to learn from, rather than be devastated by, failure is an important reason that his company has been so successful.

In 1989, Dell Computers failed to recognize how rapidly the personal computer industry was moving toward a new type of memory chip, and his company erred by having too many of the old chips. His fledging company suffered dearly for its miscalculation, and it took almost a year to recover from the error.

With Dell as its leader and his learn-from-failure abilities, the company did precisely that. As a result, Dell Computers developed a new way to manage inventory, a strategy that has helped to catapult it to its lofty status today.

Dell is not the only person within his company who is unafraid of failure. He has made this mind-set a part of the company's ethos. Says Dell as to why his company and its employees are so innovative: "We do our best to make sure that people aren't afraid of the possibility of failure."

Strategies for Becoming a Successful Failer

Dell's leadership practices have been an often-discussed subject in business school and at various professional meetings. In his role as a successful failer, he recognizes the inevitability of failure in vibrant organizations and on the part of ambitious leaders. Dell learns from his failures, and you can learn from him by answering two questions: (1) When I fail, do I learn from it? and (2) Within the organization that I lead, do others with whom I work have a comparable attitude?

If you responded yes to both questions, then both you and your organization have a framework within which failure can occur, and when it does, positive benefits can be derived from it. If you answered no to either or both of these questions, you, and probably your organization, are locked in a malaise relative to failure. We offer you several strategies to aid in moving from this negative condition to one in which success can more readily happen.

In addition to learning from less successful efforts and possessing a high value for and drive to achieve success, power thinkers use their talents and skills to (1) direct positive outcomes from their successful initiative to higher levels in ten specific ways, (2) deflect the potentially negative trappings of success before they can detract from their accomplishments, (3) initiate ten specific beliefs and actions to maximize the benefits that occur when plans of action fail, and (4) engage ten internal cognitive processes to ensure that failure does not have long-lasting negative residues to impact future goals. You can rate your own abilities in these four areas by assessing your beliefs about success and failure. If you want to become a more successful failer, we ask you to complete Exercise 8.8.

—✺— Exercise 8.8

YOUR BELIEFS ABOUT
SUCCESS AND FAILURE

For each item, place a check mark if the sentence is true for you, a minus sign if it is not true for you, or a plus sign if you wish it were more true of you.

_____ 1. In your life, fewer successes have occurred through luck, politics, inequitable standards, or injustices than through sustained effort.

_____ 2. In your life, success is not accidental.

_____ 3. A strong belief in your own abilities was an important component in past success.

_____ 4. Experiencing success creates more positive outcomes for you. It saves you time rather than increases the demands on your time because it eliminates the need for repeated trials to reach the same goal.

_____ 5. Past successes increased the quality of your life.

_____ 6. To be most successful, you have to enjoy greatly what you do.

_____ 7. When you were successful in the past, most often it was because you found your niche. You can describe exactly the special flair you contribute to that niche.

_____ 8. When you were successful in the past, you used a strategy to assure yourself that you would not accept failure. You can describe that strategy and the first action you take to implement it to peers.

_____ 9. For you, success provides energy for new challenges rather than stress and increased pressure.

_____ 10. You view success as running a race between yourself and your ever increasing ability to exceed your last level of performance rather than winning a race between yourself and others.

_____ 11. When you succeeded in the past, you expected the result to culminate in greater responsibility for developing better ideas and interacting with more challenging goals. When it didn't, you:

_____

____ 12. You have found that your success stirred up anger or envy in others. You realized that this "bad blood" existed and took action to channel it into positive directions. The action you took was to:

_____

____ 13. You found that to be successful, you had to become more capable or work harder than other people. As a result, some people became jealous. Therefore, success has taught you to forgive jealously.

____ 14. When you succeeded in the past, you did not experience an increased fear that future goals would end in failure. You were not afraid that you would be found out that you did not know all that you were expected to know for this new level of accomplishment. You did not become concerned that you would be found capable only of "talking the talk but not walking the walk." You can describe the strategy you used to avoid this fear:

_____

____ 15. After you experienced a success in the past, you knew that you had not "reached your level of incompetence," so even if success brought demands for which you had no previous experience, you:

_____

____ 16. For you, success is not measured by the critiques or compliments of others but by how successful you feel because:

_____

____ 17. You have noticed that neither succeeding nor failing causes you to become less sensitive to others, withdraw into your own goals, or overextend your ego. You can describe the strategies you use not to treat others differently whether you succeed or fail:

_____

(Continued)

Exercise 8.8 (Continued)

____ 18. Past successes increased your self-reliance because:

       _____

____ 19. It is important to you to try many things to become suc-
           cessful because doing so enables you to throw away the
           strategies that you have used that have not helped you meet
           your standards for success.

____ 20. You believe that you are in control of the level of success you
           will achieve.

____ 21. You agree that high-achieving people fail from time to time
           but that failing does not stop them from pursuing and
           achieving monumental victories.

____ 22. After failing, more so than after successes, you fulfill your
           need for introspection.

____ 23. Your failures have taught you how to adapt.

____ 24. Failures have caused you to acknowledge your mistakes
           and learn from them. Without your failures, you would
           have invested more energy in trying to disavow your
           mistakes.

____ 25. In your life, most failures occurred because you worked too
           fast, left something lacking, spent an insufficient amount of
           time preparing for the task, or neglected to do something
           you did not know how to do.

____ 26. Past failures often increased your fear of failure or made
           you apathetic.

____ 27. You have found that one of the costs of failure is the loss
           of opportunities. Failing causes you to return to the same
           goal rather than move to another goal, as successes allow
           you to do.

____ 28. When you fail, only after some time has elapsed can you
           permit the full gamut of emotions to be experienced again,
           but you do open yourself totally to feeling all emotions
           again, regardless of how painful they may be.

____ 29. Failures have increased your ability to trust the right people.

____ 30. Your failures have come from errors that led to a loss of con-
           trol or a negative momentum. When these errors occurred,

you chose to continue working toward a satisfactory result rather than abandon the effort. The strategy you used to do so was:

_____

____ 31. Failures helped you learn what can be improved to obtain even greater success in projects.

____ 32. You believe that when you take things head-on, there is always a chance that you may fail but that doing so is better than waiting.

____ 33. Failures increased your self-knowledge so that similar defeats did not reoccur. The talent you use when facing defeat is:

_____

____ 34. One of the outcomes of past failures was that you carefully reexamined your strengths and shortcomings as a leader and set higher principles, so that the likelihood of being knocked down again was lessened. You did so by:

_____

____ 35. Knowing that you survived a failure and perhaps even made something fruitful of it has increased your willingness to take risks.

____ 36. Your failures were humbling and increased the value you place on courage in yourself and others.

____ 37. You believe failures are temporary.

____ 38. Failures made you resilient to being afraid to fail and reduced your vulnerability.

____ 39. Failures have been useful experiences for you. They increased your determination and made you search for new methods of functioning as a leader.

____ 40. Failures enabled you to establish the conviction that accidents will never govern your life.

(Continued)

Exercise 8.8 (Continued)

COMPUTING YOUR SCORE
Count the number of checks, minuses, and pluses that you wrote in
the blanks that precede items 1–10, items 11–20, items 21–30, and
items 31–40. Record these numbers below.

Positive Outcomes of Success
(Items 1–10)

Number of checks   _____

Number of minuses   _____

Number of pluses   _____

Potential Negative Outcomes
of Success (Items 11–20)

Number of checks   _____

Number of minuses   _____

Number of pluses   _____

Potential Negative Outcomes
of Failure (Items 21–30)

Number of checks   _____

Number of minuses   _____

Number of pluses   _____

Positive Outcomes of Failure
(Items 31–40)

Number of checks   _____

Number of minuses   _____

Number of pluses   _____

The quadrant that contains the greatest number of checks is the
belief system in which you have the most skill and the one that your
colleagues most depend on. If you believe most strongly in the positive outcomes of success, you will be distinguished as an innovative
leader. If you believe most strongly in the positive outcomes of failure, you will be the leader whom others turn to in crisis. If you believe
most strongly in your potential to overcome the negative outcomes of
success, colleagues turn to you when they feel they have tried everything and exhausted every possibility for success. Peers think of you
to lead them into uncharted territories.

If you believe most strongly in your abilities to overcome the
potential negative outcomes of failure, colleagues turn to you above
all other leaders when courage, conviction, and high principles must
rule the hour. Successful failers possess strong beliefs in all four of
these leadership domains. Because they possess such strong, positive

convictions and strengths, they are called on to lead in a wider array of situations than nonsuccessful failers.

If the total of minuses and pluses exceeds the total number of checks in any quadrant, your internal cognitive self-knowledge process needs to be strengthened in that domain. Your existing set of beliefs relative to that quadrant is limiting your success as a leader.

In evaluating the results of Exercise 8.8, the following information can assist you to analyze your abilities as a successful failer.

Items 1 through 10 are statements about the positive outcomes of success. The more items you marked with a plus or a minus in this group, the less strong your beliefs are about the value of success compared with beliefs of power thinkers. The expectations you hold for your own capabilities may be too low, restricting your own power. Reread each item you did not check, identify why you do not believe that statement to be true of you, and use one of the strategies in this chapter to strengthen your abilities to use all of the positive outcomes of success more effectively.

Items 11 through 20 describe negative qualities of success that, if left unattended, can diminish the positive outcomes of your initiatives. The more items in this quadrant that you checked, the stronger your beliefs are about the benefits that can be derived from the demands that success places on you compared with beliefs of non–power thinkers. If you did not have many checks in this category, each unchecked item is likely to be a specific reason that you often "choke" or become stuck on the doorstep of too many potential successes. You may believe (consciously or subconsciously) that you cannot handle the negative effects of a success or the increased responsibility that a success is likely to generate. As you review each item not checked, analyze why you did not find that item to be true. You can alter your belief through the use of a strategy from Chapters Four and Five. Through practice, you can develop your skills in validly viewing the negative qualities of success.

Items 21 through 29 describe the negative consequences of failure. If you left any items in this group unchecked, you may lack confidence in your ability to solve problems. As a result, you may pretend to (or actually) lose interest in areas in which you encounter difficulties. You may also have a high sensitivity to criticism and avoid exploring new ideas. If any items in this range are not checked, you have probably reacted negatively to past failures and need new power thinking strategies before you can risk failing again.

You can become a more powerful thinker by using this chapter's strategies to overcome these and other thought patterns that lead you to overemphasize the potentially negative outcomes from failure. Again, as you review the items not checked in this quadrant, analyze why you do not believe that item to be true. Leaders who have participated in our Power Thinking for Leaders programs and who have used Exercise 8.9 to conduct this analysis found that they more readily selected new power thinking strategies, which enabled them to obtain more value from failures. As a result, they developed the abilities to become a successful failer. The strategies in Chapter Six are particularly effective in increasing your abilities to overcome the potential long-term negative consequences that can occur from failed goals.

Items 30 through 41 describe benefits that can result from failure. Any unchecked item suggests a belief that is keeping you from maximizing the potential for growth that failure provides. To overcome this belief, take advantage of Exercise 8.9 to analyze these beliefs. Those

---

Exercise 8.9

WORKING TOWARD SUCCESS

1. Recall an event or project that did not end as successfully as you desired. Describe the reasons that you believe that experience failed.

   _____

   _____

2. What could *you* have done differently in order to reach greater success?

   _____

   _____

3. Think of a problem that confronts you as a leader. How will you use what you have learned from this chapter to solve it?

   _____

   _____

who have done so learned that they could select a power thinking strategy to use in the future when failures occur.

To analyze whether your beliefs about success and failure have limited your leadership abilities, know that the most successful and powerful leaders believe that *all* the statements in Exercise 8.8 are true. By reviewing the statements with which you disagreed, you can identify the beliefs that are limiting your success. Success and failure can create positive, productive outcomes in the hands of successful failers. The ability to grow equally from success and failure comes from analyzing inadequate previous beliefs. Power thinkers value both success and failure for the contribution they can make to stronger reasoning, insight, and self-knowledge, all of which contribute to their growth as a leader.

Before our discussion closes, we caution you to remember that many people were brought up to believe that to fail is a disgrace: that your worth as a person lessens if you fail at anything. As our assessment of your beliefs about success and failure proved, this simply is not true. To be a success, you must become a successful failer. To cite only two examples to support this claim, Thomas Edison tried many times before he invented the light bulb. When asked about the 3,000 times his experiments failed, Edison confidently replied, "I never failed. Each experiment brought me closer to my success." Edison took his experience from each day's experiment with him to the next day, so he never considered any day to be without a positive result. He learned to fail without considering himself a failure. Life is a succession of trials and errors, not successes and failures.

Another man failed repeatedly, and after his ten failures, his one success placed him as one of our most admired leaders. Do you know who this man is? We give the answer at the end of this list if you have not recognized this dominant leader before that time:

- In '31, he failed in business.
- In '32, he was defeated in the race for House of Representatives.
- In '34, he failed again in business.
- In '36, he had a nervous breakdown.
- In '38, he lost another election.
- In '43, he lost a congressional race.
- In '46, he ran for office and lost.

- In '48, he ran for office and lost.
- In '55, he lost a Senate race.
- In '56, he was unsuccessful in his bid for the vice presidency.
- In '58, he lost another Senate race.
- In '60, he became president of the United States.

The answer is Abraham Lincoln.

In review, successful failers have mastered self-knowledge's internal cognitive process that enables them to produce gains regardless of the number of positive or negative outcomes that initially occur in new ventures. These successful failers use two strategies to increase and positively focus their talents, beliefs, and values to achieve productive purposes that arise from success or failure. In the process, they minimize or eliminate the potentially negative effects that could result from success or failure.

SUMMARY

In this chapter, we have discussed several facets of this complex thinking domain of self-knowledge. As we stated at the beginning of the chapter, self-knowledge has elements unique to it as well as ones in which it draws on reasoning or insight.

Because you completed the exercises and analyses in this chapter, you are more likely to:

1. Base your actions on what you believe.
2. Reinforce your reasoning and insight with the sense of stability and understanding that increased self-knowledge affords.
3. Monitor your self-respect.
4. Practice proactive repair.
5. Make appointments with yourself.
6. Turn daydreams into visions.

Other strategies you learned were to identify your core beliefs and values; evaluate and improve your level of self-esteem, self-concept, and self-efficacy; keep score; eliminate self-imposed limitations by turning self-talk into action-oriented questions; and assess your beliefs when challenged.

You also read about the methods used by Joyce Brothers, Michael Dell, Hedy White Manry, and Ken Chenault to exercise self-knowledge's internal cognitive process as a valid viewer, successful failer, receptive realist, and confident keystone. By replicating their actions, you can respond to leadership responsibilities with more self-knowledge in the future. You know that you should reevaluate your beliefs when your confidence wanes. An invalid belief confuses your reasoning and pulls your insights and self-knowledge in counterproductive directions. Alternatively, when your belief system is strong and in tune with your personal talents, needs, and motivations, your confidence increases, enabling you to reach your potential and to applaud others who do the same.

On the next two pages, we once again have provided you space in which you may write your reflections at this junction as to steps that you plan to take in order to become more proficient in each of these segments of self-knowledge's internal cognitive process.

SELF-KNOWLEDGE INTERNAL COGNITIVE PROCESS THINKING ENHANCEMENT

Valid Viewer

Successful Failer

Receptive Realist

Confident Keystone

CHAPTER NINE

Self-Knowledge

External Cognitive Process

A long-popular ballad could well be the theme of this chapter. In the "The Gambler," made popular by Kenny Rogers, a gambler explains to a boy his philosophy for success. He tells the boy about holding and folding hands of cards, as well as the right time to walk or run away.

The self-knowledge of the gambler, based on experience, strategy, and insight, apparently served him well over the years. To create organizational successes, power thinkers have used that same combination.

Our research showed that these excellent leaders consistently demonstrate four types of actions. We called these external cognitive processes to be that of principled colonel, flexible doer, inventive finisher, and reliable completer.

PRINCIPLED COLONEL

In the movie *We Were Soldiers,* Mel Gibson, who portrays Lieutenant Colonel Harold G. Moore, told his troops that he personally would be the first person to get off their helicopter to face a battle in Vietnam and the last person to board it when they returned to their base. He also stated, "We will all come home together." Lieutenant Colonel Moore meant not just those soldiers who survived but also the bodies of their slain comrades.

Moore's words were not merely rhetoric. As anyone who has seen this film or read his fine book of the same title knows, despite exposing himself to some extremely dangerous situations, all of his troops did indeed go home together.

Certainly, Moore's actions were ones of valor, but they were much more than an act of bravery: they were based on his being a person of principle. Few would argue that Moore had deeply entrenched values about things such as loyalty, and he acted in accordance with them.

Although the leaders in our study were not in situations as precarious as the one that Moore faced, we noted that they were principled individuals whose values had a great impact on how they thought and the decisions they reached. It is for these reasons that we called a power thinker with these skills a *principled colonel*.

Understanding the Principled Colonel

Items 8, 23, and 66 of the Yale Assessment of Thinking assess the degree to which you are a principled colonel. Fill out the Principled Colonel Item Cluster Graph, entering your scores for these items from Chapter Two. If your total score was 5 or under, write as the YAT score interpretation "highly skilled." If your total score was 6 or 7, write "average ability." If your total score was 8 or higher, write "need for improvement."

Item Cluster Graph.   Principled Colonel Item Cluster Graph

YAT Items	Your Response
8	_____
23	_____
66	_____
Total	_____
YAT score interpretation	_____

If you responded "very often" or "often" to item 8 ("People compliment me for aspects of my professional life that are less important to me than my other values which they do not recognize"), you may think that this attitude is of little consequence. If you hold this view, you are wrong.

Our research showed that such an attitude exists in individuals for one of three reasons. First, you have values that are important to you that should not be. For example, you may consider yourself to be witty and endeared by colleagues. In reality, you may not be humorous at all, and your coworkers do not have warm feelings about you. Second, what you value may not be important to those persons with whom you work or the organization. Therefore, you may indeed be witty, but others simply do not care that you are. Instead, they compliment you on being trustworthy because this value is more important to them. Third, what others are citing you for may be a strength of which you are unaware. And since you are not aware that it exists within you, you do not recognize it as being important.

Principled colonels are sometimes complimented for a trait or behavior that they did not know they exhibited. When this happens, they initially ask themselves if the area for which they are being lauded is important to being an outstanding leader or to organizational success. If the answer is yes, they will consider it a potential area of untapped talent. If they find that it is indeed an ability that they possess, they examine ways to nurture it within themselves so that they can use this newly discovered tool effectively.

Principled colonels also think differently about their actions in initiatives that they do not value (item 23—"When faced with an initiative that I do not especially value, I do not establish any goals relative to it"). Their less skilled counterparts do not establish goals before becoming involved in these initiatives. In contrast, principled colonels do formulate them. They establish goals because they have a mind-set about themselves and the quality of work that they produce. It is important to them that when people think of them, they will say, "When X does something, it is done well."

This commitment to quality is crucial to how principled colonels approach and implement tasks. It is equally important as to its effect on others. They reason, "Since X does things well, I too must do my part of this undertaking equally well." Thus, doing things well becomes the manner in which others in the organization operate.

Persons who respond "very often" or "often" to item 66 ("My values are not reflected in the actions I take") frequently believe this mind-set is a positive one. They contend that they act objectively as a leader by not allowing their own values to affect their actions.

If you gave either of the preceding responses to this item, we urge you to rethink your viewpoint. Our internal cognitive process occurs in a logical pattern. Values influence our thoughts, and our thoughts produce the decisions that we reach. Values are also our warning signals. It is the way that our subconscious tells us that an action that we are about to take is at odds with our values. By ignoring your values in the internal cognitive process, you are not using a significant resource that can immeasurably aid you in reaching sound decisions, solving problems effectively, and thinking creatively.

By ignoring your values, you are also sending out a negative message to those with whom you work. If your actions are not aligned with your values, you convey that you are merely playing a role as a leader. You are regarded as someone who advocates one thing and acts in a manner inconsistent with it.

Is it any wonder why people like Lieutenant Colonel Moore, whose values drive their actions, are trusted? Clearly, their colleagues have a higher regard for them than that of a leader who is perceived to be a gadfly.

In addition to being held in esteem by others, principled colonels benefit in another way by their values being reflected in the actions that they take. Their actions are appreciably better because they have used their internal cognitive process as it is meant to function: values producing thoughts, and thoughts developing actions.

An Exemplary Principled Colonel: Jim Perdue

Anyone who knows or works with Jim Perdue would agree that he is a principled colonel. He is the chairman of the board and CEO of Perdue Farms, which has consistently ranked in the top 100 on the Forbes list of the leading 500 private companies. It is the foremost poultry producer in the Northeast and the third largest poultry producer in the United States. The company annually provides more than 2.5 billion pounds of chicken and 200 million pounds of turkey to its customers.

Jim Perdue has family ties to the business. His grandfather founded it in 1920, and his father, Frank, was responsible for its products being sold in big city markets in the 1970s.

Jim Perdue's values are reflected in the actions that both he and his company take. Since the company's inception, Perdue's grandfather,

father, and now him have strongly believed in the importance of people. And this credo has gone beyond mere words. Despite a busy schedule, Perdue travels once every two weeks to visit customers and plants.

These trips go far beyond the largely ceremonial ones taken by many CEOs. Perdue uses them for two purposes. First, since Perdue Farms has historically had a strong commitment to customers, he wants to know what their consumer demands are. For example, he learned that they wanted to have precooked chicken available to them, and the company responded by creating a new line of "heat and eat" products that can be prepared in about twenty minutes.

The second purpose of Perdue's travels is to remind customers and associates of the company's commitment to quality. To that end, although he grew up in the poultry business, Perdue not only listens to what others say but also acts on their feasible ideas. Associates know that they are valued and that their ideas for making a quality product are important to Perdue. He says of the value that he places on employees and their ideas: "Nobody knows more about the business than one person doing his or her job day in and day out. They are the experts and if you don't believe that, you are in trouble."

Strategies for Becoming a Principled Colonel

Perdue is a principled colonel who knows his values. So too do those with whom he works. Perdue's actions are aligned with those values. Rather than being an enigma to others, he has established an exemplary record of valuing individuals, welcoming their ideas, and acting on them when warranted. Jim Perdue also provides a fine example of how a principled colonel acts. He is an admired leader whose employees respect him and whose company's high level of performance is the beneficiary of his acting in accordance with his values. If you would like to increase your abilities in this aspect of self-knowledge's internal cognitive processes, the following strategies can assist you: increasing your enthusiasm, actualizing confidence in your leadership role, identifying the qualities of historical figures whom you admire, and achieving self-actualization.

INCREASING YOUR ENTHUSIASM. In our research, we have surveyed thousands of leaders across the nation and around the world. One of the questions we posed was, "What is the number one quality of a good leader?" Overwhelmingly, respondents identified "enthusiasm for one's work" as most important. Ironically, employees often complain that their leaders are boring. Can you remember sitting in a meeting where the leader was not confident and enthusiastic about the company's goals? Can you recall what a difference an enthusiastic, confident leader made?

Enthusiasm demonstrates passion for your work. Passionate people enjoy what they do and are more successful. Moreover, such enthusiasm is inspiring. Consider some of the world's great leaders. They possess enthusiasm and optimism, which is founded on self-confidence. They inspire others to action because their confidence exudes strength.

Confidence is not a skill and not something that you can develop after taking a course. Rather, it is a state of mind. Confidence combined with optimism is the awareness that one can take a glass that is half full and fill it. Confidence is a way of looking at the world with the belief that one can indeed make a difference. Principled colonels have developed this attribute. Whenever your confidence falls, remember the following quotations from famous leaders:

> "No dream is too big for those with their eyes in the sky."—Buzz Aldrin, astronaut

> "Excellence! The attitude generates enthusiasm, attracts top people, and becomes the basis for real optimism."—Robert Schuller, religious leader

> "A leader is a dealer in hope."—Napoleon Bonaparte

An enthusiastic leader views the world and difficult situations not through rose-colored glasses but with an abiding sense of the positive and a belief that possibilities exist where others see hopelessness. Confidence is not generated merely in crisis situations; it is evident as leaders go about their daily work. Displaying genuine interest and dedication in their work is the first key to a successful leader's development of confidence.

Such leaders inspire others through their deeds and their words. Confidence generates the enthusiasm that resounds in their choice and delivery of words. To motivate yourself, turn to Exercise 9.1.

ACTUALIZING CONFIDENCE IN YOUR LEADERSHIP ROLE. The next step to increase your self-confidence is to raise your level of enthusiasm, defined as the state of being that exudes fervor about something of value or importance. Enthusiasm cannot be trained; it is a developed

---

——⌇—— Exercise 9.1

IDENTIFYING MOTIVATORS

1. Which leader have you heard deliver a speech that motivated you to action or energized you most?

   _____

2. What specifically about that leader's delivery or choice of words motivated you? List three qualities here.

   _____

   _____

   _____

   _____

3. How can you integrate these three qualities into your future presentations without copying that leader's delivery style? List additions that capitalize and enhance your own leadership strengths.

   a. _____

   b. _____

   c. _____

---

by-product of confidence. Although nearly anyone can feign enthusiasm for a short time, it is tough to do so over time. We can, however, enhance our enthusiasm by identifying and adhering to a strong set of values.

A genuine desire to impart what we believe to be true is the most significant impetus to generate sustained enthusiasm. This is true for you and your employees. For this reason, the next step in building self-confidence can be taken when you establish a stronger sense of self-knowledge by completing Exercise 9.2 to fine-tune your values.

IDENTIFYING THE QUALITIES OF HISTORICAL FIGURES WHOM YOU ADMIRE. If sustaining self-confidence as a principled colonel is still difficult for you, we recommend three actions that you can take:

—∿— Exercise 9.2

FINE-TUNING YOUR VALUES

1. If you have a firm set of beliefs and values, you are most likely to exhibit enthusiasm while actualizing them. Write down the four leadership values that are most important to you.

_____

_____

_____

_____

2. What do you want for your employees?

_____

_____

_____

_____

3. What values do you want to assist your company to reach?

_____

_____

_____

_____

4. List your fifteen most important beliefs from Exercise 8.1. How can you use each to increase your commitment to the most challenging task or foresightful mission that you have established for your company?

_____

_____

_____

_____

(Continued)

Exercise 9.2 (Continued)

_____

_____

_____

_____

_____

_____

_____

_____

_____

_____

- Identify the qualities of people in history that you admire.
- Find a common element among people whose company you enjoy.
- Identify the resources you most often draw on when challenges emerge.

When you identify the qualities of people in history whom you admire and think about why you admire those qualities, you can uncover additional core values and leadership talents in yourself that you may not have realized previously. This identification process increases your self-confidence because the people whom you admire possess values and skills that already exist within yourself. When you complete Exercise 9.3 on qualities that you admire in others, you can focus on and begin to nurture these undeveloped values so that they can enhance your leadership success.

Reread what you have written in Exercise 9.3. The traits you identified in these answers are qualities that you likely possess. This is true because it is easier to see in others those values that we possess than it is to analyze these values within ourselves.

When the actions of a historical or fictional character are memorable to you, it is because you have identified them with action, and you should use these same talents when you lead. For the same reason, you generally identify with people in your daily life who impress

---

⌐᷈ᷠ᷈⌐ Exercise 9.3

IDENTIFYING QUALITIES YOU ADMIRE

1. Write the names of two or three people in history (or, if you prefer, the names of characters in plays, movies, or books) whom you admire.

   _____

   _____

2. Identify the personality traits that these figures have in common.

   _____

   _____

   _____

3. Write any additional qualities you particularly admire in these people.

   _____

   _____

   _____

---

you. By recognizing that you possess the character traits and talents that you admire in others, you can more quickly analyze others' strengths and use these same virtues more frequently. The result is a greater sense of who you are and a strengthened self-confidence.

For these reasons, we recommend that you continuously add and analyze role models in your life to become a principled colonel. These mentors become wise advisers, mentors, and coaches for your newly evolving leadership skills. Principled colonels choose mentors wisely; their "teachers" hold careers that match their interests. They meet with their mentors on a regular basis and listen carefully to them. Study with them, and ask them to tell you their stories often!

ACHIEVING SELF-ACTUALIZATION. Among the most common traits of principled colonels is their ability to sustain a high level of self-actualization (the highest state of achievement in which people use all their competencies and talents to make unique contributions to events). In 1950, Abraham Maslow identified five states of leadership that are structured hierarchically from most basic to most sparse in leaders (see Figure 9.1). Taking as our goal the uppermost, self-actualization, before we can sustain this level of effectiveness, each of us has to identify into which of the four categories our self-knowledge falls.

• Sharing similar values and principles with those with whom they lead. If you are among these people, you will notice that your feelings of self-confidence rise in direct proportion to the degree to which you share beliefs, goals, and values with those whom you trust and lead.
• Sincere expressions of appreciation of themselves, their company, and their work
• Resolving or understanding a complex event, establishing the rationale for it, or realizing that they played a major role in transforming a bewildering challenge into a reliable, replicable solution
• Promoting a new concept, project, idea, person, or product that aids others or leads a group to a positive result that could not have been obtained without the leader's vision and participation

Although everyone feels good when they are in any of these situations, you will become a principled colonel when you identify the one type of situation that most consistently makes you feel most positive about yourself. Use Exercise 9.4 to determine which of the four conditions above most predictably raises your self-confidence.

Figure 9.1. Maslow's Hierarchy of Needs

⎯⌇⎯ Exercise 9.4

CONDITIONS THAT RAISE YOUR SELF-CONFIDENCE

1. Reflect on a recent situation in which the best aspects of yourself were in play: your self-esteem was high, you had increased confidence to support good ideas, you organized new information rapidly, you performed exceptionally well for your own or others' welfare, you promoted new ideas optimally, and you led others effectively. Write one sentence that captures the essence of what made this principled colonel inside of you so strong:

   _____

   _____

2. The most important component of this experience was that you created a situation in which you knew how to receive what you truly needed to feel powerful, valued, and actualized. Identify what was present in that situation that enabled your values to guide you so effectively:

   _____

   _____

By examining the four categories, you can assess what is absent in situations in which your self-confidence wanes. For example, if you notice that you become less than your best when your values are not shared, you need to use power thinking strategies from Chapters One through Seven to bolster you into self-actualized performance when others you are working with do not share your values. Similarly, you may notice that most of your negative emotions emerge when you feel unappreciated (the second category). Or you may observe that you feel least powerful and most vulnerable whenever you do not understand something (the third category) or you lose your motivation, drive, and self-esteem when you are unable to reach a new goal, promote ideas effectively, or lead others (the fourth category). In each of these circumstances, you need to rely on a power thinking strategy that you have learned thus far before you can sustain your self-actualization.

This condition is one in which you must seek to place yourself more often so that your confidence continues to grow. When you do, you will more continuously sustain the highest levels of confident performance: self-actualization.

Summary

By sensitizing yourself to these feelings and their effects on how you function, you can capitalize on this self-knowledge to maximize your power thinking for yourself and others. By becoming more aware of your needs, you can anticipate the effects of a given set of circumstances before they have a negative impact on your leadership. You can also take proactive steps to counter their negative impact by adding what you need in these situations so your self-confidence increases. For example, if you have a need to be appreciated, you know in advance that you may become scattered and unrealistic when your hard work goes unnoticed. Therefore, you can knock holes in the walls of new challenges more rapidly when other people do not acknowledge your efforts by adding a personal talent to the task that you value and appreciate. This self-knowledge enables you to eliminate the potential negative effects of your feelings and devise new ways of rewarding your personal inclinations, preferences, and strengths so that your self-actualized, confident leadership sustains.

We have found that the more successful people are, the nicer they are. The reason is that they own high self-esteem and do not feel threatened by anyone. Therefore, it is easier for them to be pleasant to everyone.

FLEXIBLE DOER

Many organizations make an effort to have employees of diverse genders, racial, ethnic, and educational backgrounds. Yet some leaders expect them to be of one mind (which coincides with that of the leader) relative to actions to be taken. Clearly, when a leader thinks this way, decision making, problem solving, and creative thinking within the unit will suffer. Here we look at *flexible doers:* they are open-minded to disagreement and equally comfortable whether they or someone else is spearheading an effort.

Item Cluster Graph. Flexible Doer Item Cluster Graph

YAT Items	Your Response
33	_____
61	_____
69	_____
Total	_____
YAT score interpretation	_____

Understanding the Flexible Doer

Items 33, 61, and 69 of the Yale Assessment of Thinking assess the degree to which you are a flexible doer. Fill out the Flexible Doer Item Cluster Graph, entering your scores for these items from Chapter Two. If your total score was 5 or under, write as the YAT score interpretation "highly skilled." If your total score was 6 or 7, write "average ability." If your total score was 8 or higher, write "need for improvement."

Those who responded "very often" or "often" to item 33 ("I find it difficult to work with individuals who have personalities different from mine") typically do not appreciate diverse thinking styles or ways to carry out responsibilities. For these leaders, style is more important than substance. Thus, they deem someone who has a different personality from them a persona non grata and do not acknowledge the ideas and outputs of these individuals.

A flexible doer not only accepts individuals who have different personalities but cherishes their uniqueness. Such leaders realize that when team members have diverse points of view, frequently richer products will result from group discussions and efforts.

Item 61 ("I find it difficult to be motivated to participate in an activity without being the leader of it") provides another example as to how those less skilled in this aspect of self-knowledge act. For these individuals, satisfaction comes from being in a position of power. Being in charge is what motivates them.

Flexible doers, in contrast, are concerned with high organizational performance rather than self-glorification. They are equally pumped up regardless of whether they or someone else is heading an initiative. What is of paramount importance is that it culminates in success because that is what motivates them.

Item 69 ("I make decisions for other people which they should make for themselves") also deals with the need of some persons to exercise power. Leaders who make decisions for other persons that they should make for themselves have a messiah complex. They believe that they alone are suited to decide what is right for an organization. Many of them think they are being benevolent because they are assuming these burdens instead of having ill-suited colleagues do them.

A flexible doer views this issue very differently. These individuals rarely make decisions for other persons that they should make for themselves. They know that such an approach does nothing to prepare these individuals to make important decisions in the future.

Flexible doers place a high degree of emphasis on personnel development. They assist others as those individuals learn the steps necessary to reach effective decisions. For a flexible doer, decision making is not viewed as a one-shot proposition but as a reoccurring action integral to a vibrant organization. They also know that if their colleagues gain skill in it, the organization's performance level will benefit. For flexible doers, immediate and long-term organizational success is far more important than their own ego need to be the sole source for decision making.

An Exemplary Flexible Doer: David Glass

David Glass's credentials as a leader are impressive. He began his association with Wal-Mart in 1964 when he met Sam Walton, the company's founder, while he was opening the second Wal-Mart store in Harrison, Arkansas. In 1976, he joined Wal-Mart as an executive vice president and later served as its president and CEO. In 2000, he was named chair of the executive committee of the board of directors.

Glass both philosophically and operationally serves as an excellent model as to how a flexible doer acts. Inclusion, rather than conformity, is important to Glass. As long as colleagues treat the customer as the boss and continue to be high achievers, their diverse personalities are unimportant to Glass. He says of these people, "Everyone's an individual and has to be treated with the dignity and respect that should be accorded to any individual. We don't distinguish between the importance of jobs."

Glass is motivated even when he is not directing an effort, and he encourages such leadership. He says, "We teach our management people that the way you can be really valuable to an organization is not by what you yourself can accomplish, because none of us can do more than a certain amount. The real measure of success is whether you're able to manifest your talents through others. That multiplies and impacts the entire organization."

Glass does not make decisions for others that they should make themselves. He believes strongly in personnel empowerment: "What you do is pick the right person, and you give them their marching orders—the overall scope of what you're trying to accomplish. And then you get out of their way and support them in ways that guarantee their success. I have often said that we have a responsibility to help people succeed rather than identify those who might fail. We have a low failure rate at Wal-Mart and a high success rate."

Wal-Mart has been a phenomenal success story under the leadership of first Sam Walton and then David Glass. Their company philosophy has embraced a diverse workforce and empowered these individuals to both reach decisions as well as to lead initiatives. Its philosophy has enabled Wal-Mart's associates' self-knowledge cognitive processes to be used optimally to attain a single purpose: the company's continuing to be a major force in the selling of merchandise.

Strategies for Becoming a Flexible Doer

You will advance your abilities to become a flexible doer by following the actions that Glass has taken. The power thinking strategies that follow can assist you in this process: identifying others' good intentions, building a strong support group, and exercising reciprocity.

IDENTIFY OTHERS' GOOD INTENTIONS. Whenever you are working with difficult people, the first clue that they are going to hamper meeting your goals is that they seem to have a lack of sense of belonging. The second is that they begin to decrease their participation. The third is that they develop a conflict of some kind. Next, they will take one of two actions: either decrease their achievement or increase their absenteeism. Finally, they will emotionally or physically leave the organization. People take such actions when they feel marginalized, perceive that few awards are in store, or do not feel as if they are part of the important impact that you are creating.

The first step that flexible doers take when working with a difficult person is to access that person's sense of belonging, so that when this belonging begins to diminish, they use this as a signal that they need to work with this person (or group) to establish a new goal or assist that person to know that his or her work is important. One of the most important ways of doing so is to develop a new company ritual. Creating a new celebratory experience enables others to feel that the company that you lead is growing and improving, and that each person's work contributes to this constant advancement. Employees want to work in an environment where new rituals are established that honor the importance of the common bonds among all of them.

Through the use of new rituals, others begin to construct positive social and professional interactions with new employees. They begin to interpret their competence as valuable and will give their own meaning to this ritual in a multitude of ways to address their specific belonging needs. As their professional needs are addressed, they become more devoted to the organization.

Problem solving requires that all dimensions of power thinking (reasoning, insight, and self-knowledge) be engaged simultaneously. Powerful problem solving overcomes challenges by first identifying cognitive reasons, subconscious insights, and personality-related influences on difficulties in the problem and then drawing on those elements to create a positive solution. In turn, effective reasoning leads to recognition of the patterns that generated a dilemma and the proactive innovations that can resolve it.

BUILD A STRONG SUPPORT GROUP. Flexible doers have special support groups that satisfy their basic needs for safety, security, acceptance, and self-actualization. This support group has members who contribute unique talents to assist power thinking leaders to overcome their own weaknesses.

To establish a comparable support group, select others who are striving for the same goals as you and have talents that you do not possess. For instance, some of your support group will build your personality as you share a relationship of memories. Some members will act as mentors, leading you to higher levels of success, while others will provide you with alternative points of view, bountiful resources, and appreciation of your accomplishments. By ensuring that you have at least one person who exhibits the strengths in each of the quadrants in Exercise 6.2, you can have a balanced foundation of support whenever you need assistance.

EXERCISE RECIPROCITY. Reciprocity is defined as an equal exchange between two people. Thus, reciprocity is equal give and take. This means that flexible doers use their strong self-knowledge external cognitive processes to develop people relationship skills in which the amount that they give to others, and to a single person, equals the amount that that group or person gives to them. Keeping the number of times that you reach out to others equal to the number of times that you allow others to reach out to you adds strength to your leadership. You can take the following steps to exercise reciprocity:

Step 1: After you say something, listen carefully to the responses that others give to your idea.

Step 2: Identify the feelings, ideas, or conflicts people have with your idea. Then restate your suggestion, including both your and other people's ideas and feelings. Explain the benefits all could receive if your idea is accepted or if other people contribute toward the goals.

Step 3: Listen to the response to your second statement to determine whether people wish to reciprocate. If they do, think of a way that you and others can use each of your talents to work together.

Step 4: If possible, give yourselves a few minutes to think about the reciprocal plan you create before you agree to do it. In this way, you can think of other improvements before you begin to ensure reciprocity.

Step 5: If possible, after the plan has been completed, discuss which parts of the reciprocal agreement benefited everyone involved. Also, identify ways you can improve your ability to give and receive in reciprocal situations.

You can strengthen your organization by providing your employees with professional development in how to exercise reciprocity. Your human resource officer can divide a sheet of paper into two columns, labeled "Give" and "Receive." Ask workers to describe relationships in which they either gave or received support, job satisfaction, and material goods. List their experiences in one of the columns as they describe them. Next, ask them to describe occasions when they gave to someone who reciprocated by returning something of similar value, and list these instances in the column on the other side of the sheet. Ask workers how they felt in reciprocal and nonreciprocal experiences, and discuss when reciprocity is most valuable.

Convey that workers will learn to improve their ability to work in groups by using this strategy and that they will know they have improved their abilities when the quality of group projects increases and all members in the group contribute willingly and successfully.

Next, ask workers to write (1) about times when they felt as if others were taking advantage of their hard work by not contributing much to a group project; (2) the reason they believe past group projects were not as successful as they would have liked; and (3) a rephrasing of that reason into an objective of something they will do in the future so that reciprocity can be used in similar situations. For example, if a worker thinks others make them do the majority of the work whenever they meet in groups, he or she might write, "I want to discover how I can help others in my group contribute more to our projects."

Another important strategy that strengthens reciprocity is to identify in advance people who would appreciate having you check to see if there are any difficulties with any task that has been assigned. By checking before a deadline is due, you have developed a strategy of positive logistics. Positive logistics means that instead of becoming upset with a person who is unable to meet a deadline, you work to help the person meet his or her objectives and thereby develop new skills.

INVENTIVE FINISHER

If you are unclear how an inventive finisher acts, we can offer a well-known character as an example: Indiana Jones. This character, portrayed by Harrison Ford in three movies, solves challenging problems, is successful in situations unique to him, and does that for which he has been hired. Indiana Jones finds inventive ways to complete tasks. So too do the power thinkers whom we studied, and that is why we call them *inventive finishers.*

Understanding the Inventive Finisher

Items 11, 26, and 59 of the Yale Assessment of Thinking assess the degree to which you are an inventive finisher. Fill out the Inventive Finisher Item Cluster Graph, entering your scores for these items from Chapter

Item Cluster Graph.   Inventive Finisher Item Cluster Graph

YAT Items	Your Response
11	_____
26	_____
59	_____
Total	_____
YAT score interpretation	_____

Two. If your total score was 5 or under, write as the YAT score interpretation "highly skilled." If your total score was 6 or 7, write "average ability." If your total score was 8 or higher, write "need for improvement."

Item 11 ("When faced with a challenging problem, I wait for events to occur that will make it less difficult to solve") describes an all-too-common occurrence for many leaders. If you answered "very often" or "often" to this item, you have created within your mind an unlikely scenario that probably will not take place.

Virtually every time that we wait for something to make a difficult situation that we are facing less formidable, these anticipated occurrences do not materialize. Individuals less skilled in this aspect of self-knowledge will view this as an anomaly and will wait again for future events when they next face a challenge. When they do not take place, they will rationalize the situation to be universal and offer that as the reason for the anticipated event's failure to materialize. The cycle will continue to repeat itself because they do not learn from it.

An inventive finisher realizes that problems inevitably crop up in today's fast-paced organizational environment. And when one does, it must be dealt with. An inventive finisher does not wait for events to occur that will make the problem less difficult to solve. These individuals identify the causes of a challenging problem and through the use of an appropriate strategy (such as the ladder strategy), they take steps to eliminate its areas of concern.

Persons less skilled in this aspect of self-knowledge wait for events, which usually never happen, to solve challenging problems for them.

Inventive finishers identify the causes of the problem, formulate an appropriate strategy for dealing with these negative conditions, and act because they know they cannot be successful without eliminating this problem. And since success is their objective, they know their decision to tackle this problem is a correct one.

Item 26 ("When told that I must perform a task for which I have had little or no experience, I find it difficult to be successful in such circumstances") also involves the rationalization of our actions. In item 11, individuals who responded "very often" or "often" justified their inaction because they were waiting for something to happen. For this item, persons who gave a comparable answer typically act in one of two dissimilar ways.

Their first response is to avoid taking any action relative to the task for as long as possible. They will tell others and themselves that they "will get it done when they aren't so busy," "when they finish doing what they are currently working on," "after they get back from their business trip," or something similar. Of course, the real reason they are not acting is that the task is in an area that is unfamiliar to them, and they have no proclivity for becoming involved in new endeavors.

The second way they might act is quite different from the former. When asked to perform a task for which they have had little or no prior experience, they will overgeneralize their capability to get the job done. They think that because they can do other things, there is no reason they cannot perform this one. They rush headlong into it even though they have had little or no previous experience relative to it. Is it any wonder that failure typically results from their ill-conceived effort?

Inventive finishers know that talent in one area does not automatically transfer to others. When they are asked to perform a task for which they have had little or no previous experience, they will assess what must be done. As possessors of accurate self-knowledge about their abilities and talents, they know what they can do successfully independently.

Inventive finishers also realize when they need assistance, and they are unafraid to ask for it so that they can realize their objective: success. Thus, if they believe that they lack an adequate knowledge base to perform a task, they will ask someone with the requisite expertise to act as a mentor as they perform this task. Or they will call others for advice regarding unfamiliar segments of the task, read about it, hire a consultant, form a team to perform the endeavor, or do whatever else is necessary to complete the assignment successfully.

In the discussion of item 26, we described the manner in which tasks in areas of unfamiliarity are not taken. Item 59 ("It is difficult to finish tasks that do not fall within my areas of strength") focuses on their completion.

Individuals who answered "very often" or "often" to this item and inventive finishers differ in their approaches to finishing tasks. During the implementation of a task that falls within an area of strength, the first group relies on persistence to see the task through to completion. When an obstacle occurs, they continue their efforts in the same way as they did before the problem emerged. If their approach fails (which is quite likely), then the organization is the loser. And even if they are able to finish the task, at what cost was it done in terms of time and energy expended?

Inventive finishers use a different strategy in this circumstance. With their strong sense of self-knowledge, these leaders know when they cannot expeditiously finish a task. Rather than continuing to butt their heads against the problem's walls, they retreat and consider what to do.

The use of this strategy enables these leaders to identify the problem. They ask themselves, "Can I alone fix it?" "Since it is not in an area of strength for me, do I need assistance from others?" "Is additional information required for me to develop a strategy for its solution?" Once they arrive at answers to these and similar questions, they develop a new plan of action and implement it with the goal of completing the task at hand.

The difference between inventive finishers and colleagues with less skill in this aspect of external cognition goes beyond style in completing tasks. Our research found one other difference. Inventive finishers' units are considered leaders. They do things that are emulated by other divisions within their organization as well as in ones external to it. Units led by colleagues who persist in using the same approach as they have used in the past when facing a problem in an area of nonstrength for them not only take longer to finish a task (if at all); their units rarely, if ever, are the first to accomplish something. As such, it is they who copy what others (those internal to the organizations or competitors) have done.

An Exemplary Inventive Finisher: Frank Batten

Frank Batten is an inventor of sorts. He is also someone who completes what he begins. It is this blending of creativity, knowledge, courage, and tenacity that sets Batten apart from many other leaders.

It is also why he so appropriately characterizes what it means to be an inventive finisher.

Batten initially gained notice as a newspaper publisher in Norfolk, Virginia. Then he added other newspapers and radio and television stations to his holdings. He is perhaps best known for creating and developing the Weather Channel.

As Batten and his team prepared to launch the Weather Channel, they did not wait for events to occur that would make the challenges they faced less difficult to solve. To achieve the goal of a station that could obtain and broadcast local weather information nationwide, they needed technology that could deliver this information to hundreds of different cable systems. Batten and his colleagues faced one problem after another in trying to achieve this objective. When they encountered an obstacle, they used problem-solving strategies to overcome it.

Although Batten was dealing with many things that fell outside his areas of experience at the time, he treated each of them as a challenge and discerned ways to deal with them. For example, his original plan to finance the Weather Channel depended heavily on selling ads. But because the fledging channel did not reach enough homes initially, the channel's capital investment outlays cost more than ad dollars generated. Batten made up for this shortfall by generating increased subscriber fee revenue.

Batten was enormously successful in attaining his goal for creating a type of channel that had been unknown in television history. The Weather Channel now reaches more than 72 million U.S. homes. Not only is it popular but it's also highly profitable.

Batten once explained his attitude about engaging in new efforts: "Not everything we have done has been a winner. But failures, in an odd way, are a mark of success in an innovator. . . ." At the root of successful innovation is a willingness to take intelligent risks.

Strategies for Becoming an Inventive Finisher

You, like Batten, can become an inventive finisher through learning to persevere and identifying your most valuable resources.

PERSEVERING. Power thinkers judge their success through consequence testing, not by imposing their own or society's criteria as a standard of effectiveness. They allocate additional effort and ingenuity to the more difficult aspects of a task, understand which factors cannot be known, and sense which method may be effective (they use insight's internal cognitive process). If these methods do not work, they change their approach. Through this process, they examine multiple combinations of consequences.

Moreover, inventive finishers know that no amount of good luck, momentum, and enthusiasm can compensate for not doing their homework. Thus, they understand the importance of perseverance, defined as continuing to work when the solution is not immediately apparent. Self-efficacy and resilience depend largely on leaders having a realistic picture of what needs to be done and pacing themselves accordingly. The dividing line between extraordinarily successful leaders and less successful ones is often a small difference in performance, multiplied by perseverance.

For example, football coach Vince Lombardi said that what distinguished the truly great running back from a good running back is that the former runs five yards per carry and the latter runs four yards per carry. This one yard of difference comes from the extra effort that truly extraordinary running backs put forth, not from their superior talent. To continue the football analogy, even the most successful quarterbacks may throw an interception on one play, but they go on to throw a long pass for a touchdown on the next series. If you develop resiliency, you can respond positively to future failures instead of being defeated by them.

The ability to persevere often begins by inventive finishers making a personal, self-knowledge-driven connection to a projected outcome. It is this intense commitment to the project—their deep, passionate care—that sustains their power thinking. As Thomas Edison once said, "My genius is sticking to it!" When inventive finishers are thrown into difficult or perplexing situations or experience setbacks, they feel a burning desire to succeed.

You may have noticed that when you persevere, you learn more about your internal constitution. This occurs because persistence can also help you develop patience toward yourself and others. One method of developing patience with tasks and other people is to develop the tenacity to perfect what you do yourself.

IDENTIFYING YOUR MOST VALUABLE RESOURCES. By identifying the talents, thinking processes, people, and other resources that help you, you can rely on them more rapidly as supports when your initial

---

〜〜 **Exercise 9.5**

IDENTIFYING YOUR MOST VALUABLE RESOURCES

1. Briefly describe a recent challenge you faced. List the supports you used to meet that challenge, and then rank them in order of the importance each holds for you (1 = most important, 2 = second most important, and so on).

   _____

   _____

   _____

2. What do the supports you ranked first and second tell you about yourself?

   _____

   _____

3. What did this exercise suggest that you need to become more productive in your life?

   _____

   _____

4. Does this ingredient exist in your life now? If so, where and how? If not, where can you develop or obtain this support more reliably in the future?

   _____

   _____

---

plans falter or go awry. Exercise 9.5 can help you identify those resources. Identifying and actualizing personal talents, motivations, and needs is the beginning of greater knowledge about your external cognitive processes of self-knowledge. When you are having difficulty achieving a particular goal, you can return to the questions in Exercise 9.5 to identify a valuable resource that can be used in your next attempt.

RELIABLE CONCLUDER

Henry Wadsworth Longfellow, the famous nineteenth-century author, wrote the poem "I Shot an Arrow," which begins, "I shot an arrow into the air, It fell to earth, I knew not where." These words are fitting descriptors of contemporary organizational leaders who lack skill in this area.

Reliable concluders know where the arrows they shot landed. They know why they take actions. Colleagues with whom they work can rely on them to fulfill promises made. For persons who answered "very often" or "often" to the items in this section, the same cannot be said.

Understanding the Reliable Concluder

Items 10, 29, and 57 of the Yale Assessment of Thinking assess the degree to which you are a reliable concluder. Fill out the Reliable Concluder Item Cluster Graph, entering your scores for these items from Chapter Two. If your total score was 5 or under, write as the YAT score interpretation "highly skilled." If your total score was 6 or 7, write "average ability." If your total score was 8 or higher, write "need for improvement."

If you answered "very often" or "often" to item 10 ("It is difficult for me to identify the reasons why I take certain actions"), be concerned. This answer reveals an important shortcoming on your part.

First, let us examine why you are unable to identify the reasons that you take certain actions. People who act in this manner do not typically have deeply rooted values. As a consequence, other persons or external events unduly affect them. Therefore, if a colleague they like is doing something, they too will "sign on" to do it with little thought.

Item Cluster Graph. Reliable Concluder Item Cluster Graph

YAT Items	Your Response
10	_____
29	_____
57	_____
Total	_____
YAT score interpretation	_____

Their inability to identify the reasons for their actions is that how they act does not emanate from reason but rather from reactions to persons or events. Although these individuals acted in a particular manner, they did not do so from personal conviction. Their actions represent merely "something I did" to them.

Also, we would be remiss if we did not point out that behaving in this way has wider ramifications beyond you. Within an organization, reactive actions like those previously described cause you to be labeled in an unflattering way: as a "loose cannon," "spur of the moment," "gadfly," and "unpredictable," for example.

If you behave in this way now, learn from reliable concluders who know what their values are and take actions based on them. If they do not believe in X, they will not do it merely because someone they like does it. Nor will they carry over their feelings (such as anger or hurt) from a prior situation into one occurring later.

Should you be unclear as to what your values are, we urge you to take the time to identify them. Devices presented in this book such as Figure 6.2, showing the components of personality, will prove helpful to you. Once this process is completed, we urge you to think before you act. Strategies in this book (for example, the weighted characteristics strategy) can guide you as you make the transition from reactionary to powerful thinking.

Item 29 ("I am late for appointments with other persons") deals with the inability to be punctual for appointments with others. Being late may seem minor, but it is not. When you agreed on a time, you made a commitment to be somewhere at a specified time, and when you are not, you are showing that time commitments have little importance to you. This lack of concern affects your stature as a leader. By being perpetually late, you are conveying that the person you are meeting is not very important to you. As a result, these others have little trust in you. And once you act as if they are unimportant, they will view you in a similar way.

Reliable concluders rarely, if ever, are late for appointments. When they are, they offer an explanation. Time is important to them. They do not expect to be kept in a holding pattern until a tardy colleague arrives or make others wait for them.

If you are frequently late for appointments, we urge you to conduct an internal audit of sorts as well as try to change this behavior. When you do this assessment, ask yourself, "What aspects of my work are important to me?" If you have trouble coming up with an answer, job burnout may be a problem for you.

You may be late for appointments and meetings, because they have become unimportant to you. Since you subconsciously or consciously consider them to be of low significance, that you are regularly late does not bother you, and you continue to act in this manner.

If you are suffering from job burnout, do something about it. A plethora of books and articles have been written on this subject, and they can aid you in getting your professional life back on track.

Another group that needs to get their professional life realigned are persons who responded "very often" or "often" to item 57 ("I do not fulfill promises that I make to individuals"). A reliable concluder who makes a promise keeps it. The individual knows that reliable concluders consider what they do to be important. Thus, they carefully think through promises before making them. Those who are given a promise by these professionals consider themselves fortunate because they know that the promise will be met. And when it is, their trust in the leader becomes even stronger.

If you responded "very often" or "often" to this item, you do not fulfill promises because what you agreed to do is unimportant to you. Perhaps you made the promise because you desire to be popular with colleagues and for them to like you. Your commitment to the promise is surface level at best, and as a consequence, you have no mental investment in what you said you would do. Since you do not, your mind will subconsciously forget what you were to do or alibi for you as you consciously neglect doing what you were supposed to do.

The irony of this pattern is that you habitually make promises in order to be well liked. When you do not fulfill them, the exact opposite occurs: others view you as superficial and not worthy of their trust. Is this descriptor the legacy that you want to have as a leader?

An Exemplary Reliable Concluder: Linda Winner

Linda Winner was truly a great leader whose actions embodied what it means to be a reliable concluder. Winner was the director of the Center for Executive Leadership at the Federal Executive Institute located in Charlottesville, Virginia. She passed away in 2003.

The Center for Executive Leadership, which operates under the aegis of the Office of Personnel Management of the federal government, provides services that include training programs, consulting, and coaching. Each year, thousands of senior executives, high-level managers, and teams of professionals from numerous federal departments and agencies enroll in programs at the center or use its staff's expertise as consultants.

Winner was appointed to this position in 1996. During her tenure, the number of programs conducted at the center increased eleven-fold. The revenue generated by it grew by 600 percent. As a result of these and comparable accomplishments, Winner was the recipient of the prestigious Office of Personnel Management Director's Award (1999), and she and her leadership team were given the Director's Award for Excellence in 2002.

It is virtually impossible to separate Winner as a person from Winner as a leader. First, she was exceptionally strong in reasoning. When she exercised this thinking skill while attempting to decide whether to make a commitment to someone, she relied heavily on her own values. Winner was very clear in her own mind as to what they were and why they were important to her as both a person and a leader. She used them as a touchstone and turned to them as she considered various options as to whether she would make a commitment. Winner would customarily submit her options to an acid test of sorts. She asked the following question of herself and those with whom she worked: "How will this action add quality to what we do?" Thus, if Winner made a commitment, both she and those with whom she worked knew that it would be fulfilled.

Second, Winner was very insightful and relied on this skill when seeking to solve a problem and in the commitments that she made. She said the following about the process that she employed to guide her actions: "I think about something for awhile, and if a solution that I like doesn't materialize, I just let the problem go. And most of the time, a solution to it comes back into my mind at an unexpected time. When it does, it seems just so obvious. Like it's been percolating in the recesses of my mind."

Third, Winner possessed a clear and accurate understanding of herself. Her self-knowledge was reflected in both how she acted toward others and how she led. She was on time for appointments and meetings and listened keenly. In the context of a conversation, she asked questions and listened for information that would give her a clearer idea of the issues and challenges facing the person with whom she was speaking. She acted in this way so that she could aid their efforts as fully as possible so that they could together accomplish the organization's goals.

Unabashedly, Winner said that subordinates care deeply about her because she felt similarly about them as professionals and as individuals. She told those who were interviewing for positions at the center, "I'll support you as you pursue things that will make us better. If you need training to become more skilled in areas, I'll work with you to find someone or a program that can provide this for you. And I will give you honest and relevant feedback often."

Success and failure were strategic weapons that Winner used as she functioned as a reliable concluder. She used her successes as "fuel for the next thing" that she believed could make the center better.

Winner had a positive degree of tolerance for failure. When she and her colleagues experienced it, she would look at what happened as a way to perform better the next time. They would discuss what happened so they could determine why they were not successful. They would then use this knowledge as they planned and implemented subsequent initiatives that they would confidently pursue so that the Center for Executive Leadership could become an even better organization.

Strategies for Becoming a Reliable Concluder

There are two important strategies to increase your skills as a reliable concluder: fulfilling promises made to others and solving problems by probing for the best pattern of interacting among the people involved.

FULFILLING PROMISES MADE TO OTHERS. To develop trust, you must learn to measure your own trustworthiness as well as that of others. As a reliable concluder, you will ensure that you are trustworthy by measuring your own level of trust of others. One means of measuring another's level of trust of you is that the person does not second-guess you. A second measure is that the person does not interrupt an action that you are in the process of implementing. The third measure is that the person does not speak on behalf of both of you. Those three measures are behaviors that characterize trustworthy people. By incorporating these traits into your leadership abilities, others will view you as more trustworthy.

Another reason you may find it difficult to keep your promises is that you are overly influenced by a negative aspect of human nature. Certain tendencies of human nature can reduce your trustworthiness. By becoming more aware of the detrimental consequences of these influences, you gain more control over your time and can fulfill more promises. The list in Exhibit 9.1 identifies the ten most prominent human tendencies that reduce your ability to become a

Exhibit 9.1.   Ten Most Prominent Human
Tendencies That Reduce Leadership Abilities

1. Non–power thinkers tend to do what they like to do before they do what they do not like to do.
2. Non–power thinkers tend to do the things they know how to do before the things that they do not know how to do. They also do things for which they have resources readily available before the things for which they have to generate or locate the resources.
3. Non–power thinkers tend to do the things that are easiest before they do those that are more difficult. They tackle small jobs before they tackle large ones and complete tasks that provide most immediate closure first.
4. Non–power thinkers tend to do things that require a little time before they do those that require a large amount of time, which often leads to focusing on the urgent to the exclusion of the important.
5. Non–power thinkers tend to do scheduled activities before nonscheduled ones.
6. Non–power thinkers tend to respond to the demands of others before demands from themselves. They do not prioritize based on the greatest positive resultant consequences that are likely to be derived by the total company goal or project's mission.
7. Non–power thinkers tend to readily respond to crises and emergencies and wait until a deadline approaches before they move on larger strategic plans.
8. Non–power thinkers tend to do interesting things before uninteresting ones.
9. Non–power thinkers tend to respond in the order of their personal objectives and to the personal consequence of doing or not doing something.
10. Non–power thinkers tend to work on things in the order of their arrival. They first address issues that "make the most noise."

reliable concluder and a method that you can use to overcome the negative effect of this tendency.

As you read each item, you may realize that you also have a different method of overcoming the difficulties associated with that tendency. If you have, describe the method in writing and review that note often. In this way, you can reaffirm its value to you and reprogram it more automatically, as a habitual function in your life.

If you do not have a method of combating a specific tendency, reflect on previous discussions in this book and mentors in your life, and use the action you observed in these leaders to help create a strategy that you can use in the future to overcome each tendency.

**SOLVING PROBLEMS BY PROBING FOR THE BEST PATTERN OF INTERAC-
TIONS BETWEEN THE PEOPLE INVOLVED.**   Reliable concluders find that the best solution to problems are influenced by many factors by using six self-knowledge cognitive processes. Non–reliable concluders use

only three. While most leaders assess (1) their own information and ideas, (2) strategies they have used, and (3) the information provided by others, reliable concluders add several more components to the problem-solving process. They weigh each of the following factors equally to the three listed.

They assess strategies that contemporaries and past leaders have employed, as well as each power thinking strategy employed by everyone associated with the problem. Next, they weigh the effects of each proaction they can take and the cumulative effects of taking several proactions. Then they evaluate the best proactions that people associated with the problem can take. The synergy between each of these components is graphed so that interactions between strengths in each of these areas can also be identified.

A sample graph that we recommend, and that has been used successfully by hundreds of power thinkers who attend our training programs, appears in Exercise 9.6. If becoming a reliable concluder is important to you, we encourage you to complete the steps described in Exercise 9.6 the next time that you must solve a problem in which many people are involved.

SUMMARY

In this chapter, you have learned about the power thinking strategies that lay behind the success of four highly successful leaders. In the process, you also rated your abilities in the subcomponents of self-knowledge's external cognitive processes of being a principled colonel, flexible doer, inventive finisher, and reliable concluder. You also explored the following power thinking strategies:

1. Increasing your enthusiasm
2. Actualizing confidence in your leadership role
3. Identifying the qualities of historical figures whom you admire
4. Achieving self-actualization
5. Identifying others' good intentions
6. Building a strong support group
7. Exercising reciprocity
8. Persevering
9. Identifying your most valuable resources

Exercise 9.6

HOW TO SOLVE PROBLEMS INVOLVING OTHER PEOPLE BY PROBING FOR THE BEST PATTERN OF INTERACTION

Think of a problem you now face as a leader. On the circle below, write the information you have to date in each section of the circle that relates to you. Then, with a second color, next to what you wrote about yourself, write what you know about others involved in the dilemma. When finished, read all your thoughts without pausing. Reread to identify interactions among problematic variables.

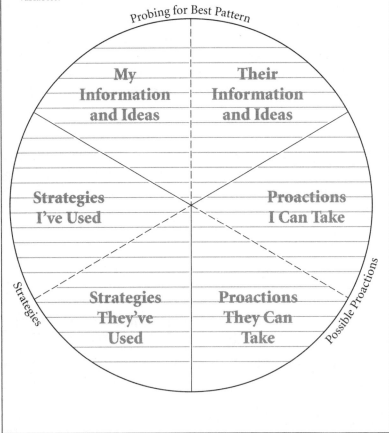

Probing for Best Pattern

My Information and Ideas

Their Information and Ideas

Strategies I've Used

Proactions I Can Take

Strategies They've Used

Proactions They Can Take

Strategies

Possible Proactions

10. Fulfilling promises made to others

11. Solving problems by probing for the best pattern of interactions between the people involved

   On the next two pages, we once again have provided you space in which you may write your reflections at this junction as to steps that you plan to take in order to become more proficient in each of these segments of self-knowledge's internal cognitive process.

SELF-KNOWLEDGE EXTERNAL COGNITIVE PROCESS THINKING ENHANCEMENT

Principled Colonel

Flexible Doer

Inventive Finisher

Reliable Completer

CHAPTER TEN

Putting Our Words into Practice

T olstoy once said: "Everyone dreams of changing humanity but no one dreams of changing himself." These words have pertinence to the very situation in which you now find yourself.

You have spent a considerable amount of time and energy on reading a book that focuses on precisely that about which Tolstoy wrote: change. We hope that you are convinced this book's content is based on sound, important, and conclusive research. The potential benefits that you can derive from implementing its content are enormous. You have the opportunity to become appreciably more proficient in decision making, problem solving, and creative thinking. You also have the chance to be a better leader and for the organization that you lead to become more successful.

Our words are based on facts, not merely hope. As you may recall, in Chapter Three, we cited research relative to 3,056 leaders who did precisely what we are now asking you to do: engage in a focused plan to improve your thinking ability. These individuals made significant improvements in their own thinking ability. They also became better leaders, and their organizations attained higher levels of performance.

The question confronting you is: Are you satisfied with your level of success, or do you wish enhance your thinking and take your efforts to the next level of success? If your answer to this question is that you are content with your ability level, then you do not need to read any further in this book. If you are uncertain or have decided to enhance your thinking skills, continue reading this chapter.

Based on the actions that you have already taken by completing the Yale Assessment of Thinking in Chapter Two and reading about your results in Chapter Three, you possess crucial data relative to your overall skill in thinking as well as your prowess in its three major domains: reasoning, insight, and self-knowledge.

In Chapters Four through Nine, you gained information about your responses. You learned why your actions relative to each item are correct or misguided. Within these chapters, we presented strategies that can improve your skill levels in the various internal and external cognitive processes where you need improvement.

THE POWER THINKING DEVELOPMENT PROGRAM

In order to give cohesion to your effort to increase your range and depth of thinking, we present three questions that are frequently asked of us when we conduct leadership or personnel development programs. Read each question and its response. Then answer each question from your perspective:

1. *What dimensions of my thinking do I wish to improve?*
Do not pursue too many goals. The experiences of other professionals who have sought to improve their thinking have shown that the best results are attained when (a) one major domain or one internal or external cognitive process is targeted and (b) no more than two subskill components (for example, judicious analyst, ready decider, receptive realist) or thinking areas contained in the items for which a response of "very often" or "often" was given.

To guide you in identifying these areas, you would do well to review the data that you derived from the Yale Assessment of Thinking in Chapter Three. It provided an overall assessment of your current thinking ability, scores in the three major domains of thinking, scores in the assessment's twenty-three subskill components, and response interpretations of each of the test's sixty-nine items.

With these data, you have several choices as to the dimensions of thinking that you can seek to improve. For the one major domain or cognitive process that you identify, your options include:

- Pick your weakest domain score, and target that as the area of improvement.
- Select the best domain score and decide to enhance it.
- If your best domain score was a surprise (because you did not know it was an area of strength), you can target it for improvement. Since it was strong without your being cognizant of it, with attention, it can develop rapidly.

You can also use these three ways to select a domain to discern an internal or external cognitive process for improvement.

You can use comparable criteria to identify no more than two subskill components or thinking areas contained in the items for which you gave a response of "very often" or "often". If the Yale Assessment of Thinking indicates that there is more than one cognitive process in which you lack strength or one item to which you gave a response of "very often" or "often," then some prioritization is needed. The most reoccurring, or crucial, of the cognitive processes (or items) should be selected initially. If you do not have any cognitive processes in need of significant improvement or you did not give a response of "very often" or "often" to an item, it would be unnecessary to target either of the preceding for action.

After identifying the aspects of your thinking to be enhanced, you are now ready to move on to the second question that will aid you in accomplishing this objective.

2. *What should I do to improve in these facets of thinking that I have identified?*
After you have selected a domain, cognitive process, subskill, or item, we suggest that you review the discussion on it in this book—either scanning it for ideas and strategies to incorporate into your thinking repertoire or reading it more thoroughly.

After you know what you want to accomplish, getting it done is the next step. Aristotle wrote, "Excellence is an art. We are what we repeatedly do." The repetition that Aristotle noted is what must occur in this step.

Skill in thinking occurs through focused practice. If something is initially awkward, you can become skilled at it if you engage in regular effort designed to acquire this facility. This skill is called automaticity—that which we can do without conscious thought.

With regard to thinking, automaticity usually takes about six weeks to occur. In order for it to happen, you must make a conscious effort to use the idea or strategy as frequently as you can in situations where it is appropriate.

As a reminder to use a strategy, we recommend that you have a visual device such as an index card on an easily seen place on your desk. The card will remind you to use this strategy whenever you find yourself in a situation where it can serve you effectively.

We offer two additional thoughts about learning to use a new strategy. First, have patience. Just as you fell from the bicycle as you were learning to ride it, your initial attempts to use a new strategy may be awkward or produce less than favorable results. Second, automaticity requires frequent use. The more often you make a conscious effort to use a strategy, the more quickly it will become entrenched in your mind. When it does, your mind will subconsciously use this strategy in situations appropriate for its usage.

3. *How long will it take me to reach my goals?*
When you begin a program to improve your thinking skills, we recommend that you write down on your calendar a date six weeks off. On that day, evaluate your progress relative to the goals that you have established.

After analyzing your response, you will have three options for the next phase of your thinking enhancement plan:

- Continue to develop the same dimensions of thinking.
- Continue to work on some of the same goals and replace others with different areas for improvement.
- Establish entirely new goals.

The thinking development program we set out here is not a one-time undertaking. You should implement it continuously for six weeks and conclude it when you are satisfied that your repertoire of thinking skills is as comprehensive and as fully developed as needed to meet your current and future professional challenges as a leader.

If you want objective data to guide you, retake the Yale Assessment of Thinking after a minimum of three months have elapsed since you initially took it. If you follow the assessment procedures correctly and give truthful answers, you will gain significant information about your progress in acquiring new thinking strategies and improving existing ones.

If you have conscientiously followed a thinking enhancement program as we have described, you should expect to see a significant improvement in the aspects of thinking that you have delineated when you retake the YAT. And because of the interdependence among thinking's three domains, you will realize gains in dimensions that were not a part of your plan.

FINAL COMMENTS

In this book, we have described thinking practices that have hindered individuals from becoming outstanding leaders. We have also presented strategies and ideas that can reverse these adverse actions on the part of individuals.

We hope that you will begin to use these strategies as you make decisions, solve problems, and think creatively as a leader. When you do so, both you and those with whom you work will be glad that you did.

—ᴧᴧᴧ— Appendix: Normative Data

The research project conducted in support of the Yale Assessment of Thinking took place initially from October 1996 until February 1998. The purposes of this research were to provide normative data for outstanding leaders who possessed enhanced thinking ability (which we have termed *power thinking*) and were employed in business, education, government, health care, and other professions and to establish the statistical reliability and validity of the assessment.

The project involved a large sampling at multisite locations in various regions of the United States. What resulted from this effort was the publication of a standardized assessment of thinking, the Yale Assessment of Thinking (YAT). Versions of the instrument have been translated into German, Italian, Spanish, Portuguese, and French.

Since its publication, over fifty thousand individuals in the United States and internationally have been administered the YAT, which had fifty-four items. The test sought to determine four types of information: (1) the overall thinking ability of the test taker, and measures of performance in the domains of (2) reasoning, (3) insight, and (4) self-knowledge.

After several years, a decision was made to produce a new version of the YAT. There were three reasons for taking this course of action. First, as a result of multiple research investigations that we have conducted, new and more highly discriminate data were found relative to the subskill components that comprise the three domains that constitute powerful thinking on the part of outstanding leaders.

Second, we sought to update the instrument's norms because the original norming sample had taken place in 1997. Since that time, many individuals had read our prior book or participated in the Power Thinking for Leaders programs that we conduct.

For this version of the YAT, we selected populations using a stratified sampling technique. We identified professionals whom supervisors and subordinates identified as being outstanding leaders and as being the person in their organizations who demonstrates excellence in the three domains of thinking (reasoning, insight, and self-knowledge) assessed by this standardized instrument. In addition, the organizations that they lead must be successful, having attained a high level of performance.

We identified 346 professionals who worked in business, government, education, health care, and other organizations who met the criteria. Business, with 181 identified professionals, was the area most represented in the normative group.

These 346 individuals ranged in age from twenty-five to seventy-one, and 53 percent were male. All but five of the group possessed a bachelor's degree, and 39 percent of these leaders had completed a master's degree (with the M.B.A. being the most prevalent degree). Forty-eight of these leaders were minorities (14 percent of the total group), with African Americans being the largest group represented (twenty-nine).

These individuals were administered items from this assessment that reflected the standards of excellence in each of the domains measured. The items depicted behaviors that distinguished them as highly skilled thinkers. We used the results of this process to establish the national norm-referenced benchmarks of thinking that this instrument assesses.

P-value statistics were computed for each item. Items that did not discriminate satisfactorily were eliminated. In addition, raw score discriminatory rankings for every item were computed. Based on this discrimination index, an item was required to demonstrate a positive correlation of .91 or higher to its area of categorization that it was designed to measure—reasoning, insight, or self-knowledge—for it to serve as an item on this assessment.

For purposes for establishing construct and predictive validation, 311 individuals were identified as being mediocre or poor leaders. None of these professionals was considered to be adept in problem solving, decision making, or creative thinking.

RELIABILITY

An assessment's reliability is the degree to which it yields consistent results. We used Kuder-Richardson procedures to provide an estimate of reliability based on the assessment's internal consistency, or the extent to which all items in the assessment are working together. The Kuder-Richardson Formula 20 reliability coefficient (r) for split-half reliability of the YAT is $r = .92$. These high reliability coefficients demonstrate that the YAT yields highly significant, reliable, and consistent outcomes.

Standard errors of measurement give information regarding the degree to which chance fluctuations in assessment scores can be expected. The standard error of measurement is 2.13.

VALIDITY

An assessment's merit can be measured by its content, concurrent, predictive, and construct validity. The establishment of these types of validity occurred throughout the years of the initial research project, as well as the psychometric procedures that we employed in revising this instrument. These procedures involved demonstrating YAT's relationship to several indexes of successful higher-level thinking: reasoning, insight, and self-knowledge. The critical aspect of validity for a thinking assessment is the extent to which the YAT's content represents an appropriate sample of strategies, knowledge, and understanding that are the goals of powerful thinking.

Content validity can be evaluated through careful examination of the objectives of individual assessment items. In order to achieve this end, a compendium of assessment objectives was created. To establish content validity, this compendium was compared to the qualities of powerful thinking as demonstrated by outstanding leaders in business, government, education, health care, and other organizations.

Concurrent validity determines the degree to which participants can improve their performance on an item after having mastered enhanced thinking strategies that are assessed by that item. Subjects who took the YAT and were instructed in one or more strategies for power thinking subsequently improved their performance on the YAT, as well as in the regular demonstration of that skill in leadership situations.

Construct validity establishes that subjects who score less well on the YAT will find it more difficult to be successful with tasks that are judged to require greater proficiency in reasoning, insight, self-knowledge, or total thinking ability. Consistently, subjects who scored least well on the YAT were those who were identified as mediocre or poor leaders.

Predictive validity is the degree to which subtests and single items separate outstanding leaders who possess strength in thinking from their less able counterparts. Median biserial correlation coefficients for each subtest were .87 to .91. These high correlation coefficients demonstrate that the YAT discerned high- from low-scoring professionals. These coefficients also documented the assessment's predictive validity. In addition, the sixty-nine-item version of the YAT contains twenty-eight of the items from the former fifty-four-item YAT that were found to have the highest predictive validity. These items were supplemented by the next fourteen highest items of predictive value on the former YAT. This second group of items was revised to increase their predictive validity as well as for purposes of clarity and pertinence.

⎯⎯ References

Block, C. C., and Mangieri, J. N. *Reason to Read: Thinking Strategies for Life Through Literature.* Reading, Mass.: Addison-Wesley, 1996.

Bradford, J., and Cohen, R. *Advanced Thinking Through Situated Learning.* Memphis, Tenn.: Center for Cognitive Development at Vanderbilt University, 1997.

Clausen, J. A. *Age Stratification and the Individual.* Berkeley: University of California Press, 2002.

Csikszentmihalyi, M. *Flow: The Psychology of Optimal Experience.* New York: Basic Books, 1990.

Comer, J. *Making Schools of Education Bridges to Better Learning.* New York: Basic Books, 2003.

Cyr, D. "How to Build a Winning Team." *US Airways Attaché,* October 1999, pp. 34–37.

Dell, M. S. "Learning from Failure." *Harvard Business Review,* Aug. 2002, pp. 34–43.

Donnie, C., and Linkie, M. *Becoming a Winner.* Fort Worth, Tex.: Harcourt Brace, 2000.

Dyer, W. "Counseling the Reluctant Client." *Journal of Counseling Psychology,* 1998, *20*(3), 240–246.

Gardner, J. W. *Strategic Thinking: The Essence of Competitive Advantage.* New York: McGraw-Hill, 1990.

Glanz, J., Grant, B., and Monteiro, M. "WHO/ISBRA Study on State and Trait Markers of Alcohol Use and Dependence: Analysis of Demographic, Behavioral, Physiologic and Drinking Variables that Contribute to Dependence and Seeking Treatment." *Alcoholism: Clinical and Experimental Research,* 2002, *26*(7), 1047–1062.

Hay/McBer. *Mastering Global Leadership.* Washington, D.C.: Hay/McBer International, 1995.

Institute for Effective Management. *CEOs and Management Study: Majority of People Were Not Taught How to Think in School.* Charlotte, N.C.: Institute for Effective Management, 1997.

Institute for the Power of Positive Students. *Research Concerning the Effects of Written Goals and Goal Setting.* Denver, Colo.: Institute for the Power of Positive Students, 1998.

Jay, M. Quotation cited in P. Fargis and S. Bykofsky (eds.), *The New York Public Library Desk Reference.* New York: Simon & Schuster, 1991.

McCullough, J. *The Life and Times of Thomas Jefferson Revisited.* New York: Dell, 2001.

Peter, L. J., and Hull, R. *The Peter Principle.* New York: Morrow, 1969.

Santayana, R. *The Life of Reason: Reason in Common Sense.* New York: World Press, 1905.

Sheldon, K. M. *Contributors to Success in Life: A Longitudinal Study of Kindergartners and First/Second Graders into Middle Age: Final Research Report.* Columbia: University of Missouri Press, 2002.

⟨⟨⟨⟨ The Authors

JOHN N. MANGIERI is the president of the Center for Leadership and Personnel Development, located in Charlotte, North Carolina. He received his Ph.D. from the University of Pittsburgh and has served on the faculty of Ohio University, the University of South Carolina, and Texas Christian University. He has also held a variety of leadership positions, including both university and corporate presidencies.

Mangieri, a Fulbright Scholar, has been a consultant and provider of leadership programs to numerous organizations in the United States and other countries around the world. He was invited to serve as an instructor in the prestigious University of California-Berkeley Worldwide Leadership Program, as well as the Center for Executive Leadership. He has been and is a member of several organizational boards of directors. In addition, he has authored or coauthored ninety-one professional articles and twelve books.

CATHY COLLINS BLOCK is a professor at Texas Christian University in Fort Worth, Texas. She received her Ph.D. from the University of Wisconsin-Madison and has been a visiting professor at the University of Notre Dame. She has been a research assistant at the Wisconsin Research and Development Center for Cognitive Development and has served as the chairperson of the National Commission to Infuse Thinking Development into the Curriculum of the Schools of the United States.

Block was recently honored as being one of the 2000 Most Outstanding Scholars of the 21st Century. She has written fifty-three research-based articles and seventeen books, including the highly acclaimed book, *Teaching Thinking: An Agenda for the Twenty-First Century.* She is a prominent psychometrician whose work includes being an author of the Stanford Achievement Test Series, now in its ninth edition.

⟶ Index